# WAITING
# FOR
# **PRIME TIME**

Marlene Sanders
and
Marcia Rock

# WAITING
# FOR
# **PRIME TIME**

## THE WOMEN OF
## TELEVISION NEWS

University of Illinois Press
Urbana and Chicago

© 1988 by the Board of Trustees of the University of Illinois
Manufactured in the United States of America
C 5 4 3 2 1

*This book is printed on acid-free paper.*

Library of Congress Cataloging-in-Publication Data

Sanders, Marlene.
    Waiting for prime time: the women of television news/ Marlene
Sanders and Marcia Rock.
        p.      cm.
    ISBN 0-252-01435-9 (alk. paper)
    1. Women journalists—United States.  2. Sanders, Marlene.
3. Television broadcasting of news—United States.  4. Television
personalities—United States.  I. Rock, Marcia.  II. Title.
PN4784.W7S26 1988
070'.92'2—dc19                                                    88-325
                                                                    CIP

# Contents

# Preface

The history of network television news encompasses a relatively short period of time, from the late 1940s to the present. My own career, beginning in 1955, covers a good portion of that history, still in the making.

I have written this book jointly with Dr. Marcia Rock, who teaches in the Department of Journalism at New York University. We have shared many of the interviews and much of the research. Much of the story is based on my experiences, so we have chosen to present it from my point of view, and often in the first person. I have talked with pioneering broadcasters such as Pauline Frederick and with many of today's network stars, women like Diane Sawyer, Leslie Stahl, and Lynn Sherr. We have both interviewed lesser-known correspondents who have stories to tell as well, along with producers, writers, and the few female news executives.

Many of the women in this book are in their forties, the beneficiaries of the women's movement of the early 1970s. Without that particular phase of U.S. history, it is doubtful they would be in television at all. Many of the younger women in the business believe there are no limits to how far they can go. Perhaps they are right, but they should understand the past that has made their hopes attainable.

Those of us who pursue broadcast journalism learn sooner or later that it is difficult to balance the work with a personal life. Some of us have managed to do so. Others have not. These personal stories may help readers to decide how much a job is worth.

I have been lucky to witness so many of the major events of the past thirty years and to have reported them on radio and television. It is one of the greatest rewards of this business to do so. It has also been a struggle to gain a foothold, and hang on to it, in a still mainly male-dominated profession. In this book, we try to explain how some of us managed to do it, and what remains to be done.

We would like to thank all those who gave of their time to be interviewed, and the NOW Legal Defense and Education Fund's Media Project for giving us access to its files.

Marlene Sanders

# Introduction: Leaving CBS

It was Friday, the thirteenth of March 1987, for the superstitious perhaps an omen, the date we all knew major cuts in our ranks would be announced. It was not possible to get much work done. I had finished writing a story on peer counseling for a forthcoming "Sunday Morning" story, but for several days I had been cleaning out my files in anticipation of being one of those fired. Others in the Northeast bureau, where my office was located, thought I was being foolish. There was widespread feeling that I was invulnerable. My outspoken sentiments on the secondary status of women in the industry were well known and often quoted. I was a pioneer in the business and firing me, some thought, would create too much bad press and the possibility, as well, of a sex and age discrimination lawsuit. My own view was that all of the above was irrelevant, and that *anyone* could be fired in the mix of more than two hundred people. Besides, the group that ruled the network news operation included not one of the people responsible for my being hired ten years before. Further, that very group had excluded me from the major broadcast of CBS News, "The CBS Evening News with Dan Rather." For someone kept off the Rather news, and not a part of television coverage of conventions, elections, or special reports, recent events could not bode well. Radio didn't count. Neither did "Sunday Morning," nor did prime-time newsbreaks, all of which I did regularly in those last years. The Rather broadcast counted for everything, and if you didn't meet its producers' standard of charisma, looks, or age, no matter how good a reporter you were, you were not part of the group that mattered. Therefore, I was emptying my files.

When the phone in my office rang around noon with a summons to see news president Howard Stringer, I had no doubt about the message. As I headed down the hall, my colleague Steve Young was on his way back. He had just been fired, he told me. He was one of the many let go even though he had often been seen on the Rather news and was regarded as an excellent reporter. The cuts had to be made somewhere. Ike Pappas, another longtime correspondent with a distinguished record, was a victim as well. For reasons best known to the news hierarchy, Pappas had not been among that favored group allowed to report on the Rather news for some time. Reasons, of course, were never given.

When I walked into Stringer's office, his first words to me were, "You're not being laid off. We want you to go to radio full time." This was an unexpected development. I was instructed to see the radio news vice president, Joe Dembo, to find out more. Our contracts specifically said that we were assignable to jobs in television or radio news or a combination of both. I was in no position to object at that time and was momentarily taken aback. It was not until my conversation with Dembo that I discovered the shifts available: the overnight, and the one he offered me — weeknights to 11:00 P.M., and weekends, with Thursday and Friday off.

As the firings continued, the closing of bureaus announced, and even radio stringers in key parts of the world were eliminated, the prospect of staying with CBS News seemed less and less attractive. Over the weekend, I considered what had been offered to me and my anger grew. No more "Sunday Morning" stories would be allowed — work I had enjoyed, done well, and felt had been journalistically sound. Instead, I was asked to fulfill a routine radio assignment suitable for someone at the beginning of her career, not at the peak of her abilities. Further, the hours were such that they precluded any kind of normal lifestyle. I had had too many years of that already.

I returned to management and expressed my reluctance to accept their offer. We reached a compromise that was face-saving for all concerned. They had not fired me, and I had not quit. We called it mutual termination, and they agreed to adhere to all union and contractual agreements.

My decision was not an easy one. In a well-paying business, it could be foolhardy to throw away a good salary. My husband had died three years before. There was no financial or emotional backup. All I had was confidence in my ability to start over. The prospect was a little frightening, but the decision was now made. As I walked down the familiar windowless corridors, I felt strangely liberated. Inside the building, the atmosphere was strained. As the firings were taking place, our colleagues in the Writers Guild were on strike, picketing outside. Those who had survived the firings and were non-union were doing scab duty, carrying out the striking writers' and editors' tasks as well as trying to do their own jobs. Many of them were suffering from survivor's guilt, looking stricken and confused as the firing victims announced their departures. The CBS News broadcast center was a tense and unhappy place.

As I headed for my office, I ran into young "Morning News" anchorwoman Faith Daniels. I told her I was leaving. "Oh, no," she said, "that's terrible. You've been my role model. You've always been there for us."

"Well," I replied, "I won't be there anymore, and I'm sorry. I don't know what that means for you for the future, whether it simply won't be possible for women to stay in this field as long as I have. Truthfully, I haven't decided yet how big a role the age factor has played in all this." We wished each other luck.

Fourteen of my fellow correspondents had been fired, and two hundred producers, bureau managers, and other news personnel had also been given notice. Warnings had been evident for weeks. The entire broadcast news industry was in a period of flux and uncertainty. The mergers and takeovers in many businesses had first been the subject of our news coverage. Now, the story hit home. General Electric buys RCA, including NBC. Capital Cities Broadcasting takes over ABC, and, at CBS, chief executive officer Thomas Wyman is replaced by Laurence Tisch.

The *New York Times* headlines tell part of the story. On 20 September 1985: "CBS Cutting 125 News Jobs in Cost Battle." Again, 17 July 1986: "At Least 70 People Dismissed at CBS News." Then on 6 March 1987, when CBS News was hit again with more than two hundred layoffs, *The Daily News* put it this way: "Ax hits CBS, 200 gone." At CBS each of the periodic dismissals was under a different news president, another reflection of the instability of the network news organization. In memos to the staff, each man cited the regrettable need to reduce costs. In 1985, the memo from news president Ed Joyce mentioned "unanticipated adverse financial circumstances," including the "consequences of successfully resisting the takeover attempt by Ted Turner, a listless economy, and a marked softness in the advertising marketplace." By the next year, news president Van Gordon Sauter reminded us of "the wrenching changes in the economy that supports our work." In 1987, news chief Howard Stringer carried out corporate requests for "streamlining CBS News" and "the restructuring of the news division to protect it from further cuts in the future and the preservation of the journalism we cherish."

The changes at CBS became inevitable in August 1985 when the corporation bought back 21 percent of its stock to prevent Ted Turner, the Atlanta television executive and founder of Cable News Network (CNN), from taking over the company. That costly purchase forced all parts of the company to slash budgets. Coincidentally, the effect of competition from cable stations and the availability of movie cassettes cut into network viewing, with losses in the entertainment divisions.

Many of us in electronic newsgathering were shocked at first by the gradual diminution of our news staffs. We were viewed by many of our print colleagues as unrealistic, overpaid, and egocentric. We were chastised in their columns for not understanding that we were merely employees of a corporation, subject to dismissal like anyone else when the budget grew too fat. But it was not our feeling that as news professionals we were immune; rather, it was that many of us veteran radio and television journalists had for years worked for companies where a different attitude prevailed. News was then re-garded as something special, and the public airwaves were a unique venue to be used by broadcasters in the public interest. For many years that goal was mandated by government regulations, and those stations that did not comply would fear for their license renewals. A certain amount of news and public affairs broadcasting was required, but under the deregulation of the Reagan administration all that was set aside, and the rules of the marketplace were substituted. Dereg-ulation was a key factor in treating news as just another profit center.

As I prepared to leave CBS I felt a rush of regret for the young women starting out today. The doors were open to them, and I felt some satisfaction with my part in that. But how long would that last? And would it be fun anymore? I had had my struggles, but there also had been wonderful opportunities to report on the major events of three decades, and to watch an industry grow. Now the business I left hardly resembled the one I found when it all began for me.

# 1

## Early Newswomen

When I was growing up in Cleveland, Ohio, in the 1940s, the only radio newswoman I was even vaguely aware of was Dorothy Fuldheim. She was a lone, disembodied voice that got lost in the sea of resonant male sounds.[1] Even if the words "role model" had been in vogue then, she would not have come to mind. But there were women radio reporters, many of whom got their start during World War II.

In many ways, my own career was as accidental as those of the women who found themselves in Europe at the outbreak of World War II when radio news, as we know it today, was being created. Their acceptance was short-lived; when the war ended, most of those early women reporters returned to print, academia, or government. They found neither the encouragement nor the opportunity to pursue a career in broadcasting. Their entrance into radio reporting was more a case of propinquity and serendipity than conscious policy on the part of the broadcast news organizations; that is, women were never sent overseas by headquarters but were hired on the spot in a moment of immediate need. It was a male-dominated profession filled with a prejudice against women. That prejudice was rationalized by the common belief that an audience did not like a woman's voice because it wasn't authoritative.

Edward R. Murrow didn't believe that. He was the first to hire women abroad. He was scrambling to get news of the European disaster on CBS radio, devising formats as he went along, and hiring staff wherever he could find them. Murrow and William L. Shirer, himself hired by Murrow in Europe, did their own hiring as the need arose. They were under great pressure to find knowledgeable people, and women would do in a pinch. Murrow and his inexperienced broadcast staff had to figure out how to use a microphone effectively, how to operate shortwave equipment, how to fight foreign governments for air time, and how to broadcast live under the most trying circumstances. They created "The World News Roundup," still on the air, a broadcast that was live during the war, with reporters never sure as they spoke whether their words were getting through. It was a conceptual and technical breakthrough, and marked the beginning of Murrow's career as a star reporter.[2] From this emerged the network reporter who was not a commentator but a person who could unite "the functions of news gatherer, writer and broadcaster . . . a figure new to communications."[3] The reporter addressed a nationwide audience directly, reaching millions with breaking news often before a newspaper could disseminate the information.[4] Suddenly the profession had clout and respect.

This new kind of reporting needed lots of correspondents — professional, experienced people with strong, convincing voices. Shortly after Ed Murrow hired William L. Shirer, he corralled an old friend, Mary Marvin Breckinridge, to work for him as well. A photographer, she had spent years in Europe as president of the National Student Federation and knew several languages. Murrow advised her only "to keep her voice low." (The advice was probably based on the common male complaint about women's voices lacking authority.) She became the first woman correspondent on staff for CBS Radio News. Murrow liked her work, noting it was "first-rate. . . . I am pleased. New York is pleased, and so far as I know the listeners are pleased. If they aren't, to hell with them."[5] She continued broadcasting from Paris until 5 June 1940, when the French government was abandoning the city. Her broadcast career ended when she married a U.S. diplomat that summer. CBS policy prohibited her from broadcasting because of a perceived potential conflict of interest.

Another woman worked for a time with Murrow. Betty Wason had a series of jobs including one with *McCall's* magazine as a food writer. She was traveling in Europe during the war, and met with Shirer in Berlin in January 1940. Although no agreements were made at that time, she must have made a favorable impression because when she was on her way to Scandinavia and the invasion of Norway began, she contacted Shirer and was put on the air. Her first broadcast was also the first report of the invasion.

But Wason's timeliness and initiative were not appreciated by the network. They were not happy with her delivery. She said she "received a call saying my voice wasn't coming through, that it was too young and feminine for war news and that the public was objecting to it."[6] There had been no objections to her writing. Wason's broadcasting career with CBS ended, even though she ran the Athens bureau until shortly after the Nazi occupation. When she left Greece she returned to the United States, and to print. She claimed her voice was perfectly all right, and that her treatment by CBS was the result of male prejudice.

Sigrid Schultz worked for a while as a translator, and in 1925 became a reporter for the *Chicago Tribune*. She was the paper's correspondent-in-chief for central Europe until 1941 and had become an expert on the Nazis. Although she did a few broadcasts for CBS, she mainly reported for the Mutual Broadcasting System's radio network. She was wounded in 1941 and returned to the States to recover. Those who heard her say she always identified herself as a newspaper reporter, and never learned to write properly for radio or master the delivery style. But she did reports of ten to fifteen minutes in length and there was no quarrel with her information.

During the same period, NBC also needed reporters in Europe and hired Margaret Rupli, then married to a British newspaperman. She spoke several languages and had worked for the U.S. Department of Labor. Even though she was going to be with a rival network, Murrow knew Rupli and gave her some advice, which was always to understate the situation. "Don't say the streets are rivers of blood. Say that the little policeman I usually say hello to every morning is not there today."[7] She reported from Amsterdam as the Nazis took over, escaping on a ship bound for England. When she and her husband returned to the United States, NBC offered her a staff job doing only one broadcast a week in the mid-morning. She decided that was inadequate and returned to the U.S. Department of Labor.

Another woman who happened to be in Europe during the early days of the war also stumbled into a job at NBC. In 1940, Helen Hiett was reporting for a small Illinois newspaper. She had been sending stories back since the late 1930s, and used some of that material and her fluency in four languages to land a job with NBC. She broadcast from Paris, alternating with the overworked staffer Paul Archinard. When the Nazis invaded, she reported the fall of France and then escaped to Switzerland and continued to report. Then it was on to Spain, where she finally succeeded in getting out a broadcast on the bombing of Gibraltar, a scoop that won her the National Headliners Club award, making her the first woman to receive it. After Hiett's return to the United States, she became a regular news commentator for NBC but stayed only for a year and a half.

She worked in academia for a time before returning to print journalism.

The Women's Bureau of the U.S. Department of Labor noted that in November 1946, one year after the war ended, women constituted 28 percent of the total employees in broadcasting, in jobs ranging from control room work to sales and directing. According to the Bureau, "as the men returned from service, women faded out of these jobs except for a few who made an outstanding success and permanent place for themselves with the networks, radio stations, and advertising agencies." However, the report on how women were faring on the air was not so good. "The public . . . turned a deaf ear to women announcers, except in certain sections of the South where 'announcerettes' [were] well received."[8]

But young Pauline Frederick was to be one of the few exceptions. She graduated from college in the 1930s, armed with a political science degree, and considered herself lucky when she landed a job on the *Washington Star.* There she found herself interviewing the wives of diplomats.

However, one of her columns was spotted by an enterprising woman at NBC who thought some of the material might make good radio features if it were recorded as she did her interviews. This arranged, Frederick made her radio debut on a free-lance basis, with traditional women's subjects. At the same time, she continued her writing career, moving on to the North American Newspaper Alliance, and for a time, phasing out of radio. After World War II ended, she approached NBC for work since they were familiar with her and had broadcast her earlier material. She also contacted CBS. Neither would have a woman on the air doing news, they told her, because women's voices were not authoritative and would not be accepted. ABC heard she was looking for work, however, and said she could do some free-lancing for them on women's stories.[9] She duly produced features they assigned. To her dismay, "women's stories" were on subjects such as the shortage of nylon stockings. Another topic, she recalls, was how to get a husband, even though she had not managed to do that for herself. When the United Nations became a reality, she traveled regularly to its first site at Lake Success in search of interviews, a trip she says few of the male regulars seemed willing to make. ABC said they would use her material, but would only include her voice if she got exclusives; otherwise only the interviewee's voice would make air. Being "on the air" was important in order to get the credit deserved for reporting the story and also to gain audience recognition.

In Frederick's favor was the fact that after the war male correspondents were in short supply. Because of that, she managed to go on several overseas assignments, but she muses that "since a mere woman was not to do hard news on the air, ABC threw junkets at me, which the men were too busy to accept." One of those was the last voyage of the Queen Mary as a troop ship before it was to be refurbished in England and turned back into a passenger ship for tourists. It just so happened that General Dwight D. Eisenhower and his wife were traveling on the ship, to a peace conference with the satellite countries. To her delight, the trip produced news, though accidentally. She was able to get an exclusive interview with Ike.

In 1947, after a couple of other trips, she went to ABC News management to review her status, once again trying to get on staff. That was still out of the question because, despite her work, women's voices were suspect. Once again, Frederick decided to approach CBS and NBC, sending samples of her interviews on "platters," 78 rpm celluloid records, the recording medium before audio tape. Edward R. Murrow was then vice president and director of public affairs, and she left the platters for him to listen to. She never saw him, but one of his aides gave her a note with Murrow's comments on her work, to the effect that while Frederick had a pleasant voice and read well, CBS had little opportunity to use women on the air.

Her rejection was probably not Murrow's doing, given his history of hiring women. He had hired Mary Marvin Breckinridge during the war, and in 1940 attempted to add Helen Kirkpatrick to his team. Kirkpatrick was then a correspondent in London for the *Chicago Daily News* and was considered one of the best reporters in London. But, again, it was the policy at the home office that quashed her being hired. Ed Klauber, the CBS executive responsible, reportedly said no more women.[10] The free-lancers Breckenridge and Wason were enough.

In 1948 Pauline Frederick was still a free-lancer for ABC when a notice appeared on the office bulletin board announcing that ABC would be covering the 1948 political conventions on television for the first time, and that any radio reporter who wanted to get into television should sign up. Apparently Frederick was the only one who didn't. There were, she says, two reasons. First, she knew nothing about television, and second, there had been a movie actress with a name similar to hers, Pauline Fredericks, with whom she was frequently confused. She was afraid that if she appeared on the screen, albeit the small one, the confusion would be worse, and that somehow she would develop an image as a performer. Frederick was a serious newswoman and wanted to keep it that way.

Much to her surprise, ABC's Tom Vellotta asked her why she hadn't signed up, and she explained that she knew nothing about television. He conceded that the network didn't either, and urged her to try. They needed someone to interview wives of the candidates and other females of note who might appear at the conventions. Reluctantly, she agreed. One of her additional concerns was how one was supposed to look on television. The only information she could get out of the network was not to wear black, white, or red. As for makeup, no one had any information at all. So she scurried over to Elizabeth Arden's to ask if they could help. They knew nothing about television either, but outfitted her with a kit of makeup suitable for still photography which they hoped would work. When she got to Philadelphia and the two conventions, she found that not only did she have to do her own makeup and interview the likes of Helen Gahagan Douglas and Mrs. Harold Stassen, but she found she was expected to do their makeup too, and she did.

One positive result of Frederick's interviews was that after the conventions she was finally offered a contract, and thus became the first newswoman to work full time, on staff, for a U.S. television network. She had a distinguished career from that day forward, joining NBC in 1953, and ending the network association with compulsory retirement in 1975. She did not stop working, however, and continued to report from the UN for National Public Radio. Her well-modulated tones and serious mien set the standard for women news broadcasters, and she was the only role model for people like me.

Frederick was one of the few correspondents to survive in broadcasting after World War II. One who didn't was Elizabeth Bemis. CBS News correspondent Douglas Edwards remembers that she came to New York from Denver in 1943.[11] CBS chairman William Paley had heard her on the air and instructed news chief Paul White to hire her. Bemis wrote and broadcast a late afternoon radio newscast, but was later fired for reasons no one can recall. In 1938 newspaperwoman Dorothy Thompson broadcast on NBC as a political commentator while continuing to write for magazines and newspapers. She didn't stay with broadcasting either.

A few women broke through the voice prohibition and did something resembling serious work on the radio. Mary Margaret McBride was the first woman talk-show host, or interviewer of any substance. Before that she was a newspaper reporter and free-lancer for magazines, but the Depression made those jobs scarce. She began broadcasting on WOR in New York in 1934, after winning an audition for a program called "The Martha Deane Show." Whoever got the job would be known as Martha Deane. McBride took on that fictitious identity, and began doing daily interviews with guests ranging from authors to local characters to heads of state. She later moved to NBC, using her own name, and remained there until her retirement in 1954. "The Martha Deane Show" continued on WOR for many years, with two other women later adopting that identity.[12]

The women who worked behind the scenes during the war and then continued afterwards to build their careers fared a bit better. They did not have to fight the prejudice against the female voice, and since female expectations of success were limited, the women were grateful for being hired at any level. They were oblivious to discrimination, which was not apparent during the war because of the absence of men. That absence was also the reason for the job openings.

Shirley Lubowitz, later Wershba, came aboard at CBS in 1944 as a desk assistant and gradually phased into a full-time newswriting job. She recalls that Beth Zimmerschied and another new hiree, Alice Weel, were alumnae of the Columbia University Graduate School of Journalism when there were few women students. Weel wrote, along with Charles Kuralt, for the nightly Douglas Edwards radio newscast, and later for the television version. Weel became one of television's first women news producers, but her life was cut short by cancer.

Ruth Ashton was another woman who benefited from the absence of men during World War II. She too walked right into a CBS job from Columbia and was hired as a writer for Bob Trout, who did a daily fifteen-minute afternoon radio news broadcast. She produced specials, and also did science reporting for Ed Murrow when he returned from London. In 1948 when she moved into television, she was one of only a handful of women in the business. While male producers of special material were allowed to voice their own reports, she had to use an announcer. The voice prejudice had transferred from radio to the new medium of television. By 1951, Ashton had married and moved to Los Angeles. A daring news director allowed her to appear on local news, doing a segment called the "Woman's Angle." There she was not only heard but seen. A year later, she moved back to radio, figuring it would be easier to raise her daughter with the more flexible and less visible demands of the medium. She continued to work, and added a second daughter to the family. Ashton recalls that in the fifties, Pauline Frederick was the only other woman news broadcaster that she knew of. By 1966 Ashton returned to television, where she continues to report on KCBS-TV. She has survived, she believes, because of her credibility and familiarity to West Coast viewers. The younger women who come along as anchors "seem

to wash out in their forties," not by their own choice. "Age, unde-
niably, is a problem," she says, adding that, "the biggest gap however
is in management, where men make policy and where few women
have been admitted."[13]

Another woman who moved out of the writers' ranks during
that period was Mary Laing, a writer and associate producer at ABC
News for John Daly's early evening fifteen-minute television newscast.
She had come up through United Press International, eventually going
into television news and then documentaries. She later moved to
Chicago, where she continued in independent production.

Shirley Lubowitz, who was working at CBS News, married colleague Joseph Wershba in 1948 and they moved to Washington. By
then, the men had come back from the war, and women were less
welcome in newsrooms. Wershba wanted a second career, as she calls
it, of motherhood, and she spent eleven years raising two children.
The Wershbas moved back to New York, and by 1962 she returned
to work as a writer for a thrice-daily, five-minute show called "Dimensions of a Woman's World," with Betty Furness. The advantage,
Wershba said, was that she could do most of the writing at home, and
the part-time arrangement let her phase back into full-time work.[14]
For four of her six years at ABC News, she was a writer on the daily
TV program "News with the Woman's Touch." She later worked for
the "MacNeil/Lehrer Report" on Public Television, and wound up
at CBS News once again in 1981, remaining there until her retirement
in 1987. Shirley Wershba believes that women had self-limiting am-
bitions back in the forties. Their expectations were low because no
one ever encouraged them to think otherwise. She feels the future
looks better for women now because the entry-level jobs are open to
them. The women's movement, in her view, denigrated women who
stayed home to raise families. She hopes that the future will bring
more genuine, guilt-free choices for women.

Betty Furness is still on the air in the 1980s, having successfully
managed several careers as actress, commercial spokeswoman, government consumer expert, and back again to broadcasting. A former
stage actress, in 1949 she became the TV spokeswoman for Westinghouse appliances. Her fame escalated during coverage of the 1952
presidential conventions when she was seen constantly opening and
closing refrigerator doors.[15] She also hosted a number of local New
York TV shows as well as radio programs such as "Ask Betty Furness"
and "Dimensions of a Woman's World." An active Democrat, she was
appointed by President Lyndon Johnson in 1967 to be his special
assistant for consumer affairs. In 1970, she became head of New York

State's Consumer Protection Board. She resigned in 1971 to join WNBC-TV in New York as their consumer reporter, and is an occasional contributor to the "Today" show. In her seventies, her authority is undiminished, and the rules which some feel require a youthful image have been waived by management in her case. But her career path, like that of celebrity interviewer Barbara Walters, cannot serve as a model for others, because of its uniqueness. The special qualities of Furness and Walters have extended their careers. Neither is a conventional newswoman. Nevertheless the survival of Walters, in her fifties, gives CBS News "60 Minutes" correspondent Diane Sawyer, in her early forties, some confidence about the future. Sawyer's hopes, she says, "are based on part on Barbara and what she's doing, but we all know she's a special case. She does it by proving herself again and again and again, proving her invaluability. . . ."[16]

One would think that today the public accepts women's voices and that the old prejudice has been laid to rest. In 1986 the Screen Actor's Guild commissioned a study to rebuke that prejudice still held by advertising agencies who often prefer men to women in voiceovers (the off-camera voice in commercials). The study, conducted by McCollum/Spielman, found that "it makes absolutely no difference whether a male or female voice is used as a commercial voice-over."[17] In fact, the data indicated that "women are more effective presenters."[18] Female reporters' voices are now accepted, and female anchors' voices are accepted on local television news. It is still being debated whether a woman's voice could hold the nation's attention in the anchor position on the main network news broadcasts.

## Notes

1. Dorothy Fuldheim did radio commentaries and later became a fixture on Cleveland television, broadcasting well into her nineties until she suffered strokes in 1984 and 1986.
2. Ann Sperber, *Murrow: His Life and Times* (New York: Freundlich, 1986), p. 116.
3. Ibid., p. 131.
4. Ibid., p. 132.
5. Ibid., p. 142.
6. David H. Hosley, *As Good as Any: Foreign Correspondence on American Radio 1930–1940* (Westport, Conn.: Greenwood Press), pp. 117, 118.
7. Ibid., p. 103.
8. Ibid.
9. Interview with Pauline Frederick (April 1979, and 12 June 1987). All

the quotes and other information from Ms. Frederick in this chapter were taken from these interviews.

10. Sperber, p. 177.
11. Interview with Douglas Edwards (7 November 1986).
12. Marion Marzolf, *Up from the Footnote: A History of Women Journalists* (New York: Hastings House, 1977), p. 125. The following women used the Martha Deane name: Mary Margaret McBride (1934–40), Bessie Beattie (1940), and Marian Taylor (1941–73).
13. Interview with Ruth Ashton (15 April 1987).
14. Interview with Shirley Wershba (4 November 1986). All quotes and information from Ms. Wershba in this chapter were taken from this interview.
15. Barbara Matusow, *The Evening Stars* (Boston: Houghton Mifflin, 1983), p. 65.
16. Interview with Diane Sawyer (15 January 1987).
17. Screen Actor's Guild, press release: "A Woman's Voice Sells as Well as a Man's on TV, Screen Actor's Guild Study Shows" (16 September 1986).
18. McCollum/Speilman & Company, Inc., "Topline," vol. 4, no. 4 (February 1986). This study was conducted by recording two commercials with both female and male voice-overs. The test audience, composed of males and females, was then asked to select a brand for inclusion in a prize market basket. Eleven percent responded to the male voice and 12 percent responded to the female voice for the Listerine product. Forty-two percent responded to the male voice and 46 percent responded to the female voice in the Nestle Morsels commercial. This study also found that the respondents were not very much aware whether the voice was male or female. The study implies that the voice could readily be female rather than the customary male voice.

# 2

## Marlene Sanders:
## The Early Years

When I was a teenager, a career in broadcasting meant being an actress on a popular radio soap opera or in a nighttime drama. Women sang, sold products, and were entertainers, not serious news correspondents. In the 1940s, young women's expectations were clear. We were supposed to do well in school, date, and go to college if the family could afford it (they usually found a way for the boys, but it was problematic for girls). After college we were expected to get married, possibly with a year or so in between when we worked at something. For people like me, whose family was a struggling middle-class one, it was also considered a good idea to learn something that, as the phrase went, you could "fall back on," something like teaching, or nursing, just in case you didn't marry. Or if you did marry you would have "pocket money," something extra, and you could survive if you were left widowed or divorced.

As a youngster I became involved in children's theater. Later I worked in community and semiprofessional theater groups in Cleveland. By high school, I was determined to become a great actress, a goal not taken seriously by those around me. It was not viewed as realistic, but it looked a lot more exciting to me than teaching or nursing, which didn't interest me at all.

At the same time, I was a good student, and, through the influence of one teacher, became interested in politics, unusual for either young men or women in the late 1940s. At seventeen, I entered Ohio State University, the only institution my family could afford. Unfortunately my college career was cut short by a lack of funds. Two years of regional theater work followed. By the age of twenty-one, I was uncertain about what to do next, succumbed to social pressures, and married a longtime boyfriend. We moved to New York. There, he enrolled at Columbia University's Teachers College to pursue a Ph.D. in clinical psychology. I determined to make my way to Broadway. It took me two years to realize it was the wrong professional choice, and that my marriage was also a mistake. At twenty-four I had to make a fresh start.

I found a summer job as assistant to the producers at the Theatre-by-the-Sea, in Matunuck, Rhode Island. It turned out to be the route to a job in television.

The Theatre-by-the-Sea was more than simply a summer theater. It also had an inn, restaurant, and bar. The theater's two producers needed an all-around assistant. My experience in the Cleveland Playhouse and also at Hedgerow Repertory Theatre near Philadelphia must have convinced them that I could do the job, and, in fact, I could.

The theater was a tryout spot for shows whose producers hoped would eventually make it to Broadway. One of those hopeful producers was Mike Wallace, a former actor who had been a radio interviewer in Chicago. The play he planned to shepherd to Broadway didn't make it under his auspices, but he had other plans as well. In the fall he was to anchor a news broadcast at a local New York television station. His producer, Ted Yates, Jr., was putting together a staff. It was going to be the first attempt at doing a television news broadcast for all concerned. On that score, I qualified, and in the fall I found myself working as a production assistant on "Mike Wallace and the News," scheduled for nightly broadcast at 6:00 and 11:00 P.M. on Channel 5, WABD-TV, in New York. My television career was launched in the fall of 1955, with a weekly salary of $75 plus overtime.

While it is now common for local stations to do their own news broadcasts, showing a nice profit in the process, that was not the case in the mid-fifties. In New York, WCBS had the only local news at 6:00 P.M., and it was billed in the *New York Times* as "News; Feature; Sports," competing with "Wild Bill Hickok," "Rocky Jones, Space Ranger," "Gene Autry," and "The Merry Mailman." At 6:45, WNBC billed "weather" before "news," and at 6:55, WABC simply had "weather." The CBS and ABC networks provided news at 7:15, and NBC came on with news at 7:45.[1] By 1957, news was carried by most stations, somewhere between 6:00 and 7:30 P.M., and again at 11:00, but no distinction was made between local and network sources in the newspaper listing.[2] The local stations that carried the networks' fifteen minutes of news considered it as public service programming. No one ever thought news would make money. The network news helped local affiliated stations satisfy the Federal Communications Commission's demand for the "presentation of programs on public issues."[3] In the late 1940s the FCC had made the point that a licensee must devote a reasonable amount of time to the discussion of issues, and that the public must hear a variety of points of view (this was known as the Fairness Doctrine) in order to have their licenses renewed every three years.[4] The three-year review process was known as ascertainment. Prior to the deregulation of television by the FCC in 1984, the commission's ascertainment policy also required broadcasters to gather information on the programming needs and interests of their service areas and to utilize this information as a basis of programming decisions.[5] In the 1970s the ascertainment requirement became a vehicle for women's groups to put pressure on stations and networks to improve their treatment of women in programming and in their hiring policies.

In 1955, television news was just beginning to develop a sense of what kind of content and structure would work on an evening newscast. Huntley and Brinkley had not yet teamed up. Cronkite was just leaving his job as host of the "Morning Show" to become the staff narrator of CBS News and Public Affairs and the host of "You Are There," "The Twentieth Century," and "Eyewitness to History."[6] The evening news at NBC, begun in 1949, was called "Camel News Caravan," with John Cameron Swayze. CBS News had been broadcasting an evening news program with Douglas Edwards since 1948. ABC was the last to start evening newscasts when in 1953 John Daly took his place in front of the cameras. None of these programs used much original film footage except for the pictures supplied by newsreel companies. Those usually showed bathing beauties, children, and dogs. There was no such thing as a correspondent. When a network did send out its own film crew to cover a story, the cameraman made the decisions about what to photograph and what the event was about. NBC didn't use reporters or producers on all stories until the 1970s. CBS differed in that when it started using its own film crews it did not rely only on the cameraman; CBS News would organize a "contact man," someone local to the area or someone who knew something about the story to meet the crew and then gather the facts.[7] The serious newsgathering was being done by the documentary units, like Murrow's "See It Now," which had huge staffs and many film crews to produce their programs. For the most part, the stories carried by the evening news programs in the mid-1950s were brief reports of breaking news, filmed human interest stories, and a few interviews. Although the concept of "anchorman" had emerged at the 1952 presidential conventions when the networks needed a strong person in the booth, that idea had not yet crept into daily news coverage. The need for personalities and stars on the evening news was not yet apparent.

At Channel 5, then WABD, named after Allen B. DuMont, its founder, there had never been a live, local news broadcast. Until 1955, an announcer read the news, voice over slides, from the booth. Our new show, "Mike Wallace and the News," had a small staff. It absorbed the station's one-man news staff, writer Bill Kobin, as one of the two newswriters, the other being Sandy Socolow. (Socolow went on to produce the "CBS Evening News with Walter Cronkite" and "60 Minutes" stories. Kobin became a news and documentary producer, and then a public broadcasting executive.) Producer Ted Yates, Jr., had previously worked at NBC for an interview show called "Tex and Jinx" (featuring Tex McCrary and Jinx Falkenburg, a former tennis star).

The station management wanted to be innovative, and had hired Mike Wallace to read the news at 6:00 P.M. and 11:00 P.M. for fifteen minutes, five nights a week. They had a sponsor lined up, Bond Clothes, and Wallace was required to wear a Bond suit on the air for the broadcast. Local news was then even lower budget and more primitive than the network evening news programs.

We began from scratch. The newsroom was tiny and bare, aside from the wire machines and the sports ticker that noisily spewed perforated tapes with instantaneous horse race results, and play-by-play reports on baseball, received through Western Union. We had to learn how to decipher the tapes and then transfer the sports scores to a "spaghetti board," a black felt board with ridges where the results were spelled out with plastic letters and numbers. We also had to create files of news pictures, the large 8″ × 10″ photographs of major public figures and events, and the smaller 3″ × 5″ pictures called telops. The large pictures were placed on an easel in the studio and flipped by a stagehand, and the telops were taken to master control and projected full screen from there. We had no film crew except the use of a free-lance cameraman from time to time. News film was supplied by Telenews, a firm which also provided footage to ABC. Occasionally, Yates would send me out with our one-man crew to cover an event Telenews was ignoring, such as a borough president holding a news conference on a local issue. No one knew exactly how to cover an event, and the first few times we did not do a very good job. Footage was black and white, and shot and edited in negative. During the film editing you could see the negative images in a viewer, but they were always hard to decipher. Even running the film on a projector didn't help much. It never reversed polarity, that is, was developed like a photograph, until it was actually projected live, during the broadcast. Even seven years later when I had my own news broadcast on ABC, we were still shooting in negative and shots remained something of a mystery until the program aired.

In the early days of the Bond News, the editing was simple. Yates would send me rushing up several floors to our film editor, with instructions to provide fifteen or thirty seconds of a fire or a governor's arrival or a departure, or whatever the story was. Most footage was silent since sound required another technician; it wasn't hard to cut, and we learned quickly. At the time we added background music from a music library, and I soon developed a list of favorite pieces, some for fashion shows, some for fires, some that was ominous and handy for approaching tornadoes or other disasters. Years later, the use of music behind news film was rejected on journalistic grounds, but in the early days, there was no set standard. As the industry matured, so did concerns over authenticity. Music or sound effects of any kind were rejected unless the accompanying sounds were actually present when the footage was shot. Today, the ambient or natural sound is an important part of the story and the sound of sirens and interviews with firefighters and victims are readily available. Good taste is optional.

In the course of putting together a fifteen-minute broadcast in the 1950s, the production assistant separated the pages of the script and found the proper visuals, either telops or 8″ × 10″ photographs. One copy of the script went to the teleprompter operator, whose large-size typewriter made an ear-splitting racket. Mike Wallace shared the office with the teleprompter, and the noise usually drove him into the adjacent newsroom at the same time he was changing into his Bond suit. He often reviewed the script half-dressed, and suffered the jokes about his legs good naturedly. Meanwhile, slides, telops, photos, and script were rushed into the studio, and with luck, the pictures were placed on the easel in the proper order. One luckless Thanksgiving, Wallace referred to "Governor Rockefeller, seen here," while the photo that came up was of a turkey. The words "seen here" were banned from future scripts, and a new system of checking the photos began.

We worked hard but enjoyed the family atmosphere. The station itself was small, friendly, and personal. Our entire staff totalled six.

We knew the names of the executives, along with the technicians and stage crew.

As I approached my first anniversary in television, things were beginning to change in our little shop. Wallace and Yates had begun planning a major effort, outside of news. With the help and support of the station manager, Ted Cott, they began putting together a late-night interview program to be called "Night Beat." It went on the air in the fall of 1956, and soon became a hit. Scheduled at 11:00 P.M., it was up against ten- and fifteen-minute news reports on the networks, the late movie, and "The Jack Paar Show." The only other lengthy interview program by a newsman was Edward R. Murrow's "Person to Person" in which the CBS cameras went into people's homes for conversations which were often limited to celebrities' personal lives and tours of their homes. "Night Beat" had none of "Person to Person's" production values but it caused quite a sensation because of its content, and, for the time, broke new ground. Until then, aside from documentary programs like "See It Now" and the Sunday programs like "Face the Nation," interviews on radio and television were tepid exchanges, mostly used to plug a forthcoming book, play, or movie. They rarely revealed anything of substance, and the interviewees were almost never challenged. "Night Beat" evolved into something quite different, and in time developed its own format: the studio was in total darkness except for Wallace facing his subject. A *New York Times* reporter noted that it was one of the few instances when an interviewer looked at an interviewee on television with the camera over his shoulder.[8] The television critic of the *Cleveland Press,* one of the many visiting critics to examine the program, described it this way in his column of 22 February 1957:

> From his uncomfortable stool, Mike Wallace has forced the TV industry to sit up and take notice. Without the fancy trimmings of "Person to Person," Wallace conducts an interview that packs immense punch, mixed with almost patronizing sincerity. Wallace breaks the rules, but with a flair that TV recognizes and applauds. There is no production—just a searching camera that sneaks up to its subject while Wallace grills him. The camera gets so close that often foreheads are cropped. . . . Wallace courageously marches where not even Ed Murrow dared to tread. He is much more personal and, thus, more exciting than "Meet the Press" reporters. Celebrities want to be on his program because it is a challenge to them because Wallace has attracted so much attention among the power elite.

Guests frequently were lulled into the feeling that they were alone with Wallace. It was late, we broadcast live from 11:00 P.M. to midnight, and people often let down their guard. The guests were thoroughly researched and interviewed in advance by a writer but they never knew for certain what they would be facing.

By the time "Night Beat" went on, I had been promoted to associate producer and that mainly meant booking guests. Both Yates and Wallace would have specific people in mind and as the program began to catch on, I had to fend off press agents and publishers, as well as go after our own choices. I became fearless on the phone. No challenge was too great, though I had many failures. Yates always wanted General Douglas MacArthur, and he'd simply say, "Get General MacArthur." I'd shrug and make the call. I never did get through to him, but we had most of the reigning show business stars, leading writers, social critics, and political figures, and a range of people from the sports world. Among those who appeared were writer Erskine Caldwell; the chronicler of the Beat Generation, Jack Kerouac; hat designer Mr. John; poet William Carlos Williams; and black historian W. E. B. DuBois. It wasn't so much that they were all celebrities, but it was the way they were handled, the subjects raised, and the probing style of the interviews that was so compelling.

In those days, before school integration was the law, civil rights issues were exotic and interracial "mixing" was a daring subject. Psychoanalysis was another area of endless fascination. Actress Elaine Stritch actually talked about her analysis and we were spellbound. Television was just coming out of the blacklisting scare, when people were accused of being communists without proof of the connection. The accusations caused many of the brightest actors, writers, and directors in the television and film industry to be fired. Television was particularly vulnerable since there was so much pressure on the industry by many of the sponsors who paid for the shows. If the sponsors exerted pressure, the executives cancelled guests and contracts. Of particular concern was a booklet called "Red Channels" that listed television personalities with questionable allegiances; included were people like Leonard Bernstein and William L. Shirer.[9] Don Hollenbeck, a television commentator and newscaster for CBS, and a good friend of Edward R. Murrow, became a victim. He was harassed by a newspaper columnist for the Hearst *Journal-American* after his salute to Murrow's McCarthy show, to the point that he committed suicide.[10] We invited onto "Night Beat" a number of those who were involved in the blacklisting as well as those whose livelihoods had been hurt by it, people like Will Rogers, Jr., who was a talk-show host; Herbert Biberman, a screen writer; and Abe Burrows, a Broadway show composer.

One of the things that used to amaze guests was the old quotes that Wallace and his successor, John Wingate, would come up with before the days of the computer. "We do a lot of research in newspaper files and elsewhere and try to find key ideas," Wallace told a *New York Times* reporter. "The guest is not rehearsed however. Occasionally if he seems a bit leery about being questioned I give him an idea of how the interview will begin."[11]

The Channel 5 library was nonexistent and the source for the gold mine of old quotes, some ten to twenty years old, was an accidental development. Shortly after the program began on 9 October 1956, Bill Lang appeared on the scene. He and his wife lived in upstate New York with several children and a garage full of old clippings filed by personality and subject. Lang had been a radio announcer for years, and to fill the hours of boredom he began to collect newspapers from all over the country. He started files never knowing just what he'd do with the material, but he found a home with us. We had eight guests a week, two a night, Monday through Thursday, and as they were scheduled, I'd call to tell the Langs who they were. If it were someone like Harry Anslinger, then the highest-ranking federal drug enforcer, Lang would look in his "drug" file, and all sorts of material would turn up. Writers who worked on the interviews went through his files, talked to the guests in advance, and constructed the interviews. Yates and Wallace worked over those scripts, and questions were carefully planned and written. Expected responses were indicated in the script so that Wallace was prepared with a comeback. No one could feign shock and surprise better, or parry his prey. What later came to be known as his "60 Minutes" style began back then.

The large calendar with the bookings was tacked up over my desk. Wallace would peer in, glare at the names in mock anger, and demand to know what we would talk to so-and-so about. As the main booker, I had to be able to tell him on the spot.

As the year wore on, I was able to take on some writing chores myself, and did quite a number of scripts in what was to become known as the confrontational, carefully researched "Night Beat" style. Again, I learned by listening, serving essentially in an apprenticeship system that worked for all of us.

Most of my colleagues were men, although we did have Ruth Cordes, another veteran of that summer in Matunuck, Rhode Island, as second production assistant. She never managed to advance past that position and disappeared within the year.

My only other female colleague in the early months of the program was Rita Quinn, who came on board as Wallace's secretary when his success with "Night Beat" provoked piles of mail. The woman question was not an issue in those days. It wasn't discussed, because it never occurred to anyone. We were a small, self-contained group of overworked but enthusiastic young people, and all things seemed possible, even to me. My models were the men around me, and I saw no reason why I couldn't do what they did, eventually. There wasn't much competition. Job seekers were not beating down the doors. No one knew the business, and journalism schools had not begun to specialize in broadcasting. On-the-job training was all there was, and those of us who got there early learned by paying close attention to those script conferences with the writers.

During one thirteen-week period, I was given the opportunity to write on my own for a new show. Channel 5, still innovative in its programs during that time, decided to do a sports interview program one night a week, hosted by tennis star Gussie Moran (who gained notoriety for wearing lace tennis panties) and called "Gussie's Corner." Moran was good-natured, but had never done this sort of thing before. Whatever she was given, she read, no questions asked. I decided to use the "Night Beat" technique on the sports figures we booked, who ranged from fight managers to ball players to boxers. The ubiquitous Bill Lang file folders were an invaluable source of material on some has-been fighter or current sports figure.

One of those interviews created a stir. Not unpredictably it was with the young, already volatile Billy Martin. The introduction went like this: "Hello sports fans. This is Gussie Moran. The man you're going to meet tonight has been called a fresh young punk, a gutsy kid, a saucy little urchin: bellicose, boisterous and brash, generally, with an affectionate tone of voice. He's Billy Martin, formerly of the New York Yankees, now of the Kansas City Athletics." Things went along smoothly, until mid-way in the interview when Martin reacted angrily to one of my "Night Beat"-style questions. Moran, unfortunately, couldn't handle his response, but I was tickled—and also anonymous, safely behind the scenes. The incident was related the next day, 31 July 1957, in the sports page of the *New York Post*. An article headed "Billy the Kid Unloads at Bat, But Not On TV" read in part: "Martin was steaming at what he called the 'Mike Wallace Interview' he was subjected to by Gussie Moran on TV the other night. 'Didn't tell her a thing,' he said, 'but she sure asked some loaded questions. If I knew it was gonna be that kind of program, I wouldn't have gone on. . . .' Martin says Gussie called him an urchin. 'So I said to her, "what's an urchin?" and she didn't know either.' "

That show lasted for only thirteen weeks, but it gave me a chance to improve my writing skills.

"Night Beat" was still the main event. Wallace opened the show with a look at "tomorrow morning's headlines," and I began writing the capsule news summaries for him. The guests were escorted to makeup and then into the studio. Yates stayed in the control room, perfecting with the various directors the use of the tight closeup, which became the show's trademark. I sat in the studio with the apprehensive second guest.

Soon after we began, in the late fall of 1956, we added another dimension — live theater criticism by Byron Bentley. Bentley had been editor of the now defunct *Theatre Arts Monthly*, a magazine I had waited for eagerly each month in the mail back in Cleveland. He would appear as Mr. First Nighter, in full tuxedo, and do his opening night reviews near our midnight signoff.

Just after midnight, I'd make a dash for the crosstown bus and head for home. By 10:00 A.M. the next morning, I was back on the job, and glad to be there. Hours meant nothing to us then. We had a hit on our hands. We were the subject of countless articles, and the phones never stopped ringing. Life outside of work went on for some of the staff. Ted Yates had married Mary Olberg, a former model who had worked with him at "Tex and Jinx" on NBC.

Yates was relaxed and good natured, rarely lost his temper, and was a true original. Wallace owed a great deal of his early success to Yates's vision and judgment. Their partnership continued for several years until Yates went to NBC News to produce "David Brinkley's Journal" and some outstanding, innovative historical documentaries. Years later, in 1967, while filming the Six Day War in Jerusalem, Yates was killed by a sniper. He was thirty-five years old. His wife was left to raise their three boys by herself. For many years afterwards she co-produced "Face the Nation" for CBS News. (In July 1986, Mary Yates and Mike Wallace — who was by then divorced — married, an event that touched all of us who knew their history.)

In the spring of 1957, Wallace and Ted Yates were considering offers to move on. They finally accepted one from ABC to do what would be called "The Mike Wallace Interview," an effort to recreate "Night Beat" during one half hour, once a week, in prime time on the network. The temptation to leave the local scene and make it big financially and by reputation was irresistible. But there would be much more at stake. Each interview would have to succeed. We, on the other hand, with eight a week, two a night, Monday through Thursday, could afford to fail once in a while. Loyal viewers would stay with us until the next interview, or the next night. Star writer Al Ramrus was going to leave, along with Wallace and Yates. Yates had asked me to come along, but I wondered how much there would be to do on a weekly show.

As Yates began to spend more and more time in preparation for the move to the network, I had more and more responsibility for the show. A certain uneasiness had begun to come into our relationship. The experience with Yates was my first painful lesson in office politics. One has to learn how to deal with a superior, and how to assert one's growing experience and authority without overstepping. He wrote me a lengthy, perceptive note which I quote in full here, spelling errors included:

> Marlene:
>
> This regards you and I would like you to reflect on it before you make up your mind on where or what you are going to do.
>
> This business has a funny chemistry. People suddenly change. They grow into a different category. Their aims become higher. Their ambitions become more defined. They want to exercise their own talents their own way for themselves. This happens to everyone that's any good.
>
> This has happened to you. You have worked hard, learned a lot, gone up in this profession fast, and have out-developed the reference of a girl friday.
>
> At ABC I want a girl friday. I want someone who's ambition is to be a good, loyal, protective, hard working, pleasant girl friday. Who'll do all the discoordinate tasks that hinge to the job. I want someone who won't be offended, hurt, or resentful by doing the dirty work. The operation at ABC initially will be smaller, tighter, more disciplined. It is essential that we have a fresh, creative, happy atmosphere.
>
> Now I think you feel . . . and perhaps are right, that you are a graduate of the Girl Friday school. You've had a lot of fast milage, you've been an associate producer on an important show, you've coordinated a complicated operation, and are now ready to fly far on your own wings.
>
> DuMont wants you, and needs you. This is a good position to be in, and I am sure you can carry it far.
>
> As for me, until recently, I felt strongly that you and I had a rapor that was good, and that you could still stick on the rolley coaster no matter how rough and rocketing. But now I think your genes have changed to the extent that you are in it for yourself . . . and that you want to parley things the best possible way. This is understandable thinking. Its developing. Its happened to me, and to half a dozen people who've worked for me from Hank Wexler to Lennie Epstein.

Because of this . . . I don't think you will be happy or content with what ever comes along at ABC. And this is essentially what the deal will be. You will be my assistant and secretary. Your salary will be one hundred dollars a week. The show will be interview . . . it will be less hetic . . . day to day . . . but the stresses will be heavier, the consequences more devistating. What the future, there holds . . . no body knows.

If you are happy to go to ABC on these terms . . . or should I say enthusiastic . . . then come on. If you are not . . . then stick to your guns here . . . and see what you can build and sustain under your own impetus.

I am writing this to you Marlene because I want to level with you. I am, of course, deeply fond of you as a person, and respect your abilities professionally. If you follow your instincts you will be much happier and much more successful in the long run. If you take on something that is unappealing to you or rubs the wrong way . . . this just causes an infection, guaranteed to fester.

On the basis of this . . . think over what you want to do . . . hassle with the brass here . . . and let me know as soon as you can so planning can be set into motion re ABC.

I put this in writing, because there are less interruptions. If you want to talk about this more . . . let's talk.

Ted

He was right, of course. I stayed, and it was the right thing to do. Our friendship later resumed, but the uncomfortable manner of our professional separation was a troubling experience for me. I did learn that there can be only one person in charge of a broadcast, and that if that authority is challenged, there are likely to be unpleasant consequences. Unfortunately, this is something most people have to learn the hard way.

Another complicating factor was that there was no clear-cut career path in news. I knew I wanted to move ahead but had no idea where or by what route. It seemed clear that going with Yates and Wallace in a less demanding job than I then held would be a mistake, even though the idea of working at a network was intriguing. After they made their move I visited them several times at ABC News, located directly across Central Park from Channel 5. The series of connecting old buildings were in no way imposing, but ABC was a lot larger than WABD, and a little intimidating.

It seemed to me that when I left it would have to be for a promotion of some kind. Meanwhile, I would stay where I was and continue to work on "Night Beat," perhaps taking on even more responsibility. I had come a long way in two years and was eager for advancement. I thought I should have been considered as the new producer of "Night Beat," but that was unrealistic for several reasons. I was still relatively new in the business. Also, it was highly unlikely that a woman would be given that kind of responsibility. I did not have close contact with the station management; although they knew me, they did not know just how large my contribution to the show had been, and probably saw me as just another girl assistant. Women have a tendency to think that good work will automatically be rewarded. I was too inexperienced then to know that one has to be sure the right people know what you're doing; I didn't realize that self-promotion and office politics are part of the game.

Before Wallace departed in June 1957, on-air auditions for his successor were held from midnight to 12:30 A.M. A number of writers and broadcasters tried out, and it was finally decided that John Wingate would get the job. Wingate was a longtime radio newsman on WOR, N.Y. He did news and interviews, and, without sacrificing his duties at WOR, moved into the new job. Leonard Zweig, a former colleague of Yates, became producer. Zweig was an outsider who had to walk into an already established production unit. He was bright but nervous, and perhaps sensed some of the free-floating resentment. The man was subtly undermined by the staff's little comments of vague dissatisfaction which were passed along to the program director or station manager, and by hints dropped about others who could be carrying out his responsibilities better. Zweig left after several months in the job. Management named two people as coproducers of the show, writer Mort Silverstein and me. We made a good team, felt well satisfied with the arrangement, and worked together easily. Neither of us had years of experience, but our combined talents meshed well. We got raises and moved into a larger, shared office.

I was satisfied with the coproducer arrangement. Silverstein had a stronger writing background than I had, though I had developed considerable skill in writing the kinds of interviews we did. Both of us worked as editors of the other writers and did scripts ourselves as well; I still did most of the booking. We began the second phase of "Night Beat" with vigor. Something had gone out of it, though, with Wallace away. We felt it, but couldn't be sure if the viewers did. The program wasn't new anymore, but it had a devoted following.

It was my third year in television, the third year of working late into the night, four nights a week, and it was becoming a grind. I felt the need for more of a personal life. Silverstein and I decided to split the night shift, and alternate being there. It was a welcome change.

The show was still important to us, and John Wingate did remarkably well, but he had a hard act to follow. Wingate was bright, but eccentric. He tended to go off on tangents, discussing things not mentioned in the script, and he liked to talk about sex. That made us all nervous.

Over at ABC, Wallace was having only modest success. The weekly interview simply didn't have the same feel to it as eight a week. He had to have a blockbuster every time. He didn't, and his tenure there was short-lived. On our side of the park, there was no certainty either about the future of the broadcast, or our jobs. We were running out of guests as well as running out of steam.

For myself, however, one negotiation over a prospective guest had long-range consequences for my personal life. In January, conversations and correspondence ensued over the possibility of conductor Leopold Stokowski appearing as a guest. He was then conducting the Symphony of the Air, an orchestra made up of members of the disbanded NBC Orchestra. The administrative director proposed that we interview Stokowski to promote a concert. The interview, though scheduled, never took place because the conductor tuned in one night and didn't like what he saw. However, the writer assigned to the interview came back with some good news: He said I should meet the orchestra's manager, Jerome Toobin. We were all single and tried to keep a lookout for matchmaking possibilities.

Toobin had been a regular viewer of our program since its inception and had been seeing my name on the credits, picturing, he later told me, "one tough cookie, hatchet-faced, mean, bespectacled." Nevertheless, having been assured by a friend that that image wasn't entirely accurate, he invited me to an upcoming symphony concert at Carnegie Hall, music for Shakespeare as I recall. He undoubtedly had to paper the house, so there was plenty of room, something I learned much more about in the ensuing years.

Jerry had large dark eyes and dark hair flecked with grey. He was slim, nervous, high-strung, volatile. Music was his passion, books next. I think he liked me as much for my library as he did for anything else. We had a lot to talk about and hit it off immediately. He too had been married before, but divorced for eight years compared to my three. We began to see each other regularly. After a brief, intense courtship, a few months after we met, we decided to get married. I was ready now and felt confident it was the right move. I was twenty-eight, in love, and ready to take a chance.

There was no question that I would continue with my work. Neither of us saw any reason why I shouldn't. At that time there were no magazines discussing dual-career marriages and how to cope. It was still the fifties and the traditional women's magazines focused on hearth and home. I knew no other women at the time who had gone the route I was about to take. Either my career had made me flexible and adaptable to change, or I had picked one that suited those aspects of my character. Even then Jerry had great confidence in my abilities, and felt that my greatest achievements were in the future, somewhere. Throughout our long marriage, his confidence in my ability never waned. No one, he felt, appreciated me enough, paid me enough, or promoted me fast enough. He fumed over my setbacks and rejoiced in my good luck. He was obviously looking for a strong woman, and never resented my ambition. Possibly because of his involvement in the arts, he appreciated my earning power, modest as it was in the beginning. We pooled our incomes over the years, and he was never resentful when I began to earn more than he did or when my hours impinged on our personal life. My salary relieved the pressure on him, and his own interests occupied him when work kept me late or required travel, as it did later on.

Our short wedding ceremony was attended by our close relatives and a handful of colleagues. It was May 1958 and the women's movement was more than ten years in the future. The attitudes we shared about marriage were not spelled out, but were egalitarian in a way that we devised on our own.

When we first married, I had to decide what to do about my air credit. I tried "Marlene Sanders Toobin" on a slide, but it took up too much space on the screen and felt awkward to me. My professional identity, such as it was by then, was closely connected to the name I started with and I was reluctant to give it up, so without much ado, I simply stayed with it. Jerry didn't care and never lobbied one way or the other, saying that whatever was comfortable for me was all right with him.

Work continued as before, but the zip had gone out of the broadcast, somehow. There were high spots from time to time, but we all began to feel that after nearly two years and eight hundred guests, it was time to abandon the program. The station management concurred. In June 1958, after an hour-long interview with the controversial congressman Adam Clayton Powell, Wingate bid the staff and the viewers a farewell from "Night Beat." He returned full-time to radio, but never reaped any tangible long-term benefits from his brief celebrity.

By then, I had learned to pay attention to the management people, and had worked out my next assignment before the demise of "Night Beat." A successor interview program called "Probe" was begun, subject- rather than people-oriented, and it worked for a while. Then there was a daytime interview program in 1959 that I produced, with a relatively unknown TV personality named Monty Hall, who later became famous as host of "Let's Make a Deal." During that time we also acquired the extensive film library of a world traveler named Julien Bryan, and I subsequently used his material to do two series, one on the Soviet Union and the other on the Middle East.

Channel 5 was still innovative, but the DuMont network had faded away and the station was now part of Metromedia, becoming WNEW-TV. The commitment to news also began to fade, and departed along with the old management. Our small news staff began to drift away as well. After four years at the station, I was becoming anxious about the next move. In a business without stability, when programs come and go, chronic uncertainty about the future was, then as now, a given in the industry.

One of my last undertakings at Channel 5 was producing a thirteen-week series called "I Speak for Myself," with author and critic Marya Mannes. It was 1959, and while there were a few women radio and TV interviewers, they rarely dealt with serious issues, or the arts, and they themselves were not taken seriously. Mannes was something else. The format was very simple: Mannes and a guest, usually a literary figure, engaged in intelligent conversation for a half hour on Sunday nights. This was conversation, not the standard interview, and the interviewer was not only female, but middle-aged.

An article about the program at the time described Mannes as "blond, junoesque and poised," all of which was true. She was also, by then, in her fifties. She considered that almost as much an obstacle to success in television as being female. At this writing, the fate of older newswomen on the air is an unresolved issue. The male authority figures who deliver the news can be grey, aging, with character lines etched into their faces. We don't know whether women will be allowed to look that way. Back in 1959, however, our main goal was to provide intelligence on the small screen. Mannes commented, "I've been criticizing television for a long time for not having enough strong adult talk. And now that I've committed myself and tried to do something about it, I have no regrets. I have always wanted to communicate with people who are starved for something to stimulate and amuse them." The program went well, and it was easy work compared to what I'd been doing in the past.

Mannes's guests, most of whom she suggested, included Virgilia Peterson, an author and participant in the long-since departed program "The Author Meets the Critics," and author-lecturer John Mason Brown, among others. In the twelve weeks that the program aired, Mannes fulfilled one of her stated goals of "proving to people that you can have a mind and a sense of humor all together, and that women do exist from the neck up."

Marya Mannes was probably the first person who served as something of a role model for me, although her personal life had not worked out well. She had been married first to stage designer Jo Mielziner, then to an artist, and at the time we met, she was in the process of being divorced from an aircraft company executive. Her professional success, too, had been erratic. She had been on the staff of the now defunct *Reporter Magazine,* and had written essays, poetry, and one best-seller, *Message from a Stranger.* For a while she was a sculptor. When she took on the television series, she was hard-pressed for money. I admired her intelligence and liked her personally, but could not help but observe that neither her career nor her personal life had worked very well, and she had no sure way to survive financially.

During the run of the Mannes series, I took on an additional chore, which, coincidentally, proved useful in the future. By now, WNEW-TV, as part of Metromedia, was the sister station of WNEW Radio, and we began to work together. I packaged something called "Newsreel 5," a weekly fifteen-minute review of the major news stories of the week, using film. We also did a series of joint newscasts read by an announcer from the TV announce booth several times a day; the copy was written by the staff at radio, a somewhat awkward arrangement. We coproduced a couple of public affairs shows for the television station, on which WNEW News executive Lee Hanna and I worked together.

I was by then the sole news employee left at Channel 5, which had abandoned any attempt at a successor broadcast to "Mike Wallace and the News." There were no other interesting projects in the works because as the station management changed, a less imaginative group took charge.

I was also concerned about my next job for another reason; I was pregnant. By then, I was twenty-nine years old, and had decided I wanted a child. Jerry did not disagree, although he already had a daughter from his previous marriage who lived in Philadelphia. Motherhood had never been one of my specific goals, despite societal pressure during the fifties. I had been too career-oriented to give the matter much thought, and after my divorce not even remarriage was high on my agenda. There was no talk then about biological clocks, but I somehow felt the timing might be right. I had no preset idea about how we would cope with a child, or where I would be working next; once again I felt we would find a way. Just as I had found no other two-career couples when we decided to marry, I found no other working mothers among our friends. Most of my colleagues were men. The few women I ran into were single, and among the young married couples we knew, the women did not work after their babies were born. I had no intention of doing that. Yet it was not clear that WNEW-TV would continue original local news programming. The place had become typical of many local, independent stations that, before the advent of cable and super stations, preferred to rerun old network programs rather than bother with the risky, more expensive business of in-house produced shows.

When I became pregnant, I decided that since my child was due in late May, I would quit and look for something else in the fall. Two weeks later, on 21 May 1960, Jeffrey Ross Toobin was born. We were thrilled, and I was overwhelmed by an awesome sense of responsibility.

For the first time since leaving Ohio State, I was not working. My son proved to be a healthy, cheerful baby, and easy to care for. There seemed to be more hours than I could fill and I became restless and concerned about getting back to work. A baby, though, is compelling and my instinct was that the longer I waited, the more difficult it would be for me to leave him. I also needed an income to pay for a housekeeper, since Jerry's salary from the symphony was modest, and sometimes nonexistent. In the middle of the summer, I found part-time work and a housekeeper who was also willing to work part-time until I found a real job.

By January 1961, Dick Pack of Westinghouse Broadcasting hired me to work on a new project. We moved to a larger apartment, and added a male Columbia University student to the household. He covered the post-dinner hours, after my housekeeper went home, in exchange for room and board. I thought it would be a good idea to have an additional male presence in the house for my son's benefit. Everything was going smoothly. Discussion of "having it all," marriage, family, and career, was unheard of then, but somehow it was all working out for me.

Other women have since told me that they were harshly criticized in those days for going to work, leaving a small child at home, when they "didn't have to." I never ran into that. For one thing, I was starting a new job and knew only a few of the people there. Dick Pack didn't seem shocked at a new mother wanting to return to work. I never hid the fact that I had a baby at home, and the group of largely single people I worked with didn't seem to care one way or the other, nor did the married men. Their wives may have been disapproving but I almost never saw them, and we soon became so busy that as long as people showed up and managed to pull together a nightly ninety-minute show, no one cared what was going on at anybody's home.

The late-night syndicated program was put together by WBC Productions. It was one of the early attempts by independent station groups like Westinghouse Broadcasting to do their own programming, instead of relying exclusively on syndicated shows or the slim output of original programs produced by their owned stations. The company felt that by producing something unique, their stations would gain distinction and, they hoped, increased numbers of viewers. Mike Wallace, it turned out, was available. His ABC series had lasted about a year and he had then gone on to other projects, including doing the "Biography" series for David Wolper. Wallace was soon hired. The five Westinghouse-owned stations would carry the show, dubbed "PM EAST: PM WEST." It was hoped that syndicating it to other stations would make the project profitable.

Wallace was to share his duties with a so-called feature editor, a former beauty contest winner, Canadian Joyce Davidson. She had her own interview program for the Canadian Broadcasting Corporation called "Tabloid" and had recently achieved local notoriety by making unflattering on-air remarks about the Queen. In the Commonwealth, that was considered quite daring.

A promotional brochure described the program, scheduled to air from 11:15 P.M. to 12:35 A.M., as designed for "nighttime people." It was "to search out the new club acts on both coasts, budding musicians, stars on the rise, up beat comers and off beat characters." It was taped at 8:00 P.M. in New York and aired unedited with Wallace and Davidson in the east, and then switched to *San Francisco Chronicle* columnist Terrance O'Flaherty for the last segment, "PM WEST." The West Coast half hour was short-lived.

I was one of the six producer-writers, the only woman among them. The rest of the staff consisted of the executive producer, an overall show producer, a talent booker, production assistants, editors, and a fellow whose sole job it was to corral a studio audience.

For the first time, I joined a union, the Writers Guild of America, East, and I was making a good deal more money than I had been earning at Channel 5.

In the "PM EAST" adventure, I was required to work late only during the one show a week that I produced. Each producer-writer was responsible for the filming, researching, writing, and structuring of his or her weekly program. It seemed like a tremendous task at first, but we gradually got into the swing of things. There were, nevertheless, signs of trouble from the very beginning. Mike Wallace and Joyce Davidson took an instant dislike to each other. It soon became apparent to us, the producers, that setting up joint efforts between them would lead to sniping, tension, and a generally unpleasant atmosphere. Mike accepted the pre-show preparation material, going over the research and questions with us carefully. The interviews were not in the "Night Beat" style, but were still prepared and were provocative when appropriate. Joyce Davidson, however, seemed uninterested in the material, and barely talked to any of us, complicating things further. It seemed unprofessional to me and I couldn't understand it. I also didn't care for her standoffishness; I tried to get to know her, but she didn't invite that sort of thing. We were miffed that she ignored us, and, worse, irritated when she refused to use our material and didn't do any better on her own. People who work in TV production units tend to form close though not necessarily long-lasting relationships, and when one key person is out of sync it throws a damper on the whole operation.

Apparently Davidson had other things on her mind, namely her romance with independent TV producer David Susskind. At some point early in the venture, he began coming to the studio at night and standing in the control room during the taping. The productions were complicated, and included not only interviews and film pieces, but also a small live combo, frequently a singer, and sometimes a comedian. The control room was a frenzied madhouse every night, with the executive producer and that evening's producer-writer worrying through every segment and dashing back and forth from the studio, the director screaming instructions, and a retinue of technical people at work. An unwelcome addition was Susskind, suggesting to the director how the shots of Davidson might be improved. Even if he didn't say anything, his presence made everyone uneasy. At first, it seemed impossible for any of us to ask him to leave, thinking, undoubtedly, that we might need to apply to him for work one day. However, the broadcast's executive producer finally firmly suggested that he depart, and he did. After an acrimonious and drawn-out divorce from his wife, Susskind married Davidson, but the show was long gone by then. Their marriage ended in divorce a number of years later.

By the summer of 1962, the television equivalent of a Broadway show closing notice was posted for "PM." As the show faded away, I began my search for work, not exclusively for the satisfaction of it, since my housekeeper had to be paid and my income was essential to the household. I looked around at the people I knew and contacted Lee Hanna of WNEW Radio, with whom I had worked in those final days at Channel 5.

While radio networks have long provided news to their affiliates, local stations at that time had no access to news services. One of the ways to achieve distinction in a crowded radio market like New York City was to cover local news with thoroughness and originality, which was what Lee Hanna set out to do. He had hired a corps of top newsmen, and I use the term advisedly. I was the only newswoman. With the exception of a secretary or two, the entire staff was male.

Hanna had begun a Sunday half-hour radio documentary series called "WNEW News Closeup," and he needed someone to produce it. Since he knew about my interviewing experience and writing from the "Night Beat" days, and was aware of the documentaries I had pieced together from film acquired from Channel 5, he felt I could handle the job. I had to learn audio tape editing, but found juggling the reels and writing connecting copy not only a challenge, but fun. My title became Assistant Director of News for Public Affairs. As I worked in the large, busy newsroom, it was easy to listen to my colleagues doing their phone interviews or planning local coverage, and I learned by osmosis how it was done. In addition to editing the work of others who did stories for the documentary series, I soon began to go out with the tape recorder myself, did the interviews, and wrote, edited, and narrated many of the programs. I never saw the on-air work as performance, but rather as a logical extension of reporting the story. Being totally involved made it easier to tell the stories, which dealt with all kinds of local issues as well as the growing civil rights movement. The work, however, was relentless and demanding, and Hanna was a tough boss. The days were nonstop work, but at last for the first time in my broadcast career, I didn't have night hours.

It was the beginning of the 1960s, and there was no better place to be than in a news organization. The country was changing, and the decade ahead would bring the civil rights and women's movements, the Vietnam War, assassinations, and student activism.

There were three key events during my two and a half years at WNEW Radio: the 1962 New York newspaper strike, the march on Washington, and the assassination of John F. Kennedy.

After my first summer on the job at WNEW, things were just beginning to settle down into a busy routine when the six New York

City newspapers went on strike. That was December 1962, and no one expected that it would last very long. The strike eventually ended four months later, in March of the following year, with innumerable casualties among the reporters, many of whom drifted off into broadcasting jobs. It also led to the demise of the *New York Daily Mirror,* and the merger of three newspapers into the *World-Journal-Tribune.*

Our coverage had to be expanded, and instead of five minutes on the hour, we added a full hour of news from 6:00 to 7:00 P.M.; we included guest columnists from the newspapers reading what would have been their columns, and stepped up reporting from the rest of the staff. I became a regular broadcast contributor, doing news stories around the city and writing material in the studio as well. Everyone apparently liked the way I sounded, and nothing was said about the undesirability of a female voice.

While my responsibilities and assignments at WNEW were expanding, the Symphony of the Air, which Jerry managed, was close to collapse. The newspaper strike was good for my broadcast career, but the orchestra's inability to advertise its concerts caused an insurmountable financial crisis. There were few government subsidies at the time, and the orchestra had never managed to attract enough backers. There were, however, bank loans and debts, and when the orchestra went under, Jerry, as manager, and some of the players were held personally responsible. My income became more crucial than ever. Modest as it was, it was enough to keep the family afloat during the difficult months before Jerry managed to find work. Ultimately, he was hired by public television as a producer of a series called "The World of Music." Nevertheless, the situation for a long time was difficult for us both. It did underline the advantages of the two-income family, particularly for people in unpredictable professions.

One of the events that distracted me from our personal financial crisis was the forthcoming civil rights march on Washington in August 1963. WNEW was going all out on that one, despite the fact that we were only a local station with no Washington facilities. Lee Hanna had big ideas, and his technical supervisor, Sheldon Hoffman, was a mechanical wizard. If we didn't have a studio, by God, he would make one. The whole reporting staff went to Washington and each person had a variety of assignments. Our headquarters were in the Hotel Washington where a makeshift studio was established in a hotel room, with wires and cables all over the floor.

I went off with my tape recorder to observe medical and sanitation preparations by the Red Cross and the DC Health Department, and did interviews with the volunteers. The day of the march, we fanned out early, while Reid Collins broadcast from the hotel room studio. The bus caravans pulling in were a new sight to Northerners like me: there were country folk, black folks from the South, big sturdy men in overalls, solemn and quiet, mixing into the crowd of urban blacks, students, and white sympathizers. The mood was serene. I moved among the crowds, carrying my Nagra, a heavy beast of a tape recorder, to the Washington Monument, where Joan Baez and Bob Dylan sang for the growing crowd. Then it was on to the Lincoln Memorial and Martin Luther King's "I Have a Dream" speech. The sight from there was overwhelming, hundreds of thousands of people as far as the eye could see. Some Southern lawmakers had predicted bloodshed, and had wanted troops to stand by. None were needed.

Once out on location, we taped interviews and something called ROSRS (running-on-scene-reports); then if time allowed, we recorded an introduction and bridges from one segment to another, and then rushed the material back to our makeshift studio. Sometimes there wasn't time to write anything in the field so while a producer or I was editing tape, one of us would write. Later when I was at ABC doing radio, we had progressed to smaller tape recorders with cassettes, and gadgets we carried allowed us to feed material via the telephone. The older model phones had mouthpieces which were easily unscrewed, and you could attach two cables to the interior, call the office, press the button on the tape recorder, and feed segments, or all, of your tape. It was disconcerting, to say the least, when you were in a desperate hurry, and couldn't find a phone that could be taken apart. Frequently we would ask people in their homes or stores if we could use their phones, and then they watched nervously as we took them apart. The process is still in use.

Some of our reporters were traveling south, as race relations became a focus of many of our news reports and documentaries. Along with the increasing number of incidents of violence against blacks in the South, blockbusting was another manifestation of anti-black sentiment in the North. Banks in their loan procedures kept blacks out of white neighborhoods, or encouraged districts to become all black. The interlude of peace following the march on Washington was over.

Then on 22 November 1963, the newsroom bulletin bells began to ring. Several people ran to the wire machines; a news editor shouted out, "The President's been shot," as he ripped the wire copy and ran to get the bulletin on the air.

Reporter Ike Pappas was told to get to Dallas as fast as he could.

Later, standing within feet of accused assassin Lee Harvey Oswald when he was shot, Pappas delivered a superb on-scene account.

We would all be going to Washington again to cover John F. Kennedy's funeral procession. This time we would report live, on the scene, without the advantage of tape editing and well-thought-out remarks. It would be my first experience with that sort of thing, and I had an important assignment, a post just outside the doors of the cathedral. From the time the cortege arrived until the mass was completed and the last dignitary left for Arlington National Cemetery, I broadcast those events as they occurred. Just before I left, Reid Collins, the anchor of WNEW's major events, asked me, "Can you handle it?" I said I felt certain I could. In truth, it was a tremendous challenge and I felt quite nervous. With all of the proper credentials, I joined the crush of reporters at the steps of St. Matthew's. I tried to be cool and calm as the riderless horse with its empty saddle and cavalry boots reversed, symbolic of the absent rider, passed by. The mournful sight of three pairs of grey horses drawing the flag-draped caisson to the sounds of muffled drums is stamped in my memory. Standing on the steps of the cathedral within arm's reach of me were the towering Charles de Gaulle, the diminutive Haille Selassie of Ethiopia, and a solemn Prince Philip. I tried to stay calm, but the emotional impact of the event was overwhelming, and my voice broke several times. Later, Lee Hanna told me that this had added to the coverage because the people listening to us in cars or at work would have to depend on us for the facts, and for conveying the grief and wrenching emotions of the event. For days the nation had been as one, in mourning, partly because television and radio brought the country together to share its national grief. The shock of the Kennedy assassination was shared by those of us in the news media, but we had little time to dwell on its implications. It was the first such event that was technically feasible to cover by both radio and television without a break. We had no time to do more than scramble to report the funeral and the change of administrations.

The funeral of John F. Kennedy was one of the first events that showed the power of television to unite the nation. The funeral brought the country to a halt, as if a family of mourners had gathered together. Television news reporting was the key to that unity. One had the sense of a new era in reporting beginning. Radio had done its share, and done it well, but pictures of the riderless horse, the widow Jacqueline Kennedy in black, and little John Kennedy's salute to his fallen father told the story better than the most vivid verbal descriptions could.

The network news organizations responded to the country's grief with control and dignity. NBC's president, Robert Kintner, ordered all commercials off the air and scheduled twenty-four hours of news.[12] Dan Rather and Walter Cronkite became America's contact with the grieving family and the new administration. Television also found what it does best—covering live, large-scale events. Barbara Matusow describes this turning point:

> As it turned out, 1963 was a pivotal year for television in more ways than one. That year, for the first time, more people said they got their news from TV than from newspapers—a shift that would grow more pronounced year by year. By this time, the transformation of America from a collection of provincial entities to a mass society— a process hastened and in part caused by broadcasting—was nearly complete. Americans were now more familiar with names and faces of anchors like Cronkite, Huntley, and Brinkley than they were with their senators, congressmen, city councilmen, and school board members. As the places of public assembly continued to diminish, and people began to divide their time almost exclusively between home and work, television news would become for many the most important link to the larger world.[13]

From a reporter's perspective, television suddenly became the medium of the future. Although I had learned how to do the live, on-the-scene reporting necessary for radio, television became the new challenge. Once again, I looked around to see if women were visible. This time I studied the television networks.

Nancy Hanschman began at CBS as a producer in Washington in the mid-fifties. She became a CBS correspondent in 1960 after several years of producing public affairs programs. She got her on-air job because the network knew by then that she was familiar with the issues and the people in the Capital. In 1963 she moved to NBC and was the first woman to have her own news broadcast, a five-minute daytime program called "Nancy Dickerson with the News." (Hanschman had married and began using her husband's name.) In 1970 she took time out to raise a family and did not return to network news; instead she would occasionally produce and report news specials for independent stations.

CBS News hired Marya McLaughlin as an associate producer in the election unit in 1963. She moved to network news as a reporter in 1965, and was promoted to correspondent in 1971. CBS News is the only network to have a two-tier category for reporters, the title "correspondent" indicating superior experience. McLaughlin appeared with less and less frequency on television in the 1980s. In the three major layoffs during those years, she was retained even though she served by then mainly as a producer accompanying crews to hearings on Capitol Hill. Scuttlebutt had it that the company was afraid to fire her because of a possible lawsuit. She was the oldest woman correspondent on staff, by then in her late fifties. McLaughlin was not a troublemaker by nature and was reluctant to make an issue of her lack of airtime, but her frustration at not being used was well known.

Liz Trotta, who had worked at the Associated Press and the *Chicago Tribune,* joined NBC's local station in New York as the first woman on its reportorial staff in 1965. By 1970, NBC News had five newswomen: Barbara Walters, Pauline Frederick, Aline Saarinen, Liz Trotta, and Nancy Dickerson. In 1971, Betty Rollin joined them.

In 1964, however, when I began wondering about my next step, Pauline Frederick, Nancy Dickerson, and ABC's Lisa Howard were the only women then visible on network news. At that time, those few of us in the business were ambitious to do more reporting, and visions of success focused on that goal. There was no thought at all of wanting a major anchor role. It seemed so out of reach as to be unthinkable.

As I evaluated the television news scene, I was hard at work doing radio documentaries. A few months after the Kennedy funeral, I was deeply involved in a major two-part effort called "The Battle of the Warsaw Ghetto." That same year I made my first move toward television and managed to get an appointment with Reuven Frank, then a high-ranking NBC News executive. He looked at my clippings and resume and dismissed me rather curtly, saying that I had a good job already, why did I want to move on? There was no pressure on the organization to hire women and the decade-old prejudice against women's voices still held in most quarters. My interview with him was not encouraging. At the same time, I could not see staying at WNEW radio indefinitely. The weekly grind of documentaries and my inability to foresee a better job in radio made me determined not to give up my search.

Later that year I spotted an item in the trade paper *Variety,* indicating that ABC News was looking for a second female news correspondent. Lisa Howard was the only one on staff. The item didn't explain why they wanted another and I didn't ask.

ABC was new in network news. Elmer Lower had been brought in as president in August 1963 with the mandate to build a news organization. There was then a nightly fifteen-minute black-and-white newscast (ABC was the last network to go to color and to thirty minutes) with Ron Cochran anchoring. Film was still being supplied by Telenews, the same outfit that had provided footage for "Mike Wallace and the News." (ABC was just getting around to hiring its own camera crews in 1963.)[14] There was a skeleton staff, and a one-man London bureau. Jesse Zousmer was brought in as news vice president from his post as coproducer of Ed Murrow's "Person to Person" at CBS. Lower and Zousmer began to put together a news department. A little later Zousmer would provide my entry to the network.

As a result of the *Variety* item, I picked up the phone, introduced myself, sent over a resume, and was asked to audition. A date was set. I was told to prepare a minute's worth of news, and be ready to ad-lib an autobiographical account of myself.

I had spent enough years in studios not to be too intimidated. The audition over, I received the equivalent of "don't call us, we'll call you," and went back to WNEW thinking that I probably hadn't made it.

About a month later *Variety* gave a glowing review to a radio documentary I did called "Portrait of a Primary," and I received a copy of the review in the mail with a handwritten note from Jesse Zousmer saying, "Marlene—good for you!" Apparently I was not out of the running, but still hadn't heard anything specific. Meanwhile, the Republican convention in San Francisco was approaching, and at WNEW we were making arrangements to go.

It was my first political convention. Our booth and Sheldon Hoffman's electronic contraptions were installed at the very top of the Cow Palace in what could not be called one of the better locations. We were so far away that a trip to the bathroom seemed like a visit to Berkeley, and food deliveries over the long days and nights were erratic because deliverymen couldn't find us.

My main function was to frantically edit tape for our broadcast which Reid Collins was anchoring from our booth. This was Goldwater country, and his followers were being widely described as little old ladies in tennis shoes, in other words, eccentric conservatives, and that was exactly how they looked to me. Nelson Rockefeller's moderate and conciliatory remarks were heartily booed. Barry Goldwater's observation that "extremism in the pursuit of liberty is no vice" was cheered.

The Democratic convention was set for August in Atlantic City. Even before then, changes were taking place in our shop. Lee Hanna had moved to CBS as head of radio news. A number of our key people would soon be going along—Sheldon Hoffman and correspondents

Ike Pappas, Jack Laurence, and Reid Collins. Hanna wanted me to go too in another administrative and production post. I stalled, waiting to see what would happen with ABC. I had never gotten anywhere before by just sitting and waiting, so I picked up the phone and called Jesse Zousmer. "I have an offer from CBS," I said, "in radio. Should I take it?" I didn't say it was not an on-air job. "Don't go there," he replied, "come with us." *Variety* reported my hiring in its own inimitable fashion on 9 September 1964 in an article headed "Tap Marlene Sanders as ABC Newshen from Among 50 Candidates." The item noted that "ABC News, which has been beating the bushes for a general assignment femme correspondent capped the hunt last week by jotting Marlene Sanders, latterly assistant news director for WNEW-NY and possessor of a string of awards. . . . She reports September 14 for assignment off the New York news desk. Web's other distaff byliner is Lisa Howard. . . ." I was anxious to get started, but could not begin until after the Democratic convention, and a vacation.

I don't remember much about what I did for WNEW's coverage in Atlantic City. I do recall being taken on a tour of the ABC television setup by one of my future bosses. It looked very plush to me. The network people had the best facilities and the best living quarters too. Hotel space was at a premium, and I never will forget my accommodations. My assistant, Carolyn Tanton, and I were housed on the outskirts of the city in the Hi Ho Silver Motel. We shared a cement-block room lighted by a bare bulb dangling from a cord. It was definitely time to go network.

In the fall of 1964, the American Broadcasting Company was located in one small building at 7 West Sixty-sixth Street in New York City. Years later the whole block would be taken up by ABC News alone and its technical operations. The handsome corporate headquarters was located down the street from CBS on the Avenue of the Americas. (Capital Cities, the new owners of ABC, plans to move the corporate offices to a new building on West Sixty-sixth Street, consolidating all the ABC operations into one city block.) Even the modest building on Sixty-sixth Street looked impressive to me, fresh from a local station. The news department, appropriate to its status at the time, was in the basement. Almost everything was in one long room: the assignment desk, the correspondents—all four of us—and our typewriters, desks, and chairs. There was a corner for the staff of Lisa Howard's daily five-minute news broadcast, and the news film operation was run out of an adjacent cubbyhole. Executives were on another floor, and the evening newscast's offices were across the street in the Hotel Des Artistes, next door to the only studio, which was in a converted hotel ballroom.

I had made the move with only a small salary increase, earning slightly more than the $350 a week I had been making at WNEW Radio, but I was assured that I would be earning more money shortly because of the fee system. Most new reporters worked for the American Federation of Television and Radio Artists (AFTRA) minimum, which back in 1964 was $350 a week. There were additional fees for appearances on the evening news, the Sunday interview program "Issues and Answers," and smaller fees for radio spots and for film pieces that were sent out via syndication on delayed electronic feed (DEF). This was the pre-satellite system of distributing news stories that did not make the evening news because of limitations in time, newsworthiness, or quality. Local stations received them early enough to integrate them into their own local newscasts. Since there were weeks when correspondents had one or no pieces on any of the various outlets, counting on fees was a risky business. Besides, you didn't get the whole fee. There was such a thing called the "recapturable," in effect, a deductible, and if a fee was $50, you only got $25. Finally, by 1981, fees were higher and the correspondent got 70 percent. Those who reported from the White House made money on the fee system because they were on television so often, as well as on radio. One could also negotiate an above money-break contract, which meant if you got $30,000 as a flat salary, you escaped the fee system, and were free of that particular pressure. Some people were able to negotiate much higher salaries of course, but you had to beat $30,000 to be rid of fees. By 1981, that figure had risen to $61,500, and by 1986 it was $75,000.

In 1964, no one really told me what I would be doing as a general assignment correspondent. By then it was no surprise to me that nothing would be explained. That's how it worked. It had always been my practice to take the assignment, nod, go off, and try to figure out what I was supposed to do, or find someone who could tell me. My first day on the job, the assignment desk editor handed me a fragment of wire copy with terse instructions to go to Brooklyn with the crew and cover some kind of school strike. I managed to locate the crew and off we went. Once there, I began to piece things together. I told Vince Gaito, the cameraman, what I wanted to do, and he told me where to stand. There were parents gathered on the street corners, and teachers picketing—the obvious interviews. Supposedly, no children were in school, but we went in anyway to show the empty classrooms. Inside, we stumbled on one child, and one child only, in class with a teacher on duty. With that angle, the story went on the Ron Cochran news that night. I soon learned that covering a story by no means guaranteed it would make air, but it did get me off to a good start in terms of morale. I also got a few pointers on television technique which I was quick to use the next time around, such as not standing next to the interviewee, but shooting with the camera over your shoulder. Interviews are still done that way, but it wasn't obvious to someone coming from radio.

Jesse Zousmer had warned me to stay away from my only female colleague, Lisa Howard, hinting that she could be troublesome. A former actress, Howard had a rather affected manner of speech and an eccentric way of dressing. However, she was a gutsy woman who gained a good deal of publicity in 1960 by getting access to Soviet leader Nikita Khrushchev during his New York visit when she was working for Mutual. She went after Fidel Castro during his September 1960 trip to New York, gaining permission to go to Cuba, and putting together a documentary which appeared on ABC. By the time I met her, she was doing a five-minute daily newscast at 2:55 P.M.

In the early 1960s, both NBC and CBS had begun to do a five-minute television newscast during the day, in addition to their fifteen-minute evening news program. ABC soon followed suit, probably at the suggestion of the sales department, former news president Elmer Lower now speculates. The five-minute format wasn't too expensive for a sponsor that wanted to target advertising to women, the major daytime audience. Purex sold Sweetheart Soap, and probably came up with the title of the broadcast which was billed "Purex Presents: News with the Woman's Touch." Despite the name, it was a straightforward news program, with the woman's touch being that of the anchor.

I saw Lisa Howard infrequently, since I was usually out with a crew somewhere and she was in the studio. But she did approach me and tried to interest me in joining her in her support of incumbent Republican New York Senator Kenneth Keating's reelection campaign against Robert Kennedy. I thought it was odd that she had gotten publicly involved in partisan politics, since everyone knew that was just not done if you were a reporter. I turned her down, but aside from that conversation, we had almost no contact.

Not only was Howard working actively on the Keating campaign, but she became its cochairman, which was widely reported. On 29 September 1964, she was suspended from her job. The network claimed she had violated its news standards policy, and she could no longer appear on the air or even report to work. She was off the payroll. For a few days a Washington producer, Peggy Whedon, was called in to anchor in her place, and then I was asked to substitute on a temporary basis. Lisa Howard was expected to return after the November election. Since I hadn't had studio experience, I viewed this as a good opportunity to learn, but thought I would be back on the road soon.

As things turned out, Howard did not come back at all. In mid-November, Elmer Lower, president of ABC News, announced that I would take over the show. "Miss Howard," he said in a newspaper account, "won't be a member of our staff." He said it was not only her political involvement that led to the decision, but "a number of difficulties of an internal and operational nature." Obviously, there were other problems only hinted at in Zousmer's warnings to me about keeping my distance from her. Her political activism, however, was her undoing.

Viewers could not be blamed for being suspicious of a reporter who took a strong public position on an issue that she was also expected to report on. How could Lisa Howard have reported objectively on the Kennedy-Keating campaign if she were part of it? It would be an impossible situation, once she had gone public. All of us have views on issues we cover, but we try to be fair. Being labeled in advance, publicly, is too great a burden for the public, the correspondent, and the employer.

It has been a long-established journalistic policy that reporters maintain the appearance of objectivity. That would preclude open support of political candidates, although no one really believes total objectivity is possible and that reporters have no personal opinions. I have run into a few journalists who say they don't vote because of their concern about being labeled in some fashion, but this strikes me as a ludicrous overreaction. There is absolutely no reason why we have to give up our right to vote, though I do agree that it is a good idea not to be openly partisan.

Network correspondents are expressly forbidden to take public positions on controversial topics. "CBS News Standards" says: "Employees who, in their private capacity, take a public position on a controversial issue, including participation in a partisan political campaign, will either be removed from handling the news involving that issue or, if such reassignment is not practical, be required to take a leave of absence. The rationale behind this policy is that an employee who takes such a public position loses, at a minimum, the *appearance* of objectivity."

Television news, from the start, has been far less open to personal opinions than radio had been. The early radio news commentators, as they were called, seemed to have no restrictions on speaking their minds. Television used its senior correspondents, like Howard K. Smith at ABC and Eric Severeid and Bill Moyers at CBS, to provide "analysis" regularly. Often those two minutes or so were elucidation, not opinion. Sometimes, but not usually, they were controversial. There is something about television that gives opinion more weight than a comparable statement on radio. Networks are skittish about antagonizing large segments of the population, and a strong opinion on almost anything is bound to have that effect.

Television was also vulnerable to criticism by the White House. This was particularly true in the 1970s when President Richard Nixon attempted to destroy public television through the Office of Telecommunications run by Clay T. Whitehead. Nixon disliked PBS's controversial programming and one of their key personalities, Sander Vanocur. Nixon felt that the government should not pay for such negative programming and put pressure on the PBS network to decentralize and stay away from "news" shows if it wanted increased government funding. PBS buckled under the pressure.[15]

The networks were also singled out by Nixon's Vice President, Spiro Agnew, in 1969. Angry over their coverage of Vietnam, he accused the press of negativism, elitism, and an Eastern bias. While Agnew did not mention commentators by name, broadcasters were sure he was referring to Frank Reynolds at ABC and David Brinkley at NBC. Although the networks researched the charge of bias and found themselves for the most part fair, ABC curbed Reynold's commentaries. Reynolds felt penalized for his views, which ironically had included the danger of muzzling the press. Reynolds was eventually dropped as ABC anchor. His removal may have been precipitated by pressure from government but it was also caused by the new pressure felt by TV news—show business. Every network wanted a personality more than a newsman as anchor.[16]

By 1987, commentary had virtually disappeared from the major network newscasts. The growing emphasis on entertainment values in the news may have also hastened its demise. The only haven left for contrasting opinions is the documentary, since there is time for a variety of views, and they are customarily "balanced." Commentaries are not. The newsroom mentality is to let those we cover express their views, and let it go at that. Twenty-two minutes of news in a half-hour broadcast, the time left after commercials, is little enough time to report on breaking events. And so "opinion" by and large is restricted nationally to radio, where CBS, for example, has a variety of people doing commentaries from differing points of view, on segments called "Spectrum," clearly labeled as opinion. They sometimes generate response from the public, though it is muted compared to the avalanche of mail that almost any opinion on television generates.

As for my colleagues who write, edit, and report the news, as far as one can tell, they appear to be a good reflection of the nation as a whole, perhaps being slightly more liberal. A few conservatives surfaced in office bull sessions during the Reagan administration, but by and large the majority have been moderate to liberal. Conservatives tend not to go into the news business in large numbers, apparently being more inclined toward business, or if they are attracted to journalism, to magazines with philosophies that reflect their points of view. Radicals of the left would also be uncomfortable in any of the network news operations. Those who have given it a try from time to time have tended to drift off to advocacy publications, or into social action of some kind. News reporting is too objective and networks are simply not a good place to be if your goal is to change the world.

Despite differences in reporters' outlooks, a disinterested observer would be hard-pressed to detect anyone's political leanings in the straightforward, noneditorial approach of network news correspondents.

After her dismissal, Lisa Howard filed a two million dollar lawsuit against ABC, but she lost her bid to force the network to reinstate her as a television reporter.

Meanwhile, in less than two months with the network, I had my own daily newscast, and because of the fee system, my salary took a healthy jump. I had no guilt feelings about the way I got the show, since I had nothing to do with the Lisa Howard affair in any way. I was anxious to improve my on-air delivery and to learn as much as possible about network newsgathering.

Jesse Zousmer instructed me to try to do at least one film piece a day for the five-minute daily program. As the news organization began to expand, our little unit operated in its own office space. We had a producer, writer, film editor, and desk assistant. I wrote my film lead-ins, but only because I liked to keep a hand in it. There wasn't much copy needed for three and a half minutes of news, especially if there was a film piece and a switch to Washington for a report from one of our correspondents there, which we tried to include every day.

By January 1965 the network was beginning to look for another female reporter, this time in Washington. A *Variety* story, dated in its use of the term "girl," put it this way:

The market in television girl reporters is still boom. ABC News, it was learned yesterday, is seeking a companion and occasional substitute for Marlene Sanders, the network's only on-camera newswoman. CBS and NBC, both network and locally, recently increased the girl power of their news staffs. "We must have seen 100 girls so far," said Jesse Zousmer, ABC News Vice President. "We think that one girl in our staff is not enough. We're not looking for actresses or television personalities. We want a working reporter, not a reader, someone who can cover a beat in Washington or Vietnam." Zousmer added that the newswoman, when found, will free Miss Sanders from the studio on the daily afternoon "The Woman's Touch" and cover events for other programs.

ABC hoped to establish that its anchors were able newsgatherers, not just pretty faces. They sent me and Canadian-born Peter Jennings, who shortly afterwards became the evening anchorman at the age of twenty-seven, out into the field to enhance our credibility. That was just fine as far as I was concerned. Anchoring is decidedly boring. Those interested in achieving celebrity may love the work. It offers high visibility and top dollars, particularly for major local anchors in good-sized cities, and for network anchors on an even larger scale. By the 1980s, there were plenty of young anchors on the local scene who had done little reporting and were mainly news readers. They often appeared to have been placed in their jobs by casting directors who mixed age, race, and sex, according to the community. That mix is fine, even desirable, if the individuals are qualified. It might be more honest to use the British system of news readers, anchors who profess to be nothing more, while others do the reporting. There is a certain schizophrenia about what an anchor represents today. Back in 1965, Jennings and I, at least, were anxious to do as much work as possible out of the studio. I also had to learn to master the techniques of anchoring.

I was fortunate that the director of our broadcast, Sonny Diskin, was a kind and helpful man. Every day after the program, for several months, he made me watch the playback on tape. People usually hate the sound of their voices on a tape recording, but it is far worse seeing yourself than just listening. Little mannerisms are magnified, and flaws leap out at you. Diskin showed me that instead of turning pages of the script by flipping them in a distracting manner, I should slip them over to the side. He also showed me how to use the teleprompter smoothly and how to turn from one camera to the other by looking down at the script as a transitional movement. A representative of the agency that handled the Purex account suggested that my very short hair would look better longer, and she was right. No network news executive ever commented on my appearance, however, or my hairstyle. Years later when the Christine Craft case made news, I was often asked if anyone had ever suggested a "make-over," or had been critical of how I looked. No one, aside from the advertising agency representative on that first show, ever did. It may have been because I learned what was required myself. In later years it also occurred to me that it might have been because the network brass didn't bother to watch the broadcasts I did. News during the daytime hours was never considered important, more a throwaway than anything else. Women, to this day, are by and large in the same category.

I began keeping a day-to-day list of what I wore on a yellow lined pad at home so that I would not repeat myself too often. In the days before color it required a little practice to find what looked best in black and white, but it wasn't a tremendous problem. Clothing worn on television is not a tax deductible expense, I learned, to my regret, unless it is a costume or uniform, something one can't use in daily life.

Toward the end of that year, only a few months after I had begun the daytime anchor chore, Ron Cochran, anchorman of the fifteen-minute nightly news, lost his voice, and I was asked to replace him with very little notice. Perhaps I was chosen because I already anchored another newscast and knew how, but no one ever told me exactly why. I didn't have time to build up any anxiety, only enough time to run home and pick out something to wear. I was concerned about "image," and I knew in this instance it would be important since I was certain no woman had ever anchored at night. I picked a blue wool blazer and a yellow wool, high-necked jersey top. I never liked to draw attention to what I was wearing on camera, preferring a conservative image, and I didn't want to wear anything too severe or too overtly feminine either. I wanted to be straightforward and unfussy, which is the way I always thought of myself as a broadcaster.

The broadcast came and went all too quickly, but the event was acknowledged the next day by Jack Gould, TV critic of the *New York Times*, in his column of 3 December 1964, under the heading "A Precedent Is Set":

> The masculine evening news line up received a temporary female replacement last night on the American Broadcasting Company when Marlene Sanders stepped in at 6:45 P.M. for an indisposed Ron Cochran. People who should know report that never before has a distaff reporter conducted on her very own a news broadcast in prime time.

For the record then, the courageous young woman with a Vassar smile
was crisp and businesslike and obviously the sort who wouldn't put up
with any nonsense, from anyone.

Her 15 minute show was not spell-binding, but that could have
been because her delivery was terribly straightforward and her copy
somewhat dull.

I was not unhappy with the review. "Crisp and businesslike" was
what I intended to be. As for "straightforward," I was somewhat
baffled. Was coyness or cuteness preferable? Who, delivering news, is
spellbinding? Appealing, convincing, authoritative, yes. But I couldn't
think of anyone then or now who does the news in a spellbinding
fashion. Most days the news itself, unless it is calamitous, isn't spell-
binding either. Gould was right about the copy. It probably was a little
dull, but I didn't write it so I didn't take it personally. It may also
have been a dull news day, which happens often enough.

I had been under a great deal of pressure to do well, most of
it self-imposed. No one told me I was a stand-in for my sex, or that
a big promotion was at stake, but I knew I had to do well, first of
all, so I would have another shot at it. I was not particularly nervous.
The studio was the same one that I used for the daytime news broadcast, but there was a different set, and three cameras instead of two.
I knew the stagehands and technicians and that helped make me feel
comfortable. I also tend to be calm under pressure and that quality
served me well. Mostly I worried about flubbing, which I rarely did.

Within a matter of a few weeks, in January 1965, I was again
selected to substitute, this time for anchorman Bob Young, who did
the network news on Saturday and Sunday nights. I sat in for him
for two weekends. The Republic did not fall on those occasions either.
Aside from my family and friends, no one at the network made much
of the event. Naturally I entertained fantasies of doing the weekend
regularly, even though I had been a network correspondent for only
a few months. As for evening anchor spots, there are few and they
don't change hands very often. There was only a handful of women
doing network news as correspondents, and I am certain no network
executives even thought of a permanent female evening anchorperson.
Several years later, I made an effort to get ABC to let me co-anchor
at night on a permanent basis, but that was not seriously considered.
To ABC's credit, however, they broke the ice in 1964, and showed
it could be done. No one else followed suit for many years.

A shocking footnote to that year was the suicide of Lisa Howard
in the summer of 1965, by an overdose of sleeping pills. She was only
thirty-five. There was a good deal of speculation of course about why

she had done it. Newspaper accounts reported that she had recently
suffered a miscarriage. No marital discord was discussed or was considered a factor, and Howard had been about to begin a new job as
publicity director of a New York anti-poverty program. But the loss
of her television job undoubtedly was a major contributing factor in
her death. Howard had been ABC's first newswoman. She not only
did the daytime program that I inherited, but was an aggressive
reporter. Newspaper reports of her dismissal from ABC said she refused to accept the network's reasoning in firing her, though most
news professionals felt it was legitimate. Though socially useful, her
new job must have been disappointing after her network exposure.
But Howard will be remembered as a pioneering woman in the network news industry and for proving to all those around that women
broadcast reporters could get exclusive interviews with world leaders.

Most of the other women in TV news in the late 1960s were
relegated to "women's stories," the traditional women's-page fare.
Food, fashion, child-rearing, decorating, social events, and the entertainment scene were all you could expect. The men on the assignment
desk were not consciously discriminating. The soft stories assigned to
women were an automatic reflex. That's what the newspapers were
doing after all, and that's what they thought most women viewers
wanted. Women like Nancy Dickerson in Washington, who had long
off-camera experience with politics, had somewhat better luck, but as
a rule only men had the top beats in Washington.

Daytime newscasts, which one could then assume were watched
mainly by housewives, were not regarded as important. Story assignments for our 2:55 P.M. broadcast rarely came from the assignment
desk. Ironically, because of our unimportant status, we had the most
freedom. We generated our own stories, and many of them dealt with
serious women's issues. We covered birth control controversies, and
a wide range of legitimate women's stories. Occasionally, the assignment desk did call on me to cover stories for other ABC News programs since ABC was short staffed. And, after all, a woman correspondent was better than no one at all. That's how I happened to
get some campaign assignments, mostly temporary, relieving my male
colleagues from time to time.

Campaign coverage is still grueling, but 1980s campaign managers often organize a candidate's appearances according to network
deadlines since they know how important it is to get on TV. In the
sixties, with the technical complications involved in filing stories, it
was in some respects worse than it is today. Covering the wives of
candidates isn't done much anymore. Now women are out actively

campaigning for themselves. I was given the chore of reporting on Pat Nixon's role in her husband's campaign, which was incredibly difficult because she really didn't do anything. But Lady Bird Johnson did, and I was always delighted to be assigned to her, largely because of her imaginative and amusing press secretary, Liz Carpenter. Those trips were always newsworthy and an excellent way to see America.

My first campaign trip for the evening news was a short one and it involved following Lady Bird Johnson around Ohio. Correspondents were their own producers most of the time, so this involved staying in touch with the home office, telling them how the story was going, and finding out if they wanted a piece for that night. If so, that meant making arrangements at a local affiliate for film-developing facilities, an editor, and feeding the film from there, or shipping it in time for air.

Although it was rare to have a producer along then, some stories could not be done without extra assistance. Lady Bird Johnson was unusual in that she campaigned alone, and was not simply a smiling presence at the side of her husband. In the upcoming election, it was important for the President to carry the South, Lady Bird's home territory. It was decidedly newsworthy that she would undertake a major campaign trip through the South by train. You could be sure of good pictures and occasionally something of substance. Coverage of Lady Bird's "Five-Day Whistle Stop" Southern campaign trip required a producer and another correspondent besides me. Logistics demanded that the producer and one correspondent leave the train, feed the story, and then catch up with the caravan later. The remaining correspondent would continue coverage with the crew, and we would leapfrog back and forth. On this trip, there were eleven campaign stops each day, and each time, a recording blared out of the back of the train playing "The Yellow Rose of Texas," which all aboard grew to loathe. Local dignitaries boarded one stop ahead of their locales, and when they pulled into their stop, they appeared with Mrs. Johnson on the platform at the back of the train; they disembarked there, while the next set of politicians got on.

We slept on the train, each person having a cramped room with bunk, sink, and toilet. Fortunately, the train stopped at night, giving those who had the time the chance to shower, if they could find a hotel.

Television was well represented on the trip. The crews consisted of three hard-working men who lugged heavy equipment on and off at those eleven stops a day. We had to decide what was worth filming and what wasn't, and to edit in our heads before we set out to the nearest affiliate to make a feed for the evening news. Some of those trips weren't easy either. The train did not necessarily stop in a town that had an ABC affiliate, and we often had to charter a small plane to get to one in time. Sometimes we discovered that the affiliate was nothing more than a quonset hut. A film editor met us at various pre-arranged stops. It was a desperate race against the clock to get the film processed, the piece cut, narrated, and fed. Then we had to figure out how to catch up with the train. Someone had to be on the train at all times, "protectively," a euphemism for "in case of violence, or in case the candidate is shot." My colleague on this trip, David Jayne, was a well-liked, hard-working correspondent who rose to responsible producing jobs at ABC. In 1978 he was killed in a plane crash, on a jet that was chartered to take film out of the Middle East while he was there as a producer on assignment with Barbara Walters.

Trips like Lady Bird's through the South were hard work, but fun, as those things go. There was time for a happy hour on board at night, and most—not all—of our colleagues were good company.

One of the reasons that Mrs. Johnson's trip got such good coverage was that her press secretary, Liz Carpenter, a lively, rotund pro, knew just how everyone operated, what the various deadlines were, and what was needed to get the stories out, or on. She was an early image-manager; the stops were designed for color, with picturesque scenes, good locations, and motley crowds.

Mrs. Johnson was not easily accessible, though you could get plenty of good film of her visiting historic sites, making speeches at the back of the train, or mingling with the crowds. We began making requests for an interview as soon as we got on board, since we needed it to cap the trip, and Mrs. Johnson knew, too, that all three networks would want to talk to her. Finally, on the last day, individual interviews were granted in Mrs. Johnson's private car as we lurched along the southern coast of the United States. On such occasions, the First Lady was formal and guarded in what she said about her husband's chances and about her own impact on the campaign. She was knowledgeable and smart, but cautious, and far more attractive in person than her pictures and television appearances revealed. Finally, we pulled into New Orleans for an overnight stay in a real hotel, a good meal, a little sight-seeing, and then a flight back to New York.

After a White House trip was over, a bill arrived at the network. Travel was usually at first-class rates, or more, and by the time you calculated the hotels and meals, the bill mounted up. Newspapers and magazines may have sent only one person. But in the case of television when there were one or more correspondents, a news film crew of three, and a producer, costs were substantial. Tape crews today are smaller, only two people, and film processing costs don't exist. Occasionally, networks send several crews, depending on the story; one for news, one for documentary or for the morning news. It's an expensive business, a point CBS chief executive officer Laurence Tisch learned quickly about newsgathering, and which led to the drastic cost cutting in 1987.

Not much was said about our coverage of Mrs. Johnson's trip when I returned, which proved to be typical. In broadcasting, an executive once told me, you are expected to do a good job, so compliments are not in order. That particular philosophy, unfortunately still observed, is bad for morale. On-air people put everything on the line and a good word is worth — well, almost worth — a raise in salary.

By the fall of 1965, young Peter Jennings had replaced news veteran Ron Cochran on the fifteen-minute, still black-and-white, evening news. Jennings was under thirty and had been hired at about the same time as I was. We were both part of the so-called "youth movement" at ABC, although I was by then thirty-four. Management was trying to attract a younger audience and wanted to give us both good exposure and publicity.

Jennings and I were sent to co-anchor Lyndon Johnson's inauguration from the booth opposite the White House, in ABC's first competition with the other networks in a major political event. Howard K. Smith and Edward P. Morgan, two veteran reporters, would handle the anchor chores at the Capitol for the swearing in, and would relieve us at the White House from time to time. This must have irked them considerably. I, of course, was thrilled with the opportunity. Jennings, who was Canadian, and then New York–based, knew little about the Washington scene. I didn't know much more and worried about being able to engage in the knowledgeable small talk required for such an interminable occasion. We were supposed to provide color during the long parade, and we were both buried in research for weeks ahead of time. Inauguration Day was brilliant and clear. The White House and the white snow all around meant that very bright lights had to be thrown on us to compensate for the bright background, and the strong quartz lights actually burned our faces.

I had to watch myself with Jennings. He liked to upstage and would seize the initiative whenever he could, trying to dominate our end of the broadcast. Although he was personable and pleasant, his ambition sometimes got the better of him. Earlier I had worked with him, co-anchoring a New York charity ball for local WABC-TV, and at that time he usurped material specifically designed for me, a move that only I was aware of. There were similar incidents during the inauguration, but not much that could be done about it. It is not acceptable to show hostility to your partner on the air, as the short-lived anchor team of Barbara Walters and Harry Reasoner would prove years later. Jennings's conduct with me was not necessarily the rule in those dual roles. Later, when Frank Reynolds and I co-anchored a special after Lynda Bird Johnson's White House wedding, he was cooperative and helpful, and never seemed to have the need to dominate.

Financially, things were looking up for me in the mid-1960s. The network instituted another five-minute program called "Feature Story" that I anchored. It was fed to affiliates who for reasons best known to them did not want to carry my afternoon news program. This new show filled the gap in their programming, and allowed other correspondents besides myself an outlet for longer stories, or stories without a hard news edge. Because of the fee system, my salary increased significantly. With that knowledge, perhaps, management in my next contract talks offered a salary "above the money-break," that is, a flat salary without fees, which I accepted, knowing full well that the feature program might not go on forever.

It was good to be busy and productive, but most of the reporting I was doing at the time was for the Purex news and "Feature Story," both broadcast during the day, a second-class assignment. Viewership is highest in the evening, the time when more men are watching. The early morning news broadcasts can catch the nation's movers and shakers as well before they leave for work. The daytime viewers were "only" women, the elderly, and shut-ins. If you worked exclusively in that time period, you were not in the mainstream. So while anchoring during the day produced a good paycheck, it made getting out into the field difficult, and the team that ran the evening news tended to forget your existence.

In February 1966, when there was an opportunity for someone to fly to India to interview Indira Gandhi, it was Peter Jennings who went. When I pointed out that I had interviewed her the preceding year during her visit to the United States and felt the assignment should have been mine, Elmer Lower said he had just not thought of me. He also pointed out that contractually, Jennings, now anchoring the evening news, was required to get out of the studio and cover at least one major story every six weeks, and that management still wanted to build his image as one of experience and credibility. I never thought that thinking would apply to me. So, I was not prepared for a conversation in my studio one day in February 1966 when Jesse Zousmer took me aside. He explained that the network wanted to send its major anchors for brief Vietnam tours, and he asked if I would be willing to go for about a month. Zousmer had been following my progress at the network with a certain amount of pride, since he had brought me in, and apparently had confidence in my ability. He also stopped me from agreeing to the Vietnam assignment on the spot, saying I should sleep on it.

At home that night, my husband and I discussed it and it was clear I was eager to go. Jerry was concerned about my safety, but recognized the temptation to cover the major story of the day. Jeffrey was six, and because of our household arrangements, no special preparations were needed at home.

Once it was determined that I would go, the network worked out a substitute for my broadcast, and I began intensive reading, as well as securing the proper documents and the fourteen inoculations needed.

On the day that I went to the U.S. Public Health Service for my yellow fever shot, there was terrible news. Jesse Zousmer had been away for several weeks on a tour of the Far East bureaus, accompanied by his wife. On the approach to the Tokyo airport, their plane crashed into the sea, killing all on board.

Jesse's death was a shock, and a dreadful loss. He was a warm, energetic, dynamic person, the closest thing to a mentor I ever had. He had hired me, and had a stake in my success. That I was a woman never seemed to concern him. Under his leadership I never felt any discrimination. I worked hard and was recognized, at least by him, for my efforts. During our short professional relationship he had been enormously helpful, always accessible and full of good advice. His death was a personal loss to me; only later would I find out how much of a professional loss it was as well.

## Notes

1. *New York Times* (19 October 1955).
2. *New York Times* (17 October 1957), p. 51.
3. Eugene Foster, *Understanding Broadcasting* (Reading: Addison-Wesley, 1978), p. 322.
4. Ibid.
5. Theodore Schneyer, "An Overview of Public Interest Law Activity in the Communications Field," *Wisconsin Law Review*, no. 3 (1977): 640.
6. Barbara Matusow, *The Evening Stars* (Boston: Houghton Mifflin, 1983), p. 124.

7. Matusow, p. 101.

8. *New York Times* (18 November 1956), p. 13.

9. Erik Barnouw, *Tube of Plenty,* revised edition (New York: Oxford University Press, 1982), p. 124.

10. Ann Sperber, *Murrow: His Life and Times* (New York: Freundlich, 1986), p. 469.

11. Ibid.

12. Matusow, p. 77.

13. Ibid., p. 106.

14. Ibid., p. 135.

15. David M. Stone, *Nixon and the Politics of Public Television* (New York: Garland, 1985), pp. 43–71, 87, 106–20.

16. Matusow, pp. 150, 151.

# 3

## Covering the World

Traveling on campaign trips was one thing, but going overseas was another. "News with the Woman's Touch," like all other newscasts, reported daily on what was euphemistically, and legally, called "the Vietnam conflict." In reality it was a war, and the major story of the day.

If the presence of women in war zones was not greeted with unalloyed joy by rival colleagues and some members of the military, there was at least a grudging acceptance. What we had to face was far different from what women encountered reporting from Europe prior to and during World War II. Just as television news found its national recognition in covering the 1963 Kennedy funeral, it found its international role during the Vietnam War. Vietnam has been called, accurately, the first television war.

Television had few correspondents overseas in its early years. The news programs of the early fifties were primitive, and by and large the networks depended on the wires, and stringers. Film was usually dated by the time it arrived on propeller planes. Most of the film crews were ex-newsreel men. In the 1950s CBS and NBC had crews in major U.S cities, but few overseas. For the June 1953 coronation of Queen Elizabeth II, all three networks made a huge effort to get their film back first; NBC even rented a DC-6, removed much of the interior, and set up a flying laboratory on board. They developed and edited the footage on the long flight home. In spite of NBC's efforts, ABC won the race by minutes. They picked up the BBC feed sent to Canada that arrived before the NBC plane. ABC then took the Canadian Broadcasting Corporation feed via a cable link.[1]

By the time of the Vietnam War, broadcasters had the equipment and the technology to cover war on a daily basis.

As the war dragged on, it was common practice for the networks to rotate correspondents in and out. Some were sent for a year at a time. Others went for six months, and star reporters often spent only weeks or days on special assignments. Unlike World War II when women had to be on the scene to get hired, by the time of Vietnam, the picture had changed somewhat. There was no longer the prejudice against a woman's voice but rather a paternalism that was hard to break through. Traditional male management was reluctant to send women into danger zones, even close to home. There had been fights over assigning women to cover riots and domestic trouble spots, as well as late-night assignments with no specific threat attached. The men in charge regarded women on staff protectively, much as they would their wives or daughters.

That is why I was so surprised by Zousmer's request that I go to Vietnam. But daily reports of the war were included on my daytime newscasts and the network was anxious to publicize its anchors, even a woman.

There was no discussion of what kinds of stories I would do in Vietnam so I made my own list, choosing to cover the human side of the conflict and not combat. The plan, such as one existed, was for me to work things out in Saigon with the bureau chief. No research material was provided, but I knew which books to read and I had been saving wire copy. Once again, it would be another case of winging it. I had only a vague idea of what was in store.

The first indication that our plane was approaching a war zone came as I observed the other passengers on that long flight. Boarding the Pan Am commercial flight from Honolulu, from Wake, Guam, and Manila were mainly servicemen, State Department employees, and those working for the U.S. Information Service or other civilian agencies. There were only three or four women. One of the men seated near me pointed out some of the cities of Vietnam as we followed the coastline. He also warned me we would make a sharp descent, rather than a gradual one, "to prevent snipers from hitting the plane as it makes its approach."

When we finally landed in Saigon, I remember seeing a delegation near the plane, including a young woman with a bouquet. My seatmate and I wondered who was being greeted so ceremoniously. We hadn't noticed anyone famous on board. I was terribly embarrassed to see that the reception was for me. Bob Lukeman, of our bureau, also arranged for that greeting to be filmed, and a day or so later, viewers of "News with the Woman's Touch" witnessed my arrival. My relatives, at least, were pleased.

Security restrictions at Tan Son Nhut Airport in Saigon were strict since it was the major military as well as civilian airport. Premier Ky's home was also on the grounds. Some days, depending on which South Vietnamese official was running things, no Vietnamese were permitted inside the airport. Other days, no American civilians could board either civilian or military planes. Since I traveled with a Vietnamese film crew once inside Vietnam, we never knew whether we were actually going to leave Saigon or not. Sometimes we did, and sometimes we didn't. It was always a relief to leave the airport, anyway. Rumor had it that the Viet Cong had been tunneling underneath it for years. Shortly after I returned home, the airbase was hit by mortars and several U.S. soldiers were killed.

The ABC News bureau was located in the Caravelle Hotel, a sturdy survivor of the French era. The Saigon bureau office was a converted hotel suite, with an editing room off to the side. A large jar of malaria pills was prominently displayed with a sign "take on Wednesday." The windows were criss-crossed with tape to prevent them from shattering following shelling. At night you could see lights in the sky from artillery fire.

During my stay, I used a room already rented to a member of the camera crew who was on the road, but I paid in full for it. Often, it turned out, several people were paying rent for the same room, not to the hotel but to someone in the bureau. I moved in and out of several such arrangements. Later, at least two bureau chiefs lost their jobs because of financial manipulation.

Running the bureau included juggling film crews and correspondents who came and went. Aside from the Vietnamese, most of the staff lived at the hotel, and the financial arrangements were largely incomprehensible. Later, ABC rented a house and presumably that removed some of the temptations.

As for currency, there were three rates of exchange; the official rate at the time was 74 piasters to the dollar, the military gave you 118, and the black market ranged from 150 to 175. Money was usually changed by a Vietnamese staff member in the black market. No matter what rate the staff got, expense accounts were scrupulously figured at the official rate. Presumably they knew back in New York what was going on, and the extra earnings must have been written off as hazard pay. Stateside ABC staff, as a rule, were sent to Vietnam for six months or a year. The bureau coordinated all coverage and worked closely with New York. In addition to shipping film to San Francisco for fast editing and transmission, some of the time the bureau had to arrange for satellite feeds of breaking news which was handled by the Tokyo bureau.

In addition to television, all correspondents fed radio spots. We made the radio feeds from an obscure location in a private house somewhere in Saigon. Our Vietnamese driver could locate it, weaving in and out of crowded streets and back alleys. On arrival, we went up a few floors in the creaking elevator and into an anteroom. Correspondents from the other networks were usually there, waiting their turn. Feeds could be made only at specified times during the day, inexplicably through Paris. You could hear the broadcasters trying to make contact, shouting "Ici Saigon. Où est Paris? Où est New York?"

Life at the Caravelle was hardly a story of wartime deprivation. A continental breakfast arrived from room service on request; tea and coffee with croissants, butter, and jam. French sufficed quite well for communication, and I was grateful for the two years I had studied it in high school.

Fortunately, the hotel had its own generator, since power failed in the city almost daily, and when that happened elevators stopped functioning, as did the air conditioning in the few buildings where it existed.

The sights of the city overwhelmed me. The Saigon marketplace held stall after stall of fruits, cakes, household goods, handicrafts, and tobacco, and everywhere there were barefoot children. An entire section of the market was devoted to chickens. Anything you bought, you bargained for. The black market was in another part of town. It was a big structure with an inside court. Every kind of military garb was for sale. No one knew exactly how these goods made their way there but it was assumed they were stolen off ships or from the bases. There were also stalls set up along the road, mainly run by women. They sold everything from Nestles chocolate bars to Crest toothpaste. In 1966, Nuygen Hue, or Street of Flowers, was still full of fresh flower stands, with gladiolus and other colorful flowers trucked in from the city of Dalat, despite the war. A semblance of normal life went on, but there was also evidence of war everywhere; restaurants put up grenade shields over their entire fronts to protect them from thieves and from exploding grenade fragments. One of the rumors going around Saigon was that restaurants paid off representatives of the Vietcong to prevent bombings. The Continental Palace Hotel must have paid a sizable sum; they had no grenade screens and one of the last open-air restaurants.

Paint was chipping off the European-style buildings put up by the French, and when the red roof tiles fell off they were replaced with tin. Lepers roamed the streets, which were always full of sick, dirty children. The heat was fierce. The workday for the city people of Saigon was then 9 to 12 and 3 to 6. Anyone who had any means of transportation went home for lunch; the streets were clogged with jeeps, foreign cars, and cyclopousses, three-wheeled vehicles with a chair in front, pedaled by a driver.

I roamed around freely during the day when I was not working, although Americans were advised to stay away from public places because it was an invitation for an attack. I found the roads were piled with garbage. Americans had hired most of the available Vietnamese men to work on the docks and in construction projects and depleted the ranks of the garbage collectors. So the piles just grew and grew. My walks gave me a sense of stories not being covered by the news crews, stories that would show American viewers what life was like in Saigon.

What I would do in Vietnam was left up to me and the bureau chief. I decided to spend five days in Saigon shooting there and getting acclimated before venturing out into the field. My two Vietnamese crew members had never worked with a female correspondent before. They spoke some English and very good French. My high school French along with English and lots of gestures had to do. We managed, somehow. I wanted to personalize the war if possible and deal with the country and the people who lived there. The first stories we did dealt with so-called District 8, Saigon's worst slum, and the Hoy Bin orphan home, then ten miles outside the city. The children, orphaned largely because of the war, had been adopted by the 578th Ordnance Company, and a flow of clothing arrived regularly from families in South Orange, New Jersey. The GIs spent their spare time building swings, and trying to make improvements in the children's living conditions. The irony of the situation was clear.

I was to discover on my return to New York that the local ABC affiliate in New York had used the orphanage story because of the New Jersey "hometown" angle. Most of the other Saigon stories got short shrift from the evening news. There was little interest in the Vietnamese people except for their politicians. Stories that told about the life of the people in whose interest we were supposedly fighting were ignored.

Once I felt comfortable enough with the country and with my crew, Mr. Tung, the cameraman, and Mr. Minh, who doubled as soundman and electrician, we set off on a trip to the Central Highlands. I was hoping to do stories on what it was like for the U.S.

military there, and left the question of covering combat for later. Our
first stop was Pleiku, about thirty miles from the Cambodian border.
All travel was with the Air Force, in C-130's, big cargo planes used
to carry troops and equipment. There were places to sit along the
sides of the plane, with room in the center for people to sprawl on
the floor and stack their weapons. Aside from press and an occasional
Agency for International Development (AID) worker, no one but the
troops were on board.

Before you arrived at a base, it was advisable to let the public
information officers know ahead of time, so you could be met. Our
little entourage carried very few personal belongings, but we were
loaded with film equipment, tape recorders, battery packs, and so on,
and we needed a truck or jeep to get around. This arranged, and
allowing for late flights, which were routine, we moved to the II Corps
headquarters. The country was divided into four corps areas.

Pleiku, near the Iadrang Valley, was the scene of frequent bloody
battles. It consisted of about six blocks of one-story open-front shops,
a few small houses, and a street of bars; the rest was rice paddies,
villages, and Montagnard tribes. Once we had been briefed in the
press tent—a tent with about twenty-two cots and gaslight only—I
was assigned to a room about a quarter of a mile away in the headquarters building.

The press tent was full of male correspondents and camera crews.
Unfortunately for me, it was directly opposite the latrine and every
time I entered the tent to use the typewriter, they had to roll down
the flaps facing the always busy, open facilities. This provided a good
deal of amusement among a rather grubby, tired bunch of reporters.
Since I appeared so infrequently in the press tent, no one bothered
trying to move the typewriter to the other side. That would have
been difficult anyway, as the tent was overcrowded with cots, and the
typing table was loaded with reporters' gear. I felt some guilt about
the sleeping accommodations I had, which were in a regular prefab
one-story housing unit, but at least there was a bathroom available.
On my forays out into the field, no such amenities existed. Vietnamese
in the countryside used ditches behind their housing, an altogether
unacceptable choice as far as I was concerned. At one army camp, I
was offered the opportunity to go into an empty tent and presumably
use the ground as the toilet facilities. I turned that down, too. Ultimately, I learned not to drink coffee in the morning, to drink sparingly
from my canteen during the day, and to wait, if possible, for a hospital
or some kind of indoor facility to turn up. If it didn't, the high reeds

that grew along the roads, which often sheltered enemy Vietcong, were the last resort.

The captain with whom I worked arranged for me to go out with the First Airborne Calvary at their base called Oasis. On the next day out in the field, my crew and I traveled by Huey—an open-sided helicopter that flew at about two thousand feet—with a watchful machine gunner at my side. A seatbelt was all that separated us from open space, the whipping wind, and the enemy somewhere down below. When we arrived at Oasis, the major who ran the civil affairs unit arranged for us to go out with the unit that day. The civil affairs teams were made up of a doctor, an interpreter, and sometimes an engineer.

The American forces had two functions in Vietnam: military operations directed against the organized communist armed forces, and civil action operations directed toward the rural civilians in an attempt to win them over to the cause of Western democracy, popularly known as "winning their hearts and minds."[2]

The futility of such a dual purpose took far too long to sink in. Certainly, the Montagnard tribespeople, many of whom did not know that Saigon was the capital or what an American was, were not good candidates. They took the soap and medicine and accepted the medical attention gladly, however. Quonset huts served as the Pleiku Provincial Hospital. Relatives of the Montagnard patients camped outside the hospital, cooking their own and the patient's meal over charcoal fires. There was a well, at least, that provided clean water. Inside, things weren't much better. There was electricity and running water in the one structure that contained the operating room and a functioning bathroom of sorts, a welcome sight to me in any case. One ward held mostly families suffering from the bubonic plague.

Later in my trip, I spent several days with the Marines in Da Nang, filming in the Da Nang Surgical Hospital, also staffed by Americans (civilian doctors brought over under the auspices of the U.S. Agency for International Development). Again, the beds were crowded, this time with surgical patients, two and three to a bed. Amputations were considered minor surgery. These were the daily casualties of the crossfire of war—six civilians to every serviceman lost.

Stories that involved the suffering of the Vietnamese or the Montagnards, however, didn't sell in New York. News management was interested only in the American presence and the effect of the war and its conduct on Americans. Fortunately the "Feature Story" program was an outlet for some of my footage, but that had very few viewers. My efforts to report the human side of the Vietnam War, at least in connection with the Vietnamese people, were not what they were looking for at that time.

In the early 1980s, when Betsy Aaron first went to Afghanistan for NBC News, and then later, in 1986, when she returned there for ABC, there was a market for other kinds of reporting. The interest in that war largely focused on the Soviet presence and influence. Since no Americans were directly involved, stories on the human interest aspect as it involved the Afghan people were salable to the news broadcast. Aaron was the only correspondent to her knowledge who talked to the Afghan women as well as to the men, and she tried both times she was in that part of the world to humanize the story.

I spent a great deal of time in Vietnam doing a story on how a U.S. Army base camp was established, complete with a huge laundry. That was edited in New York and almost made the 7:00 P.M. news. It "sat on the shelf," as the expression goes, for quite a while, waiting for a news peg, an event that would make the story newsworthy. When none turned up, it went to syndication and to our affiliates. We all preferred the network's nightly news, obviously, but syndication was better than nothing, and better than my own daytime broadcast which reached a limited audience. I thought the stories I was sending back had good human interest value and that it was a mistake not to include that kind of coverage. However, I had grown used to that brand of frustration and simply looked for stories that appealed to me.

I finally lucked out and ran into breaking news in Da Nang in April. The Buddhists had been involved in protests against the government, and several big demonstrations were being talked about. There was to be a general strike, and the day before, I covered a city-wide work stoppage, doing my narration from the top of parked trucks and showing traffic stopped in all directions. The people wanted free elections. The next day, we shot a march involving some ten thousand people, including yellow-robed Buddhists and uniformed Vietnamese soldiers, some on crutches. The entire city was shut down by a general strike. My crew translated banners for me, some expressing anger at the lack of American support for national elections. Finally, we had the elements they were looking for in New York: color, action, political content. Both stories made the news, but unfortunately over the weekend.

After returning three hours late in a jam-packed C130, with Vietnamese and American soldiers filling the rows of seats against the side of the plane and sleeping on the floor, I found mail in Saigon with news from home. My son Jeff had gotten the mumps.

A child's illness compared to the pain and suffering endured during the Vietnam War may seem insignificant, but as a mother I regretted not being home at the time. I was to return soon, and I was sure my husband and housekeeper could cope with the situation, but it made me aware of the extra pressures women face on overseas assignments. Male correspondents, then and now, often have their families nearby on a foreign assignment. Their presence provides a refuge and helps make a stressful life bearable. The women they marry seem willing to follow them as they move around the globe to changing home bases. When women began to cover foreign news, few could find that kind of comfort. The women who become foreign correspondents are almost always single.

It was hard for me to plan on an exact departure date, since Premier Ky often commandeered Air Vietnam planes for his own government's use. While I was waiting for a flight, I decided to restore my appearance after weeks in the field, and our bureau secretary, Miss Hien, directed me to her local beauty shop. She explained in advance how I should pay, escorted me there, and told a gaggle of young women what I wanted. The equipment was modern but there seemed to be only one towel which was shared by all the customers. The only other problem, from my point of view, was whether the electricity would stay on long enough to run the hair dryers.

After several cancellations of my flight, I finally left for Hong Kong on an Air France plane. I was relieved to depart in one piece. On the other hand, on returning to the States, the lack of concern and the indifference to the war seemed criminal.

Before the flight for Hawaii, I did several stories in Hong Kong. One was about "press widows," the women and children of the U.S. correspondents who lived there, and who saw their husbands only during "R & R" (rest and relaxation) breaks when they came home.

While it might be said that I broke ground for other women to go overseas, a short stint hardly qualifies me as a foreign correspondent. The first woman in television news to claim that distinction was Liz Trotta, then at NBC News. In 1968, she called me for advice on what to pack and to find out what it had been like in Vietnam. She became NBC's first full-time woman foreign correspondent, serving three tours of duty in Vietnam, first in 1968, then in 1969–70, and again in 1971 when she also filed stories from Laos and Cambodia. She was Singapore bureau chief from 1971 to 1973, and an NBC London-based correspondent from 1973 to 1975. By then, there were a few other women abroad. The first real move in that direction was a direct result of the women's movement and affirmative action, and because of what some of us managed to accomplish within our companies.

It was in the early 1970s that a sprinkling of women began to be sent overseas. Hilary Brown, a Canadian reporter on public radio and television, decided by 1971 that foreign news was what she wanted to cover, not the provincial Canadian beat where she found herself. Her efforts to find an overseas job in either a Canadian or U.S. news organization had failed. She did manage to get an assignment to cover the Shah of Iran's celebration of the 2500th anniversary of the country for radio, and after that stint, decided to stay overseas and free-lance on her own, moving on to India and Pakistan. It was 1971, and war there was imminent. Brown waited and reported on radio for the CBC when war finally broke out. It was at that time that she met a BBC television correspondent, John Bierman. They fell in love and decided to become a reporting team, living together when they could. He was then assigned to open the first BBC bureau in Teheran, and she went along continuing to report as a stringer, now for CBS radio in the states as well as for Canadian outlets. Two years later when Bierman was expelled from Iran, both moved to Israel. There was plenty of news there, including the Yom Kippur War, and her U.S. employers had an appetite for spots. It was by then 1973, when the effects of the women's groups and affirmative action coincided, and the networks were finally actively looking for women. ABC radio knew Brown's work because of her CBS reporting, and she was hired as their first female television foreign correspondent. She was offered a position in the London bureau, a plum assignment. Bierman, still with the BBC, was also able to make the move. They decided to get married while they were in London. Shortly afterwards, however, he was assigned to Cyprus, a jumping-off point for covering the Middle East. During the first year of their marriage, they saw each other only six times. Hilary Brown had been moved to Paris, a departure point for wherever news broke out. At first, the network was afraid to send her to a war zone, pulling her back at the last minute from covering the Portuguese revolution. But by 1974 when the war of attrition was underway in Israel, she insisted on going. She did well, and after that ABC was "perfectly willing," she says, "to let me risk my life along with the guys."[3]

The Paris assignment should have been considered ideal, but Brown found it increasingly difficult to see her husband only every few months. As a young woman, she had thought she would never marry, wondering if any man could put up with her goals and her determination to have the vagabond life of a foreign correspondent.

Now that Brown had found someone who accepted all of this, she found it increasingly intolerable to be apart so much. Brown then decided to accept an offer from NBC which had an opening in Tel Aviv. That way she knew they would at least be able to get together on weekends. It was then 1977, and Roone Arledge had become president of ABC News. No one knew what he would do, and in that period of uncertainty, she decided to make the move to NBC. She had earlier turned down an offer from ABC to return to the States and anchor the news portions of "Good Morning America," newly on the air, with Ted Koppel, because she wanted to stay overseas. Another negative development coinciding with Arledge's arrival was the change in Peter Jennings's role. As chief European correspondent, he began to usurp the work of other correspondents, arriving late on the scene, and using their footage. One day, after Brown had covered a story all day in Paris, Jennings arrived and, with a "here, hold my trench coat" gesture, did the story. This tactic became an increasing area of frustration for correspondents. For Hilary Brown, it wasn't so much the ego trip; rather it was professional pride. When you're out there covering a story, you want to be the one who reports it. Besides, the measure of correspondent productivity consisted of counting how often you got on the air.

So when NBC offered Tel Aviv, and a hefty salary increase, Brown moved. It was a time of constantly breaking news in the Middle East, including the Sadat visit to Israel. She had had a lean year at ABC, but now was getting on the "Nightly News" three nights a week, along with appearing almost daily on the "Today Show."

Life in Israel had other advantages. The bureau was not over-staffed, so one's work got used. It was before the era of video tape, and a reasonable lifestyle was still possible. Film went out on a charter or commercial flight and afterward one could go out to dinner or meet with a source. Later, when immediate transmission of tape became possible via satellite and more broadcasts had to be fed, there was no time to relax. There was also less time for checking facts, since competitive pressures were intense and speed was vital.

Those considerations had not yet changed correspondents' lives. During the two years the Biermans were in the Middle East, their son was born. Brown was anxious to have a child, and knew that at least in Tel Aviv both parents would be at hand; but Jonathan's birth was in London, a deliberate move on the Biermans' part so that their child would not have passport problems in later life. When they returned to Israel it was with their baby and an English nanny. Hilary, a mother at thirty-eight, went back to work, and all went well for nearly two years.

Brown was unusual for a female foreign correspondent in that she was married. The work and a normal social life are simply incompatible. Having a rewarding personal life is not the only challenge for a woman correspondent. She must also face the prejudice against women in the office.

Juggling one's personal and professional life is difficult for national network reporters but it is even a greater challenge for foreign correspondents. First, one must fight the competition to get the choice assignments, decisions that are often influenced by the reluctance to send a woman into danger and by the fact that women are usually not the favorite reporters in the bureau.

Susan Peterson joined CBS News in 1974 after having jobs in Chicago, Minneapolis, and Washington. Eight months into her employment, she was offered the London bureau. It was the first time CBS had given a woman a job as a foreign correspondent. Until then, the London posting was a reward to male reporters who had been to Vietnam. Two were already there: John Laurence and Bob Simon. Those two colleagues, at first, were unfriendly to Peterson, regarding her arrival as an intrusion and questioning her qualifications. The bureau chief, an unmarried man, appeared to hate women. He regarded her as a spy for the new vice president of news in New York, Bill Small. Peterson was indignant, since she didn't know Small any better than the others did. Worse yet, the bureau chief refused to assign her an office, which both of her colleagues had. It was the first time she felt anyone was against her solely because she was a woman, and she did not know how to deal with the situation. The first problem was the lack of an office. She was given only a desk near the door, so that she looked like another secretary-receptionist, and deliverymen and messengers constantly approached her. The chief would not even issue her a file cabinet and so she finally picked up an apple crate from the street and put it prominently in view on the desk. To complain to New York just after arriving, she felt, would look small and petty, so she decided to try to do the best she could. In the beginning, she got secondary assignments, but slowly began to prove her worth. She felt, however, that it took two to three years longer to prove herself than it would have taken a male correspondent. During the first year she almost went home, her frustration was so great. However, Bill Small fortuitously paid a visit to the bureau and found her without private space to work in; he sized up the situation, and ordered that she be given a regular office, with a door and a real file cabinet.

As time passed, Peterson's two male colleagues became more friendly and tried to help when they could. Nevertheless, assignments were often given to her at the last moment, when the chief knew she had theater tickets or another engagement. These were instances when he had been aware of the particular assignment well in advance. Fortunately, he departed after two years, and her situation improved when a more reasonable person was put in charge. During her four London-based years, she covered the South Molluccan hostage crisis, the Iranian revolution, Franco's death, and the installation of two popes. She made friends, and describes the time as a stupendous opportunity for covering the world.[4] But she was in what she calls her crucial thirties with a sporadic personal life. She had to be ready to hit the road within half an hour, and then possibly be gone for a month. Susan Peterson didn't worry much about it then. Work was her priority, and being a network foreign correspondent was the front-burner item. It was clear that her lifestyle could not take in another person or a lasting relationship. Gradually, however, her perspective began to change. It was supposed to be a glamorous life, but she began to question that when on one occasion she arrived in Paris late at night and had to eat toast and beer in her room because that was all room service had at that hour. Also in Paris, she found herself recording a narration voice track in the only quiet place she could find—a dirty broom closet. It wasn't the Paris she envisioned. Her life, she says, began to feel like a big lie, and she found she was becoming embittered and wanted to go home.

By the 1980s more women were sent overseas, but usually no more than one from each network. Most of the women reporters overseas are stringers, women who are already abroad and work on a per diem/per story basis. The practice is similar to the haphazard hiring of women during World War II. Women were still fighting the battle to prove they could handle dangerous and exhausting assignments. But one thing happened that opened the door a crack and allowed some women to go abroad. There was a change in the type of stories required from a foreign correspondent. Battle footage was no longer the mainstay of overseas coverage. Magazine programs, latenight specials, and morning news were clamoring for a variety of feature and background stories from abroad.

Betsy Aaron grabbed at that new interest at ABC and in the early 1980s did a number of in-depth foreign stories, including several from Afghanistan. Several men had turned down the Afghanistan assignment, feeling, she says, that the assignment would not do anything for their careers. It was also an arduous, dangerous story. If a woman turned it down, she would be regarded as a sissy, unwilling to take the risks of a real correspondent. For women, the business of proving oneself never ends. As things turned out, Aaron and her crew had to walk most of the 150 miles they finally covered, in order to report on the rebels' resistance to the Soviets.

In Lebanon, and in other parts of the Middle East, Aaron tackled the plight of Amerasian children among other stories. While she was praised for her work, she says it never seemed to earn her the right to go back without having to fight for the opportunity. The men who get the good foreign jobs go automatically because they are members of the club. Women have to argue their way there. One factor, Aaron believes, is that there is still a lingering fear on the part of management that the death of a female correspondent would be more embarrassing to the network than the loss of a man.[5]

Paternalism surfaces in a variety of ways. Despite Aaron's track record of dangerous overseas assignments, before she left for Lebanon, Ted Koppel asked her if she had her husband's permission to go. Aaron wonders if he would have called her under reverse circumstances, to ask if her husband, correspondent Dick Threlkeld, had her permission to go.

Female correspondents, domestically and abroad, have not been afraid to face danger. In 1977, when Aaron was a CBS news correspondent out of Atlanta, she was seriously injured during a Klan rally in Americus, Georgia, when a sports car plowed into the crowd. Her knee was badly damaged and surgery was required, followed by years of physical therapy at the Rusk Institute in New York. Despite residual leg problems, she did not hesitate to trek through Afghanistan. She willingly went to Iran to cover the revolution that led to the Shah's downfall.

Martha Teichner, a foreign correspondent for CBS posted to South Africa in 1987, recalls her network's earlier resistance to sending a woman to a danger zone. Vice president John Lane did not want to send her to El Salvador in 1979, because sending a woman to the civil war was too risky. He also warned he would deny ever having said that to her if she ever repeated it. And, as a matter of fact, he added he didn't particularly want to send a man who had three children to war either, that a single man was his first choice for such assignments.[6] Nevertheless, Teichner did finally prevail and made three reporting trips to El Salvador between 1979 and 1980 before being posted to London.

An additional barrier to women is favoritism which determines the choice of what Aaron calls the "correspondent du jour," who is almost never a woman. When management wanted to send someone to the Middle East, they did not approach her first, but would not level with her about why. She believes they are constitutionally unable to evaluate the women using the same standards as they do for the men.

Martha Teichner looks back on her years in Europe with mixed feelings. She had been working for CBS News in its Atlanta bureau when she was asked to replace Susan Peterson in 1980 in the so-called "woman's slot" in London. John Blackstone was sent there in the "man's slot." By then, the practice of favoritism, of featuring star correspondents, had become common, notably at CBS, but not exclusively there. In part, it developed because of the increasing role of the anchorman in determining who would appear on his broadcast. Teichner found that Blackstone was assigned the best stories, including the Iranian hostage story. While she was eventually sent to report on the hunger strikes in Northern Ireland, it was only after he had been there first, getting on the air when the story was fresh. She was always the "other person" assigned. She did take her complaints to news vice president Ed Fouhey, who acknowledged the truth of the situation but said anchorman Dan Rather preferred to use Blackstone, and wanted to make him a personality.

Frequently Teichner found herself in the midst of violence on the streets, but her coverage would then go into stories fronted by Blackstone. Earlier, Hilary Brown found herself in the same boat, feeding material to Peter Jennings. By the mid-1980s, the technique was used frequently not only overseas but on domestic stories as well, with favored correspondents on air while the others served in invisible reporting roles. During Teichner's London stint, Tom Fenton was designated chief European correspondent, and at times, everyone reported in the field for his pieces.

In most bureaus, the problem of being second or third in stature is tough to live with. Teichner says there are compensations; the money is good, the stories are there. The foreign assignments were exhilarating, great experiences. One's fate depends, however, on many different people: the bureau manager, the news vice president, the evening news anchorman.

Again, as in Betsy Aaron's case, Teichner faced a battle to get the go-ahead on such assignments. And with the constant change of news administrations, one could have no confidence that the point had been made. A new man would have to be reeducated. It was not only top management that had to be won over. The same VP who fought Teichner on the El Salvador assignment also resisted sending her to cover the Jonestown massacre. He was well-meaning, protective, but a negative factor in her career. Such attitudes, more prevalent in the over-fifty set of executives, protect women only from getting ahead since a foreign assignment is often a prerequisite for moving up in the organization. Rather and Jennings both developed their reputations as star journalists overseas. The bureau chief is usually the person who holds that power of assignment.

When Martha Teichner wanted to go to Beirut she pressed the bureau chief to allow her to go and to grant permission to apply for a visa. Her request to go was never put into telexes to New York, because the bureau chief told her "they" didn't want women in Beirut. At the same time, the men in the bureau were being rotated to Poland, where the government was involved in street battles with the union Solidarity. The women were not assigned there either, and the male correspondents resented it. There was more than enough violence to cover to go around. The men felt the women should take their turns, but the system, for the moment, wouldn't allow it. Finally, assistant foreign editor Don deCesare, on duty in New York in place of his boss, gave Teichner the okay to go to Damascus, and then on to Beirut. Teichner distinguished herself in her reporting and made several trips to Lebanon between October 1983 and March 1984. Her excellence there paved the way, some months later, for her former London producer, Lucy Spiegel, to be assigned as Beirut bureau chief. Back in New York, management was now bragging about what a good job their women were doing in that part of the world.

By 1983, Teichner was asked to return to the States, where she was assigned to the Dallas bureau. Once again she had to play second fiddle to a newly hired, younger, less-experienced male correspondent. New York management could not bring themselves, she says, to name a woman the senior correspondent there. By then, at thirty-eight, she felt she had reached a turning point in her personal life. In London, it was possible to have friends, since many single people worked there. But Dallas turned out to be a couples kind of town where it was impossible to meet single men and women—all in all, a bad work environment. She traveled constantly and was home only a day or two a week, mainly to do laundry and rest. Life became a series of trips to the airport, and work totally enveloped her life. When she was transferred there after four years in London, she felt her chance for a personal life had ended; she felt devastated at the thought of being alone forever. She believed she would never marry or have children. That was always a vague goal, but the excitement and challenge of the work had compensated and pushed it into the background.

Suddenly, as she neared forty, she was concerned about the future. Would the network keep an older woman correspondent, and what kind of life would that be?

Teichner has, however, thought about the future in some practical terms, having bought a house for her mother, whom she helps support. The house is in a college town, and Teichner thinks about living there some day and possibly teaching. She is sure she could not go back to working in local news.

Apparently that decision is still years away since Teichner was assigned to South Africa in 1987, probably for two years. In that bureau, they work seven days a week. There are constant problems with the authorities, but it is a major hot spot, sure to generate news. Martha Teichner tells those who ask about the work and the life that it's a non-personal life, that you might as well join a convent. The men seem to be able to manage marriage because their wives are willing to go along bodily and emotionally, putting up with the deprivation. The men manage to have that support and companionship. Teichner says that the dominant feeling of most of the women correspondents is concern over their work's reception back home in the "fishbowl" or the "rim," the little group of news executives who run the evening news. Every story is like your first. You have to prove yourself anew each time.

Hilary Brown found that out when she returned in 1980 from her ten-year stint overseas. The new NBC News president, Bill Small, and others felt she should return to the States, and she became convinced that would be a smart move. Her husband would go too. She said later that this move proved to be a disaster for her career. The return to home base is a common problem, it turns out, for foreign correspondents. While overseas, it is often difficult to keep track of office politics back home. It is easy to be unaware of where the good assignments are.

Unfortunately, management assigned Brown to the Pentagon, where there happened to be an opening. The family was to move to Washington later, if things worked out. It was a post, she says, that she was totally unsuited for. Her competition at ABC and CBS were seasoned Washington reporters who had been on the beat for five and seven years respectively and had all the contacts. She did not even know where the washroom at the Pentagon was and within a short time was regarded as a failure. Before taking the post, she had tried to find out what would happen if it didn't work, but was reassured and her doubts swept aside. It was a sink-or-swim proposition, as it usually is, and when she did not come up with exclusives within a month, Paul Greenberg, then executive producer of "NBC Nightly News," turned against her, she says, and she found herself in an impossible situation, in a job she never should have held. She hung on for less than a year and was then moved to general assignment.

By 1981, it appeared to be time for Brown to change networks again. The family moved to the New York suburbs, nanny and all, and she returned to ABC News. By then, her husband was writing a book. She traveled in and out of the country, doing a number of stories in South America, including the Falklands War. Male stars, however, were regularly preempting the big stories, and her professional frustrations increased. In the New York bureau, which had six correspondents when she first joined ABC, there were now twenty, and not enough work to go around. News President Arledge had overexpanded, and the other networks had done the same. She pressed for another overseas assignment, and was promised Rome, where there was about to be an opening. A date was set. The family started packing and selling household appliances. Their house was on the market. Then, suddenly, the move was cancelled. Roone Arledge, absent much of the time and distracted for several months while obtaining a divorce, had returned to work, reviewed the staff situation, and cancelled all foreign relocations. This time, there seemed to be no U.S. solution. Brown accepted a local television anchoring job on the "News Hour" for the Canadian Broadcasting Corporation in Toronto. Her husband continued work on his book, and also became editor of *MacLean's*, a prestigious Canadian weekly news magazine. They bought a house, and live comfortably.

When Susan Peterson said she wanted to go home, CBS wanted her to stay in Europe. NBC, meanwhile, had made her an offer to anchor a proposed hour-long daytime broadcast called "Our World," from Washington. She felt a desperate need to go home, the show sounded good, so she packed up and left for NBC and the USA.

The program never got on the air. Budget constraints forced its cancellation. Peterson found herself in Washington without a special beat, in a bureau with twenty-eight other correspondents. After covering much of the world, she now felt in limbo. She had a great deal of independence overseas, but as others before her discovered, she found in the new setting she got no credit for the past.

After six years of covering the Middle East and eastern and western Europe, she found herself at stakeouts on the 11:00 P.M.-to-4:00 A.M. shift at the State Department during a hostage crisis. Even if something happened, there was no broadcast to report on. The men, she said, did not get those assignments. She was assigned the

third position at the State Department, which meant she never got
on the air. The question then became, "Why am I doing this?" Her
unhappiness with the business grew. There was frustration with the
brevity of the reports, which just amounted to doing headlines. "After
a while," she said, "it was hard to go home, hold up my head and
say, 'Didn't I do a good job today? Didn't I cover that story fairly
and well?' And the last few years I couldn't say that with any pride."

Peterson began to consider leaving, and started to think about
what skills she had that would transfer to something else. A decision
did not come easily. She talked to people, and suffered at the thought
of leaving news and starting something else. The biggest moment,
and one of the toughest, was telling her parents of her decision. She
flew to Florida, saying, "I can't take it anymore, my contract is up
in ten months and I'm going to leave and start my own business." To
her surprise, they applauded her decision, observing that her face
was stressed, and that they noticed that for some time she had seemed
lethargic about what she was doing.

Increasingly, her life had seemed out of control, a common
complaint of many women in broadcast news. There was no way to
meet anyone for dinner without taking a phone number so she could
reach them if she had to cancel. As she neared forty, a personal life
now seemed important. The four offers of work from private clients
she had solicited, she felt, could all be hers if she began her own
business. She finally quit NBC in 1983 on a Friday. On the following
Monday, Susan Peterson Productions came into existence. She now
makes films and tapes for health associations, foundations, industry,
and academic institutions, and counsels politicians and business people
on how to handle the media. She worried that the change would be
difficult, that she would be overwhelmed with nostalgia for the business she once loved. Much to her surprise, she says she has never had
one single moment of regret. She is happier and says her sense of
humor has returned. She found she is doing new things, exploring
other facets of herself she never knew existed, and is using her skills
by writing, conceiving, and executing projects from start to finish.
Four months after she left network news, she met a man she cares
about, and they plan to be married. She had had no time in her life,
she felt, for this kind of relationship, until then.

Is it possible for men, this kind of gypsy existence? Peterson
thinks it is. They have wives, who are there when they need them,
who pack the suitcase and unpack it, who take care of the children,
and who are there for them emotionally. But the men are not in
control of their time either, and have the same inability to plan ahead

the simplest thing, from having dinner out with friends to attending the theater or a school play.

Peterson says her fiancé has observed that the network reporters he's met radiate feelings of insecurity. Peterson says, only partially in jest, that sometimes when she sees bag ladies talking to themselves on the street, she's convinced one of them was once a network correspondent.

For Peterson it came down to thinking about the future, and wondering if at sixty-two she would be on a stakeout somewhere in the middle of the night. She decided there were other choices. There is life, she says, after "a minute twenty," the usual length of her stories.

Neither Hilary Brown nor Susan Peterson had contemplated early marriage, or thought much about it. Work was the goal, and both resemble other correspondents, male and female, in the hard driving, tireless approach common to the breed. Hilary Brown now regrets that she did not have a second child. She felt they could have handled two. She was thirty-eight when the first one was born, her husband thirteen years older. Their efforts to have another failed. At forty-five, she values her family life, while still being uneasy about her local anchoring job. Now, it seems difficult to leave a comfortable home in Canada. They have a predictable and, at least for her, undemanding way of life. She still hopes that they can all return to Europe at some future time. And if her age is a negative factor by then for television, there is still radio. On the other hand, she sometimes thinks about a total career change. Such decisions are in the future.

Betsy Aaron knows her jaunts overseas have been easier to manage for her than for some of her colleagues because she has no children. Her marriage to Threlkeld is her second, and his children from his previous marriage live with his ex-wife. Aaron's first marriage was to John Aaron whom she met early in her career while she was working as a secretary for ABC News. He had been coproducer of Edward R. Murrow's "Person to Person," and was a partner of Jesse Zousmer in that enterprise. At her first husband's death, Betsy Aaron was in her early thirties and she remained single for the next nine years. She says her generation got a heavy dose of the message that women's lives were only validated if they became wives and mothers. Aaron wanted to be a reporter as well, but still feels somehow incomplete because she did not fulfill those expectations of motherhood. After John Aaron's death, she moved to Philadelphia to a reporting and writing job for a local station, becoming a network news producer, and finally a network correspondent in New York. Aaron was unmarried during the crucial child-bearing years of her thirties. Now, at fifty, the issue is moot. Aaron feels that women often have to compromise if they want to have it all.

## Notes

1. Erik Barnouw, *Tube of Plenty* (New York: Oxford University Press, 1975), p. 171.
2. See James Wilson Gibson, *The Perfect War: Technowar in Vietnam* (Boston: Atlantic Monthly Press), 1986; General Bruce Palmer, Jr., *The Twenty-five Year War: America's Military Role in Vietnam* (Lexington: University of Kentucky Press), 1984.
3. Hilary Brown interview (23 November 1986). All other information from Ms. Brown in this chapter was taken from this interview.
4. Interview with Susan Peterson (13 November 1986). All other information from Ms. Peterson in this chapter was taken from this interview.
5. Betsy Aaron interview (14 October 1986). All other information from Ms. Aaron in this chapter was taken from this interview.
6. Martha Teichner interview (9 October 1986). All other information from Ms. Teichner in this chapter was taken from this interview.

Pauline Frederick reported for ABC radio in the late 1940s. She made the transition to television broadcasting during the 1948 political conventions, and became the first newswoman to work full time on the staff of an American television network. (Photo courtesy of Lee Silvian)

Pauline Frederick joined NBC in 1953 and had a distinguished broadcasting career with the network until her retirement in 1975. She is shown here in Washington, D.C., in the late 1950s with David Brinkley, Chet Huntley, Ned Brooks, and Bill Henry. (Photo courtesy of Lee Silvian)

In 1957 Marlene Sanders was the associate producer and Mike Wallace the host for the successful "Night Beat" interview show on WABD-TV in New York. (Photo courtesy of Marlene Sanders)

Marlene Sanders covered the civil rights march on Washington in 1963 for WNEW radio. (Photo: Planned Photography, Vince Finnigan and Associates)

ABC News hired Marlene Sanders as a correspondent in 1964. Within months, she had her own daily newscast and soon became the first woman to anchor an evening television news broadcast. (Photo: ABC News)

Peter Jennings and Marlene Sanders co-anchored the ABC News television coverage of the 1965 presidential inauguration of Lyndon B. Johnson, ABC's first competition with other television networks in covering a major political event. (Photo: ABC News)

Marlene Sanders was sent to Vietnam by ABC News in 1966 to cover the war. Working with cameraman Mr. Tung, she was based first in Saigon. (Photo: ABC News)

Visiting a Vietnamese refugee camp, Marlene Sanders interviewed a U.S. soldier about conditions there. (Photo: ABC News)

Liz Trotta became the first full-time woman foreign correspondent in television news when NBC sent her to Vietnam in 1968, 1969, and 1971. (Photo courtesy of Liz Trotta)

ABC News correspondent Mal Goode and Marlene Sanders interviewed New York mayor John Lindsay for "Issues and Answers" in 1967. (Photo: ABC News)

Muriel Humphrey campaigned for her husband, Hubert Humphrey, in the 1968 presidential race. Marlene Sanders covered her role for ABC News. (Photo: ABC News)

In 1974, Susan Peterson joined CBS News and covered events at the White House. She moved to the network's London bureau eight months later, the first time CBS had named a woman as foreign correspondent. (Photo courtesy of Susan Peterson Productions)

After several years at CBS, Susan Peterson moved to NBC, and by 1983 had begun her own firm, Susan Peterson Productions. (Photo courtesy of Susan Peterson Productions)

# 4

## Struggling to Make It, Juggling to "Have It All"

Not only foreign correspondents face difficult compromises. National network reporters and producers travel often and have unpredictable schedules. They also complain of feeling their lives are "out of control." They must consciously decide if they will have children, and when. Concomitant with that decision is the question, "How important is this job to me?" The answer can be difficult for those who thought they could have it all.

I was twenty-nine when I had a child, and I never really thought about the pros and cons. I just assumed I would make it all work. Organizing child-care was my main concern. The emotional problems didn't really come into it. My husband was always supportive of my work and my income. His schedule was such that he was there to take up the slack. Besides, I couldn't imagine myself being satisfied with staying home all day.

As a working mother I did not lose out on all the joys those dedicated to full-time motherhood assume we do miss. One weekend just after he turned one year old, our son walked on his own, as both parents watched. Time spent with him was a treat, and we both looked forward to seeing him at the end of the day. Quality time a myth? Not in my book. When we were with him he got plenty of attention, and our various housekeepers over the years followed the rules we outlined.

In the early sixties, there was no public discussion of the child-care problems of working couples. Middle-class women were apparently staying home. If working-class women needed child-care, which they no doubt did, it was not a public issue. I never felt guilty about working since all concerned seemed to be thriving as far as I could see.

My son never felt cheated, a fact he confirmed as a young man when he wrote a letter to *New York Magazine* from Harvard University where he was studying law. He was responding to an article the magazine had run about career women who were also mothers, by then not a new phenomenon. It read:

> Fortunately the "New York Mother" was old news to some of us, the hearty band of young adults who were raised in New York by two working parents. We know that two, caring and compassionate and (by necessity) well-organized parents are far more important for kids than omnipresent maternal hovering. My mother (CBS News correspondent Marlene Sanders) was in Vietnam when I got the mumps, but Dad holding the thermometer left no scars. Working mothers, then and now, means liberation for women, men, and their children.[1]

As TV newswomen struggle to make a personal life (including motherhood) and a demanding career possible without sacrificing success, some are finding Washington assignments most compatible. The job of White House correspondent is the most desirable because of its high visibility and generous amount of air time, but covering Congress or government agencies can also be rewarding. All Washington assignments offer at least the possibility of a reasonably predictable home life. By 1976, a number of women were being featured as Washington correspondents, including Lesley Stahl, Judy Woodruff, Cassie Mackin, and Ann Compton. None of those women were still in the same jobs by 1987. Compton, of ABC News, was the first broadcast newswoman to be assigned as a full-time White House correspondent. When she had her children she felt even the White House beat demanded too much travel and she gave it up to work on Capitol Hill so she could be home with her growing family more regularly. Judy Woodruff was NBC White House correspondent but left NBC after she had her first child. She ran into problems at the network not related to her recent motherhood and now has found a comfortable home as a featured correspondent for the "MacNeil/ Lehrer NewsHour" on PBS. In 1986 she took a maternity leave to have her second child and was back at work in a few months. She rarely travels. Many network women envy her lengthy interviews and long reports on issues, as well as her control of her hours, and time for a personal life. Mackin of NBC was a rising star, well regarded by everyone, and later was lured to ABC by Roone Arledge. Her promising career was cut short by her early death from cancer.

Lesley Stahl of CBS News worked the White House beat for eight years. In 1986 she says, "I was saying to myself, I've seen this before, it's the same thing, here's what they'll do, here's what they won't do. In a way that made me valuable, but I was losing my edge."[2] When the idea was proposed that she become national correspondent and do analysis, it appealed to her; that was coupled with hosting "Face the Nation" on Sundays, which she had begun to do in 1983. Stahl joined CBS News in 1972 as a Washington-based reporter. At forty-six, she is married and the mother of a daughter who was not born until Stahl was in her late thirties. In a sense, she says, that decision has had an effect on her career. "I cannot go after things like '60 Minutes' because I have a child and it would be a sacrifice, but I have my child and it's wonderful, it's my life." The "60 Minutes" correspondents are on the road about 70 percent of the time.

Stahl admits that many women are workaholics. She's not sure what the reason is, conceding it might be insecurity because of women's late arrival in the business. "I don't know," she says. "It's inside though and even when the evidence is out there that you don't have to be, it's one reason we do succeed in this business. We just give it everything. . . . Maybe it's because our kind of personalities are attracted to this industry, compulsive, deadline-oriented people who keep pushing ourselves to see how much work we can do. We love work. . . . It's not just a symptom in the early stage, it goes on."

NBC White House correspondent Andrea Mitchell agrees. In part, she says, it's because she is responsible not only for "Nightly News," where she is second to Chris Wallace, but also for the "Today Show." She says her routine often runs like this:

> I have to be here on the phone, working an extraordinary number of hours every day. It generally means I have to be at the studio at 5:30 or 6:00 in the morning, work the entire day and then after the evening news, talk to the "Today Show" producers about how we can advance the story beyond the "Nightly News" version. So when I get home, I read the early editions of the newspapers when they come out around midnight so I can follow up any stories that my print colleagues have developed. I often call White House officials at one or two in the morning to prepare for going in live at six A.M.[3]

This is not a daily routine, but happens more often when her colleague Chris Wallace is on vacation or out of town.

Mitchell admits to being ambitious but does not consider that pejorative. "Sometimes I think women get criticized in subtle and not so subtle ways for being aggressive or ambitious. We're called pushy, bitchy, if we pursue a line of questioning at the White House aggressively. I get dumped on by the press secretary, but if Bill Plante [CBS News] or Sam Donaldson [ABC News] do it, it's okay. It's really a matter of male expectations that we behave in a certain way." She said that covering the Reagan White House was not much different from the Carter days.

> I don't think the Carter White House was any easier for women because of the particular personalities of the people involved. No matter what Jimmy Carter's view of women in authority might have been, with the exception of Anne Wexler, he didn't have any women around him in the inner circle. This president [Reagan] has the kind of men around him that are used to working with women. There used to be greater sensitivity during the first term. There were several people in the White House who were more even handed, but that's not the case in the second term.

People on the White House beat are often reluctant to be away for any length of time. Is it insecurity? Mitchell explains:

> I think that's bred into us. Sure I felt insecure. Partly it's my own fault because I wouldn't want to be away during a major story. So you're always afraid to leave town because you could miss THE big story. That means you have to take every Reagan trip, miss every holiday because you're in California during major holidays. It's not something that was demanded of me except that I noticed a lot of other women tending to work harder to reach a certain level. . . . When I came to the White House and worked weekends, I found I couldn't take days off during the week and follow the flow of information, especially as you're learning a beat. I literally worked seven days a week the first two years. It takes its toll. I finally realized that I had proved myself, and there are times when you have to step back and find a little peace and quiet. I took my first real vacation last summer, a vacation that was not interrupted by being called back to work. I was completely out of pocket for two weeks in Tuscany and I really discovered that one can live without the *New York Times.*

Mitchell, at forty-one, is single. Her six-year marriage ended in divorce in 1976. She says she would like to have a child, but has no plans at the moment to remarry. "I guess the bottom line is still that if it's a choice between an important personal commitment and being at a presidential news conference, I'm going to still choose the presidential news conference."

Those women who have made time for personal lives appear to be most happy with their careers and most optimistic about their futures. CBS correspondent Susan Spencer is one of those confident and uncomplaining newswomen. She joined WCCO-TV, Minneapolis,

in 1972, remaining for five years, as a reporter, co-anchor, and producer. It was not her first job, but she was lucky to be at the CBS
affiliate formerly known as a farm team for male network correspondents. Her job there coincided with affirmative action and the push
for women to enter the business. In 1977 she joined the CBS News
Washington bureau. She covered Senator Edward Kennedy's bid for
the presidency in 1980, and drew coverage of the Democratic nominee
for President, Walter Mondale, in 1984. She is also one of the few
women regularly featured during the political convention coverage,
and often anchors the Sunday 6:00 P.M. "CBS Evening News." She
says she doesn't worry about the future, which is always uncertain
anyway, not because she is a woman but because of the vagaries of
the business itself. She feels she has a good job, is in demand, and
hopes it continues. Spencer says, however, that her competence would
stand her in good stead if she had to look elsewhere. She would like
to see more women in management where she thinks more balance
is needed, and where there would be less of a macho syndrome. She
feels women are less likely to do things just to impress others and are
less apt to flaunt or abuse power.

Spencer is married for the second time, again to a newspaperman. She says she thinks about becoming a mother, but that's as far
as it's gone. She cites several Washington colleagues who have successfully managed the dual role: Rita Braver, Lesley Stahl, and ABC's
Ann Compton. But she travels a good deal and knows a child would
complicate her life. She concedes she could afford it, between her
husband's salary and her own. However, as the 1988 election campaign
approached and as Spencer neared forty, the motherhood decision
remained in the future.

Rebecca Bell began her career as a newspaperwoman, moved
on to writing TV news, and then worked as an assignment editor. For
a while she left the business to raise her two children. Returning to
work at WCAU in Philadelphia, she ran into problems because of her
children. By then she was a single parent. She remembers:

> I came into work late, having phoned in that my son had hurt himself
> and I had to take him to the doctor. When I walked into the office
> the news director looked at me and said, "you're going to have to
> make a choice between your career and your children." I quit two
> weeks later and joined PBS. That was my choice. And people said to
> me, "you're working for 'New Jersey Nightly News?' Oh, how pa-
> thetic." And I thought, damn it, my kids come first. As a single mother
> there was no question that I had to do it. I had no backup except

whatever person was helping at home. . . . I used to live in dread of the housekeeper calling up ill.[4]

Later, when her children were high-school age and in boarding school, Bell took a network job. She worked overseas for a time for NBC News, an experience she describes:

> I was doing some very big stories in Europe, the hunger strike in Belfast, it was the time of the Charles and Diana wedding, the time of the race riots in London. I was doing a lot of that work that I was really fascinated by and enjoyed. But the realization hit that I did not want to travel anymore. I traveled 300 thousand miles my last year reporting for the magazine show "Monitor" [later called "First Camera"]. I think it's two things that happened. I think it's a young person's business because you can't have much of a personal life in it. It's very difficult. It's a trade-off, isn't it? I no longer wanted to work twelve-, fifteen-, eighteen-hour days. I had a successful run when I made the decision to go into management. I was forty-one. I had been on prime-time TV once a week for two years, and a funny thing happened. I noticed it didn't boost my self-esteem. Being on camera no longer became that important and in a funny way I think I outgrew it.

For a while Bell had a management job at NBC in New York. When she decided to remarry, her fiancé was working in Washington for the BBC. Bell quit her New York job, moved to Washington, remarried, and is now working for Stanley Hubbard's satellite news distribution system, CONUS (Continental U.S.). She notes:

> I don't feel bitter. I really had the best of all worlds. I have children. I had a fascinating career that aided my children both financially and emotionally, which was necessary to do and that was tricky. I've had a fascinating life. I'm now starting a new phase of life, a new marriage. You can have it all, but not at the same time, is what I figured out. If you do it sequentially, you can do it.

But the biological clock ticking away panics many young women working their way up in the industry. Their plight is not unusual. According to the *New York Times* only 35 to 40 percent of successful women over forty have children as compared to 93 percent of their male colleagues.[5]

The greatest complaint by young women correspondents and producers is their feeling of being out of control. After facing incredible competition to get into their positions and after working hard to get promoted, they find themselves having to make difficult choices between their careers and their personal lives. Lori Hillman, a CBS News producer, says the job poses many dilemmas:

> ... when you decide to work in hard news you make a choice; you
> agree to work on weekends and late at night; it's terrible for your
> social life. . . . I think if you get into this business in your late twenties
> and you haven't developed any really significant relationships, or got-
> ten married, you're going to be in trouble. Even though you're out
> in the field most of the time meeting all sorts of interesting people,
> it's not easy. I mean, you might be lucky, but breaking plans all the
> time and getting called at three in the morning and being sent out of
> town, it's very hard to keep people interested when you have those
> kinds of limitations. . . . I think what happens in this business is you
> get entrenched, it becomes consuming, work consumes so much of
> your time.[6]

While still in her twenties, Hillman left the network and her New
York–based job because she met someone she wanted to marry who
worked in San Francisco. After her marriage, she was able to switch
to local news, landing a good job as executive producer of special
projects at the CBS affiliate, KPIX-TV. She misses the professional
rewards of network news but likes her work. She says local news allows
her the great advantage of being able to control her life both professionally and personally.

Some women decide to give up their careers in favor of the
family which is what Peggy Stanton did in 1967. It was so difficult to
get into the business then that her decision took me by surprise. At
the time I was anchoring "News with the Woman's Touch," and ABC
was looking for another woman correspondent so that I could get
away and go on the road more often.

Stanton (who was known as Peggy Smeeton before she married)
was in her twenties, based in Washington, and in 1965 the only other
female correspondent besides me on the staff. She traveled on some
of the trips with Lady Bird Johnson, and also with President Lyndon
Johnson. Shortly after she joined the network, she met Congressman
William Stanton from Ohio, and they became engaged. They planned
a gala engagement party, and had the invitations printed, the envelopes
addressed. The afternoon the invitations were to be mailed she was
told she would be traveling with the White House press, and found
that the trip would extend through the time of the scheduled party.
She was out of town on assignment at the time she got the news, and
she immediately called her fiancé's office from a phone on the highway,
shouting over the sound of truck traffic that he should not mail the
invitations, that the party had to be cancelled. As things worked out,
her trip, originally scheduled for five days, lasted closer to two weeks.

When she returned, with the wedding date now in sight, she

was informed she would be accompanying the President on a trip to the Far East. No way, she said. She marched into the bureau chief's office and told him she was not going, that he had cancelled her engagement party and "I'll be damned if you can cancel the wedding." She didn't go, and the wedding duly took place six months after she joined ABC News. By the summer of 1967 she was pregnant and still subbing for me on the "News with the Woman's Touch" show, as my travel increased. Meanwhile, her husband's political career had its own demands, with his base in Washington and his district in Ohio. She described a typical week during that period like this: Saturday night they were together in Ohio. Sunday night he flew to Washington while she flew to New York to substitute for me, where she remained for Monday and Tuesday nights. Wednesday after the broadcast she flew to Washington to be present at a dinner party at their house, returning to New York the following morning. Thursday night her husband came to New York, Friday morning he flew to Ohio. Finally Friday afternoon, she flew to Ohio. This kind of routine continued through August, when I was away on assignment and then on vacation. Finally having spent less than two years at the network and seven months pregnant, she quit.

News, she says, is more like a calling than a profession, and in her case she felt she couldn't have everything. After working in small stations in Milwaukee and then in Washington, Peggy Stanton felt she had fulfilled her goal of making it at the network level. The demands of her husband's political career, she found, were not compatible with her life. After her only child, a daughter, was born, she felt that if she continued, then neither parent would ever be at home. She feared that the last-minute assignments and the disruption of her home life implicit in her job would make the success of her marriage doubtful.

Stanton does not regret her choice. She became a free-lance feature writer for the *Washington Post* and other newspapers, and co-authored two books. Now in her late forties, she is free to travel with her husband, who after a long congressional career joined the World Bank.

It's not only the travel by choice that she likes, Stanton says, but her "superb quality of life," a happy marriage, a daughter in college, and the satisfaction of working when she wants to. The things that attracted her to news—the issues and concern over public policy—continue for her through her husband's work. The main plus for her, however, is that she, not an organization, controls her life.[7]

But in network news, some of the best jobs involve constant travel. Correspondents, producers, and bureau managers figure that two or three years in a city may be all they can count on. For field producers attached to bureaus, and correspondents assigned there, home may be a place to do laundry, repack, and pay bills. Living out of a suitcase is a routine part of almost every week. In one's twenties, that prospect is exciting. It's why people want to work in news: to see the country or the world, to report on its problems, hoping by that work to leave the world a little better place than they found it. By age thirty, the passage of time becomes a reality. People in their twenties seem to feel that time stretches endlessly ahead and all things are possible. At thirty, life has a sharper focus. Marriage, if you care about it, may slip out of your grasp. Childbearing years do not last forever. Parents are aging and their death becomes a reality. The questioning about where work figures in a life scheme, if there is one, becomes more intense.

Lesley Stahl remembers that some of her best advice came from a male: "He said the secret was to . . . never forget which are the rubber balls and which are the glass balls. Obviously, the glass balls are your family and your health, and some of the rubber balls have to do with the job, let's face it."[8] NBC White House correspondent Andrea Mitchell agrees. "My generation has not handled these things very well. Those of us who are single have probably made the choices in terms of career and not in terms of our personal [needs]. . . . I am just hoping that we can start holding back something, and not being so available."[9] Those struggling with this issue now are part of the first generation of TV newswomen who were brought in when the FCC added women to the Equal Employment Opportunity rule in 1971. They have often delayed having children or did not have any at all because of the intense struggle to prove their worth in the workplace. There was also a feeling that the "new" career women had to dispel the stereotypical fears of employers who thought women were a bad investment since they expected that after women learned the job they would get pregnant and leave. Therefore, women in broadcasting who decided to have both career and family were pioneers, breaking new ground and old ideas about how job and family life should work. Most of these newswomen have worked for five years or more and were married for three to five years before they even considered having a child. Their one advantage in making their family situation work is that they were with their organizations long enough to have moved up in the professional hierarchy to positions that allowed them to have some control over their professional and personal lives.

Amy Entelis recruits producers and correspondents for ABC

News. She tells women to "get as much accomplished as you can before you have a family. The higher position you have, the easier it is to come back without losing anything."[10] She believes that the more status you have, the more power you have to work out arrangements for maternity leave and job assignments. She uses herself as a model. She worked at ABC as a producer, but after she had her baby, Luke, she managed to move from the unpredictable schedules of producing to a management job with a fixed schedule. She has also noticed, as she screens hundreds of audition tapes, that most of the female applicants are single. When she sees a woman in local news who has children and also has network potential, the woman often does not want to make the switch to the network but prefers local news because although the hours are long, she will always be able to go home at night.

Renée Ferguson worked in local news for nine years before she became a CBS network correspondent. After she had her child, Jason, she was able to switch to the Northeast bureau and have a home in the New York City area. She covered the states from Pennsylvania to Maine, all within a few hours' plane ride so that she could often be home at night. She also had her mother living with her to look after Jason. Ferguson's husband, Ken, worked all day at the magazine *Black Enterprise*. Although Ferguson is devoted to her work she thinks she would give it up if she had to make a choice between her career and her son. But she didn't have to make that choice because her mother came to live with her. Her mother believes strongly in Ferguson's working in a job that has high visibility for women and for blacks. Ferguson says her mother "knows how tough it was being out there in a male-dominated workforce and that's why she's here . . . to support me in what I'm doing."[11] Ferguson grew up in a segregated community in Oklahoma. She always knew she'd have a career because all the women around her worked. But her parents had never seen a black journalist so they made sure she had a teaching certificate when she graduated from college, just in case.

Although Ferguson was pleased with her assignment to the Northeast bureau, she feels more can be done to accommodate women with children. She notes:

> My dilemma is every time a network reporter has a child she sees the option of going to local news. But that doesn't solve the problem at the network. The standard [at the network] is that you're expected to go anywhere, any time, for as long as it takes. If you want to get ahead, you really have to do that. And then women come along and

they have children and they don't quite feel the same way about that. I don't want to be sent away from my child for six months at a time.

Ferguson sees some solutions in part-time and flexible schedules. She realizes these accommodations might hold her career back but says, "I don't want to be punished for it. For all these years I've been clawing my way up, then what's there when I get there? What price? I'm not willing to sacrifice Jason or my relationship with him." Ferguson hopes that when women finally filter up to management, some basic child-care issues will be addressed. "We need women who believe stories on day-care are hard news. We need women who are in the board rooms and can make decisions on maternity leave, and are flexible on how to use women." She left CBS News in 1986, in part because of a contract dispute and in part because of the travel, to work as a local reporter at the NBC affiliate WMAQ-TV in Chicago.

Not only on-camera women face these problems. Producers are on the road as much as, if not more than, the correspondents. Betsy Rich was a producer for ABC News at the time we spoke to her in 1986. She worked for the network for nine years and, with a nine-month-old baby, juggled home and work by having live-in help and a husband who works close to home. In many ways she and her husband, Jamie, reversed traditional roles in order to maintain their family life; Betsy Rich brought home the larger check but she had little control over her schedule. Her husband, on the other hand, could be home by six o'clock and get dinner started so that when she arrived home at eight they could eat together. Like, Ferguson, Rich feels that motherhood changed her outlook on her career:

> Having a baby has really changed some of my goals. Having a job is very important to me, it always will be. It always will be more than a just a job because it requires more than most jobs. I think eventually I'd like to get off the road. I'm finding it more difficult to travel. I feel ripped apart. I'll call home and Jamie is feeding the baby and I hear her little noises and I just fall apart. I feel emotionally raw when I'm away.[12]

Rich realizes, though, that the news is unpredictable and that's part of the job.

> Basically, you give the control of your life to someone else. People don't see that side of the news business. They see the being a part of history. They see the luggage tags that say ABC News, they see the famous people, but they don't see hours and hours of waiting around; they don't see the being away and staying in hotels night after night.

The news business by its very nature makes it impossible to be sympathetic to people as human beings. If a plane goes down the story has to get on the air. And that's hard, especially if you have a baby.

Rich also knew it was hard when she looked around the office and saw few women with babies. "It's a hard job. A lot of people I work with either aren't married, or have failed marriages." Sometimes Rich feels the women's movement put too much pressure on young women to prove that they could have it all. "It sounds strange, but I feel I was sold a bill of goods to come to expect I could have everything. I don't know if it's possible to have everything and I don't know if it's fair to think I can and should be able to do it all. It puts too much pressure on us as women." But the job also helped her cope. Rich says, "TV news producing teaches you not to be defeated by anything. You can always find another way around it. You don't let yourself get stopped by anything."

Since then Rich has left ABC to work in a public relations firm. She described one incident that led to her decision to leave the network. She had been on the road for over a week and arrived back at the office in New York on Friday at 5:00 P.M. She immediately sat down and worked on the script for a story that was to be edited and aired on Monday. When she handed in the script she was told by the senior producer, a woman in her late thirties with no husband or children, that she would have to go to Washington D.C. to edit it. Infuriated, Rich reminded her that she'd been on the road and needed to go home to see her child; Rich told her to find someone else to edit in D.C. The senior producer was enraged that Rich refused to go because of the child. Rich wonders how women in TV news are going to balance career and family life if no understanding or help can be expected even from other women.

The theme I have found throughout these women's thoughts on career and family is that having a family is a normal desire and should be possible even for a television newswoman. Faith Daniels, "CBS Morning News" anchor, had a child in 1987. She stayed on the air until two weeks before she gave birth. She remarked, "I don't think anybody would say [I'm] less professional because I'm having a baby."[13] When Daniels looks around the newsroom she feels she deserves the same as the men. "Certainly you don't think Peter Jennings is less professional because he has two children, and Dan Rather has a family." But obviously women need special treatment as mothers with infants. Accommodating women with children must be supported by an entire news team because relieving one woman of traveling puts more pressure on management to reschedule, and often means single men and women are asked to do the longer and more distant assignments.

Some managements are responding well to this challenge. At the local news level, executive producer of WNBC's "News 4 New York" Tina Press believes that, "if you are sympathetic when you need to be, they'll give something back to you. They realize there is a debit in the account."[14] And she tries to be sensitive to the needs of both women and men. "I've always felt if a person is not happy or healthy they're not going to do a good job. I also feel the same way about men who have to run home too because their kid is sick." Press is aware that "you can't say sorry, you don't have a private life anymore just because you're in the news business." She also sees a slow change occurring in the attitude toward maternity leave and scheduling flexibility. "It used to be that the people who made policies tended to be male with wives at home. It's just not the case anymore." Press also sees the women now coming up through the ranks having new priorities. "For a while nobody was having children. Women concentrated on their careers. There's anecdotal evidence that women are realizing that children can be a part of their lives. Parenting is an expertise one brings to the job."

This management attitude at WNBC-TV positively affected one reporter, Magee Hickey, when she discovered she was pregnant the day before the July Fourth celebrations in 1986. There is a potential health hazard for pregnant women who are subjected to the intense microwave penetration propagated during live shots. This has been a source of conflict between reporter and management. For example, WABC-TV's "Eyewitness News" has no policy on whether pregnant reporters should be exempt from doing live shots. A reporter must negotiate each assignment with the news director each day. This is an extremely difficult situation and often forces pregnant reporters to do the live shot or to take an early medical leave. But when Magee Hickey went to her news director, Jerry Nachman, to tell him she was pregnant he immediately said she'd do no live shots. She recalls, "And then he thought about it and thought, oh no, this weekend, I'm one of the two reporters on duty for all the Statue of Liberty festivities and he had to bring in a replacement. But there was never any grudge or question of professionalism or what is this going to do to your career."[15] Perhaps she was surprised about how easy it was, and she "started to make little speeches about how this will only strengthen me as a female reporter because so many of the women in the viewership are mothers and this will give me a new dimension to my life." But he stopped her and said, "You don't have to tell us that. We know

that. Have a great pregnancy and a wonderful child and we expect
you to come back to work full force."

Hickey is very confident about her decision to have a child now,
in her early thirties with over ten years of work behind her. "I really
love my work and that was always number one. I made a conscious
decision not to get married as long as I was in TV news outside of
New York. I very rarely saw those marriages work when you don't
know where you'll be the next year. I could have made so many
mistakes by getting married early on or having children early on, in
terms of my career and what I was ready for emotionally, and professionally." But now she's ready for a change. "I'm beginning to slow
down and let more of the emotional, family side take over." She knows
that she is able to feel so confident because of the example of others.
"I'm constantly comparing myself to women who are a few years older
and the choices they made." Those choices were perhaps not the best
because "you can't let your job be everything. You can get fired
tomorrow." In the job reductions in 1987 at the networks these words
may have rung even more true.

Magee Hickey does not want to be a network correspondent,
because of the unpredictable schedules. She prefers local news as many
women do today. There are other avenues for regular though strange
hours in the television news business, such as anchoring morning news
shows. Joan Lunden, Jane Pauley, and Faith Daniels all have children.

Daniels worked in local news for six years, moving around from
Wheeling, West Virginia, to Pittsburgh, to Peoria. She came to New
York to anchor the CBS Morning News. Although she doesn't do
much traveling now, she must contend with an unusual schedule. She
gets up at 2:30 A.M. and goes on the air at 6:00. She had a baby boy
in November 1986 and went back to work in six weeks. She decided
the timing was right to have a baby because of her regular, if early,
schedule, and found she never had morning sickness because she never
had a morning. Like Hickey, she felt she had put enough time into
the job to be able to slow down and not jeopardize her career.

Daniels's husband is a senior producer for the "CBS Evening
News," so he is sympathetic to her scheduling problems, except that
when he gets home, it's time for her to get back to work. But Daniels
feels that they will each have time with the baby and that their careers
are important. She has full-time help to care for the child. Daniels
says, however, that it hasn't been as easy as she thought—leaving the
baby and going to work every day. Most days, when things are going
well at work, she finds being away from the baby easier to deal with.
But when there are difficulties at work, she wonders why she's there

when she could be at home with the baby. It's days like that when she asks herself, "Should I chuck it all and go home? Is the baby being cheated?" The mental process is different for her, she feels, than it is for her male colleagues. She doubts that they ever think that way. She wrestles with the conflict often. "I thought about this in advance by looking through rose colored glasses," she says. "I'd done the story so often I thought I knew it all, but living through it is different." Daniels is not about to give up her work. The family needs two incomes, and the work is rewarding. Still, she says, "It's tough to say goodbye" when she leaves for work.

Daniels followed a path similar to those of the other women in broadcast journalism. She worked for about five years, and was married for at least three years before she finally felt settled down enough to have a baby. An advantage she has is that the atmosphere at "CBS Morning News" is very supportive. Many of the men working on the show are new fathers, and her senior producer, Pat Shevlin, was also pregnant when Daniels was. Shevlin also fits the same pattern as Daniels in that she worked for over five years and is in her thirties. Shevlin sees a change in the newsroom and recalls a Joycean epiphany of the changing newsroom when "Faith and Missy Rennie [another CBS Morning News senior producer] and I were standing in the main newsroom and all of us were pregnant and it didn't seem odd."[16]

What is odd is that corporations and the government have not kept up with the changing workplace, especially in the area of maternity leave. Daniels says, "I don't feel there has to be a policy just for women but I think there has to be a policy." Daniels is sympathetic to the feminists' desire to establish a national maternity and paternity leave policy, but thinks "there has to be a policy, for pay or not, just so that a woman can take the time off, be with her child, and have a job when she comes back. There has to be something to protect women. There are too many women who go on leave with no guarantee of a job, no benefits. Women are put in a terrible position of having to make a choice between career and family, and in this day and age, it should be possible to have it all."

Women working for the major networks do get maternity leave benefits that in New York State fall under short-term disability. The formula for each person is different because of the variables used to decide the benefits, including years with the company, vacation, and compensation time for extra hours worked. CBS has guidelines for determining these benefits. Renée Ferguson found them out easily and had so much compensation time owed her, she was able to take eight months off. The clarity of the CBS policy, Ferguson explains, is due to the women's group, "who ten years ago went to the chief executive officer of CBS and insisted on a written maternity-leave policy. The women formed a group to decide what that policy should be so there would be a clear-cut defined policy you can find out the day you know you're pregnant." This is not the case at ABC. When Betsy Rich found out she was pregnant it took her almost five months to find out her benefits. Rich thinks, "if ABC had one person you could go to it would be easier." But she also sees no pressure on ABC to provide this service since "there just aren't a lot of pregnant women in the news business." There is little hope for improving the personnel department and providing more service since all the networks are looking to make budget cuts. Helping pregnant women most likely has a low priority. The ABC women's group, though, says a clear maternity-leave policy is one of their goals.

Not only did all these women have to negotiate their maternity leaves, and resolve any job hazards such as exposure to microwaves, but they all worked while pregnant. Most of the reporters chose to hide their pregnancy by having their on-camera reports shot from the shoulders up. Faith Daniels, who appeared on the "CBS Morning News" set which included a couch, played down her growing waistline. "Most times they do shoot closer in those situations. It's just a little less distracting if you do shoot closer. The director strategically placed pillows on the couch. I would like to think barriers have been broken for pregnant women in all aspects. Since we don't have a woman on air [as anchor] in the evening news, that barrier has not been broken."

It wasn't until the late seventies when local New York reporter Pia Lindstrom worked during her pregnancy that there was no attempt to hide it from the public. But by then more women were on the air and the attitude toward pregnancy had changed. It was not considered something that was unaesthetic, or that had to be hidden. This was a triumph for women who had previously had to leave jobs when they became visibly pregnant. More openness about sex and reproduction was part of the sexual revolution, and that contributed to more acceptance of pregnant women continuing with their jobs, whatever they were.

Although women now work and appear on camera while pregnant, there are other problems women in this industry face during pregnancy. Ferguson found that she did not feel she was as strong a presence in an interview because of her being pregnant. "When I go on a story I approach people with a certain strength, power that's important to me. I felt more vulnerable while pregnant, less powerful. It changed the way I'd walk into the room." But she overcame that and worked as long as she could. Ferguson also advises pregnant women to "tell people if you don't feel good right away." She was pleased that people were so supportive. "I never felt I was imposing on people." She took an early maternity leave though because, "near the end I didn't want to travel, schlepp luggage. People started to cover for me. I felt I was imposing, so I left."

Betsy Rich worked as long as she could as well. She found the most annoying thing was constantly finding a bathroom. But the crews were very sympathetic and never let her carry anything. Because of complications she had to stay in bed for the last two months. Faith Daniels found her staff to be overly protective when they wouldn't let her go out on an assignment on a drug story. Fortunately, the reaction is no longer shock over pregnant women working long hours, or fear of hurting the child. Daniels's obstetrician recommended staying active. Still, one pregnant assignment editor overheard remarks such as, "Why don't you just go have a baby and get out of here?" But, on the whole, Amy Entelis feels, men's attitudes are changing. "As more women in the workplace are having children, there seems to be a feeling among men, that they're starting to emphasize their families more. They're placing more of a value on it." From her viewpoint of both producer and management, she sees ABC as "not either supportive or unsupportive. It's not a big issue. But people personally are supportive." She found individually that "I didn't ask for anything and I didn't expect anything. I cut my last story for 'World News Tonight' eight hours before I had a baby." She warns against antagonizing "women and male counterparts who have to pick up the slack."

Hickey disagrees with Entelis's attitude that pregnant women need to prove themselves as equals. "For people to say, well, we should just treat you like anyone else, just isn't true. There has to be special consideration. You don't feel the same as you feel when you're not pregnant." But she also knows that women have to fight the response of "oh, no, another female reporter pregnant. When she comes back to work her commitment will be divided. When we ask her to work weekends or late it will be a problem." But Hickey also reminds us that, "news organizations want normal people who have to have a life."

All these women would agree that having a family and a job in television news increases the pressure on one's life, especially financial pressures. Even the women with the best salaries find day-care, live-in help, and nursery school a huge drain on their income. But most agree that their jobs are very important to them and worth the effort.

Most would also agree that the women's movement made it all seem possible. Although Rich feels one's expectations of one's self might be unreasonable, Daniels is more optimistic: "There was never any other way to do things. I was always going to work, have a family and a husband. My generation always felt we would grow up to have it all. Women have come a long way in a short period of time. We still have a long way to go, but yes we can do it. It's a very demanding job but you can have a life on the side. For me, my family comes before work, although it is nice to have both."

Quality-of-life problems, Cable News Network's anchor and vice president Mary Alice Williams concedes, can be a problem in this business. She finds the choices are never easy. Williams, divorced and now in her late thirties, would like to have children. She's toyed with the idea of single parenthood and adoption, but has not considered it seriously. She is aware, though, that whatever she decides to do in her professional or personal life will affect others as well as herself because her high visibility makes her a role model for others. She says:

> That finite group of us who are on the air are now in the position of being the standard bearers and having the responsibility to masses of total strangers who come up after us. But aren't we allowed choices in our lives? There's a woman at ABC radio in Washington who was offered a vice presidency in New York. She has a husband and two small children and she turned it down. A lot of people, mostly women, said, "how dare you? Here was our chance to get someone in the board room and you loused up." Well, come on, can't we make a decision, once we pass the cub status, on our quality of life? I'm sorry I don't have children, so I make quality-of-life decisions, but not on the same basis.[17]

Diane Sawyer, at 42, is still single but she does not blame that on her job. "There's always been a man in my life, always. I guess the reason I haven't married probably has to do with me and my quirks more than it has to do with the job I'm in. I think it probably would have been true no matter what kind of work I did. . . ."[18] She admits to mixed feelings about never having had a child. "Sure it bothers me. You think about it a lot. And I always thought I could do it, and I would have if I'd gotten married. . . . I would have loved it a lot. Having said that, I don't know how on earth I could have done it. I cannot imagine having this job and having to pick up and go to Russia and then go straight on to Zaire and then come back here, and having a child at home. You would have to be so unfeeling and selfish to do it happily." In terms of our business, she sees no easy way around that problem. "It has no solution. You know it has no solution. And we can say all we want, if we had a more equal distribution of labor and guilt and domesticity, that it wouldn't be as big a problem, but it will be. It will always be a woman's problem. You can't breed that out of women in generation after generation."

Sawyer thinks the issue is one not restricted to women in news, but to all contemporary working women. "We are in evolution of some kind and we feel the conflicts and the geotopographical plates scratching back and forth as the earth shifts one way and the other, and we're right there at a time that it's shifting. So to me, the question is, is the next group, the women in their twenties and thirties, going to be more like the men or is there going to be some sort of backlash and they'll be more like our mothers?"

In the early 1960s it was clear to me that I would not follow the traditional pattern for women, but combining a demanding career and a family life was not the subject of public debate. It took the civil rights and the antiwar movements of the late 1960s, a period of rapid change and turbulence, to stir the emerging women's movement, and bring these issues to the forefront.

## Notes

1. *New York Magazine,* October 1984.
2. Interview with Lesley Stahl (19 November 1986). All other quotes and information from Ms. Stahl in this chapter were taken from this interview unless otherwise noted.
3. Interview with Andrea Mitchell (18 November 1986). All other quotes and information from Ms. Mitchell in this chapter were taken from this interview unless otherwise noted.
4. Interview with Rebecca Bell (18 November 1986). All other quotes and information from Ms. Bell in this chapter were taken from this interview.
5. Barbara Basler, "Putting a Career on Hold," *New York Times Magazine* (7 December 1986): 159.
6. Interview with Lori Hillman (19 December 1986 and 4 January 1987). This quote and other information from Ms. Hillman in this chapter were taken from these interviews.
7. Interview with Peggy Stanton (20 October 1986). All other quotes and information from Ms. Stanton were taken from this interview.
8. Eleanor Randolph, "Women Sharing Their Story," *Washington Post* (15 November 1986).
9. Ibid.
10. Interview with Amy Entelis (3 October 1986). All other quotes and

information from Ms. Entelis in this chapter were taken from this interview.

11. Interview with Renée Ferguson (8 November 1986). All other quotes and information from Ms. Ferguson in this chapter were taken from this interview.

12. Interviews with Betsy Rich (30 September 1986 and 21 February 1988). All other quotes and information from Ms. Rich in this chapter were taken from these interviews.

13. Interview with Faith Daniels (8 October 1986 and February 1987). All other quotes and information from Ms. Daniels in this chapter were taken from these interviews.

14. Interview with Tina Press (24 October 1986). All other quotes and information from Ms. Press in this chapter were taken from this interview.

15. Interview with Magee Hickey (9 October 1986). All other quotes and information from Ms. Hickey in this chapter were taken from this interview.

16. Interview with Pat Shevlin (8 October 1986).

17. Interview with Mary Alice Williams (4 December 1986).

18. Interview with Diane Sawyer (15 January 1987). All other quotes and information from Ms. Sawyer in this chapter were from this interview.

# 5

## The Winds of Change

Signs of social change were beginning to emerge when I returned from Vietnam in 1966. The war spawned an antiwar movement, and many of its leaders came out of civil rights. Students would join in denouncing both the war in Vietnam and inequality at home. A growing questioning of the war that had begun within the major political parties would culminate in the challenges to President Lyndon Johnson's renomination in 1968 made by senators Eugene McCarthy and Robert F. Kennedy. The women's movement, nascent still, was soon to emerge as an outgrowth of the secondary position women had in both the antiwar and civil rights movements. It was a time of unrest, a time poised for change.

The ABC News organization was in the throes of change too in the late sixties. Zousmer was gone, and although news president Bill Sheehan and I were friendly, he had no personal stake in my success. Our relations were cordial and I had no reason to expect trouble from him. Other factors, however, can also affect the progress of one's career. My tour of duty in Vietnam in no way improved my status with the news desk. The trip was little noted by my colleagues and I returned to the routine of the daily program.

In March 1967, "Feature Story" was cancelled. Economically the arrangement had not worked out for the network. Then in May, after five years of sponsoring "News with the Woman's Touch," Purex withdrew, informing the staff that the marketing people had decided to "change the mix of time on network TV in order to tell our story to more people." Another sponsor was found, however, and we moved to a morning time period. At the same time, ABC had been negotiating a merger with International Telephone and Telegraph (ITT). The network anticipated a large infusion of cash into the news department if it went through. However there was great consternation among the staff about how such a merger with ITT would affect news gathering, since that company was involved in a number of controversial, and potentially newsworthy, activities in various parts of the world. In the end, the merger failed. Instead of more money coming into the network, cutbacks were ordered. Our five-minute newscast became a casualty.

We hated to break up our unit, but everyone was ready to move on to other things without the confining schedule that a daily broadcast imposed. I moved to the correspondents' quarters off the main newsroom, sharing a cubicle with a series of colleagues, all male. Some became close friends, and we learned about each other's families, professional anxieties, and struggles with the management. All of our careers hinged on where we stood with whoever was in charge. One's reporting and writing skills were always a factor, but increasingly performance judgments seemed to overwhelm professional considerations. Air presence, charisma, star quality—whatever the phrase of the day—became more and more important.

I joined my associates as one of the "firemen," the workhorse reporters who run, like firemen at the sound of the bell, to cover breaking stories of any kind. General assignment reporting is where most reporters start, and most local reporters today do nothing but spot news. In a sense, the work is rewarding because of its variety. It can also be journalistically troubling because of the brevity of reports on the air and the shortage of time available to get the facts. When film footage had to be hand carried to a transmission point the reporter had a brief respite to think about the script. With the pressures of instantaneous transmission of tape from the field, the process leaves more room for error.

Still, those assignments were preferable to other kinds. Whoever was lowest on the favoritism totem pole drew stakeouts, those interminable waits for either an announcement of some sort or someone's arrival or departure, usually outside in bad weather. You never knew when you went to work in the morning whether you'd be reading newspapers and making phone calls in search of story ideas, or sent out of town for hours or days. Getting a decent assignment depended entirely on one's standing with the evening news producers or on the absence of their current favorites who were on other assignments. I had my share of the poor stories, along with a mix of good ones. In December 1967 I was assigned to cover the White House wedding of Lynda Bird Johnson and her Marine captain husband-to-be, then referred to as Chuck Robb, not Charles, as in his later job as Governor of Virginia. I spent a week in Washington attending White House briefings and doing a number of "advancer" stories on the event, including interviews with the couple. After coverage of the wedding itself, Frank Reynolds and I cohosted a special. He was ideal to work with, well-informed, gracious, and never one to try to usurp someone else's role.

Along with the many forgettable stories, one other challenging assignment was a mine disaster in Farmington, West Virginia, where I spent more than a week. There was an attempt to rescue trapped miners which went on for days, guaranteeing airtime, the equivalent of newspaper space for print reporters. The question of how reporters should handle people involved in personal tragedies is often raised. Critics are quick to condemn, and rightly, the "how do you feel?" kind of question. My own approach has always been to circle the issue for a while, to try to get legitimate information, and to quickly attempt to change the subject if the interviewee begins to break down. Truthfully, genuine emotion will always make air, but a sensitive reporter knows when enough is enough, and learns how to pull back. It takes experience to handle a delicate emotional moment, and actually doing those interviews is the best way to learn how far to go.

No one I know likes to talk to people involved in disasters. It's the kind of task you steel yourself for, and you try to be as detached as possible. If you need the story, you do what has to be done, with taste and, if possible, with compassion. Our needs are different from those of the individuals involved. If people refuse to talk with us and all attempts fail, so be it. We tried. But if we can get those interviews, painful as they might be, that's part of the job. We can't afford to miss out if the competition succeeds. Some people have said that talking to reporters has helped them handle their situation, and it makes our job easier if we can believe that.

There were few pleasant distractions in the news in the late 1960s. Even before the student protests and anti-Vietnam War sentiment grew, there were stories that hinted of things to come. One of my assignments was to cover a precursor of the germinating women's movement. I ventured to rural Georgia to interview Jeanette Rankin, the first woman elected to Congress around the time of World War I. She and others were to march in an antiwar parade in Washington in what was being called "the Jeanette Rankin Brigade." She was eighty-seven, and part of the advance guard of women who would be marching often in the years to come. It was those women working for peace and civil rights who eventually got fed up with their subservient roles in both efforts and formed the women's movement that emerged in the early 1970s.

During the spring of 1968 I became a substitute political reporter, relieving the regulars. I would have preferred to be assigned a candidate of my own, but the men got those jobs. I spent a good deal of time with the campaign of Senator Eugene McCarthy, who had begun to develop a loyal following. My resentment at not being assigned a candidate full-time was tempered by the knowledge that my family life would have been disrupted if I had been gone so much of the time. Campaigns are strenuous and exhausting, but everyone, including me, wanted to go. If you had a good candidate, it was guaranteed air time—the only reward for all the time and hard work.

By spring, antiwar sentiment was growing, and the campuses began to erupt. In April of 1968, students at Columbia University occupied five buildings after four student leaders had been suspended. The disruptions began as a protest over Columbia's increasing incursions into adjacent Harlem, and ostensibly concerned the building of a gym there. Various people had covered the story until then. The occupation of the buildings had been going on for days and no one knew how it would end. My New York apartment was twenty-five blocks from the campus, and when the overnight assignment editor got word that the police were going to invade the campus, he called the person closest to the scene: me. It was 3:00 A.M. By the time a film crew could be put together and we could meet, it was 4:30 A.M.

For weeks I spent most of my time at Columbia, becoming the resident authority on students by virtue of the luck of where I lived. The most harrowing night was when the police were ordered on campus at 4 A.M., breaking down makeshift barricades and attacking students and anyone else in the way with clubs. My one regret was that the film technology of the day could not capture enough of that activity in the darkness.

Some of the mail we got as a result of my reports on Columbia reflected the hostility such demonstrations generated in large segments of the population. One letter said in part:

> What a joke was the sob-sister act of Marlene Sanders on the news last night as she tried to put on a tear jerker for the poor dear Columbia University student who got his nead bloodied and a black eye from the police who ejected him and his ilk from the buildings of the University where they had been defying authority and the rights of others for days. . . . From one woman to another in my opinion Marlene Sanders was plain *DISGUSTING* and it is no wonder more and

more people are getting better acquainted with the OFF button on
their TV set and finding out more reliable news sources.

That, from Arlington, Washington. Another, from Toledo, Ohio, in
a similar vein said that "when these Communist bums dared to fly
red flags from within a democratic university, etc. then they deserve
to have their heads clubbed. God bless the police." We had shown
and interviewed the students but had not editorialized in their favor.
The mail was just the beginning of a "shoot the messenger" attitude
that grew gradually worse.

Only the civil rights coverage generated more hate mail than
the student riots, that is, until the 1968 Democratic convention in
Chicago.

In late May, the primaries were in full swing, particularly the
contest between senators Robert Kennedy and Eugene McCarthy. I
had covered both of them sporadically, and for several weeks I was
assigned full-time to the California primary campaign. It was customary to keep a crew around Bobby Kennedy "protectively," the euphemism for "in case the candidate is shot." After President Kennedy's
assassination that coverage seemed like a good idea.

The Kennedy group always included staff from Ted Kennedy's
office as well as from Bobby's. They knew their way around, and they
knew how to get along with the press. After facing a particularly bad
crush of people in Santa Barbara at the courthouse square, in sizzling
heat, we piled back onto the bus, to be followed by a case of ice cold
beer. Not too long afterwards, box lunches appeared on the scene.
Such expensive amenities were unlikely to appear with Senator
McCarthy and his group. There was a confidence within the Kennedy
team. These people were used to winning; they knew the ropes. Most
of us were somewhat incredulous—at least I was—with what the
candidate had to endure, and how he didn't seem to mind. The
tugging at Bobby Kennedy, the grasping of hands, the pushing and
shoving of kids too young to vote, reflected people's adulation or at
least the curiosity of celebrity hounds.

During the time I was assigned to the Kennedy campaign, it was
customary for correspondents to be their own producers, except in
unusual circumstances. During his campaigning in the San Francisco
area, as elsewhere, it was usual to have the candidate's press staff tell
the media when it was safe to let their crews take a break, either for
meals or for time off. One day, after a morning of campaign stops,
the staff assured us that there would be no further activity until mid-
afternoon, that the candidate would be resting. I gave my crew time
off, arranged when to meet them, and set off for a walk toward

Fisherman's Wharf. About a half hour later, I heard a voice over a
megaphone from a passing car announcing that Bobby Kennedy would
be heading this way momentarily, and inviting citizens to come and
hear him. I was stunned, and rushed up to the car asking how this
could be, we had been told there would be no campaigning until later.
I was informed that Kennedy had changed his mind. I tore to the
phone booth and tried to locate my crew, without success. In this
crazy world of news, I was thinking that if this afternoon someone
tried to shoot Kennedy, I wouldn't have it on film. Fortunately nothing
happened.

A few days later, Kennedy and McCarthy were scheduled to have
a debate. There was a sharp division between Democrats who were
followers of McCarthy, the first to come out against the Vietnam War,
and those who favored Kennedy, thinking he had a better chance to
win if he became the Democratic candidate. On primary day and that
night I was assigned radio coverage from McCarthy headquarters,
and at the end of a long day the TV and radio crews planned a late
dinner.

It had been a grueling day and night, and the results of the
primary were incomplete. I climbed aboard the remote truck, and
watched the screen for about ten minutes. Our sign-off theme music
came on, but there seemed to be a problem. The mobile studio at
Kennedy headquarters, a good distance away, called and informed
the producer that the assistant director there, Billy Weisel, had been
shot by a stray bullet [fired by Sirhan Sirhan]. We greeted this news
incredulously, and waited tensely for further information. The faces
on the screen began to change and register shock. It was not until
Bob Clark, the ABC correspondent covering Senator Kennedy, called
New York to confirm the news, that the network announced that
Bobby Kennedy had been shot. By now, we were transfixed in states
of disbelief. When it became clear where the injured would be taken,
we were ready to move. I was told to get to the hospital, and I jumped
into a cab. By the time I got there the streets were blocked by police.
I clipped on my press credentials and rushed to the front of the
hospital. The press was starting to gather. The police held us back,
and we could learn very little. The pushing and shoving of camera
crews and still photographers continued until we moved behind hastily
set up barricades. The mobile truck I had left earlier arrived at the
scene. The phone company arrived as well. Telephone lines were
being installed and additional lines were set up going into the hospital.
Finally, Frank Mankewiecz, Kennedy's press secretary, came out and
gave us the first official word that the American public would hear.

Kennedy had been shot in the head; brain surgery would follow, and they expected to complete the operation in forty-five minutes. This sounded implausible, but it was all we had. In the meantime, the network was coming to Bob Clark and me for reports. The night was clammy. The chill added to a kind of numbing fatigue that was beginning to settle over all of us. At 3:00 A.M., I roamed around the periphery of the hospital to see what was going on. Acrid-smelling flares had been set up in the street. Clusters of people were sitting on the curbs or standing and talking in groups. There were members of various religious sects giving the small crowd their versions of the meaning of life and death. All around the hospital there were people waiting. Some were praying. These groups remained throughout the ordeal. It was 6:00 A.M. After a number of live broadcasts, I was sent to my hotel for a few hour's sleep. When I returned to the hospital, a press center had been set up inside a gymnasium adjacent to the hospital; there most of the press sat, partly dazed by events and fatigue. Then press secretary Frank Mankewiecz appeared and briefed us, his face strained and lined. He said Kennedy's condition was "extremely critical as to life," the first time he had incorporated those last three words. I knew then that we were on a deathwatch. He said he would not be back with normal bulletins until 8:00 A.M. By then, it was close to 7:00 P.M. In the next few hours, we had three false alarms. Someone would cry, "He's coming," and we would rush to our positions near the podium. The still photographers were poised; the print journalists were waiting; I grabbed a microphone and stood waiting. Sometimes it took half an hour before we realized it was a false alarm. Three times I thought about what I would say when the word of his death came. Three times I collapsed into a chair, emotionally drained and physically whipped. Jim Burnes came to relieve me at 1:00 A.M. Kennedy died during the night.

The next day we were told to get back to New York. Our coverage continued later as the funeral train chugged from New York to Washington.

There was barely time to recover from the exhausting emotional events of June. It was a turbulent time in this country and vacations for us were out of the question. We went from story to story not often stopping to reflect on the emotionally wrenching repercussions of what we were reporting, but continuing on the kind of adrenalin high reporters get when directly involved in the major events of the day. Before we knew it, it was July, and we were off to Miami Beach and the Republican convention. For the first time, ABC planned to carry a ninety-minute wrap-up of events each night, rather than the gavel-to-gavel coverage of the other networks. This practice was not abandoned until 1980. The rationale was that much of what goes on in the convention hall is not worthy of coverage, and that highlights could be culled. The company also believed that many Americans did not want to watch convention coverage all evening, preferring their regular program fare, with an end-of-the-evening summary. It was also cheaper. While CBS and NBC sent approximately eight hundred and seven hundred people respectively, ABC made do with four hundred.

It was the first political convention to be carried in color, and the equipment and logistical problems were tremendous. All three networks had booths in the hall, plus mobile units and trailers parked outside. We had thirteen trailers and three moving units.

That was the convention that nominated Richard Nixon and Spiro Agnew. There were sidebar stories having to do with the Poor People's Caravan, and the courtship of Julie Nixon and David Eisenhower. Governor Ronald Reagan was there, making a play for the Presidency, but failing that time around.

When it was all over, there was a short turnaround in New York before the trip to Chicago for the Democratic convention.

We had all been covering aspects of the Yippies and the youthful McCarthy campaigners. There were rumors of trouble. Labor problems had already developed in the city, seemingly masterminded by Mayor Richard Daley who did not want coverage of demonstrations. An electrical workers' strike was preventing Illinois Bell Telephone from installing the necessary cables and wires TV needed. Up until the last moment, the networks hoped the Democrats would change their minds and meet in Miami Beach, where everything was set up. But they refused to change.

There were ominous signs about Chicago from the very first. A number of us were sent there a week early to do preparatory stories. The first sign of difficulty was that there was a taxi strike that began before the convention and lasted throughout. To no one's surprise, the strike which made it so hard for delegates and reporters to get around was resolved the day after the convention ended. It was suggested that Mayor Richard Daley wanted delegates confined to their hotels and to the buses that took them to the hall.

The Mayor had made it known that the demonstrations planned by thousands of troublemakers would not be welcome. Large numbers of protesters of all kinds were expected. Permits for sleeping and rallies in Grant Park had been granted, however. The parks were filled with young people, clean-cut supporters of McCarthy, Yippies, and, some thought, provocateurs.

During the week before the convention we were busy doing stories on what was going on in the city, as well as on the upcoming convention where Senator Hubert Humphrey was expected to be nominated.

Most of my assignments were outside the convention itself. One of the pieces I did took several days and was a portrait of the entertainment figures working for the various candidates. Shirley MacLaine and a host of others were on hand, doing their part and staging a number of events. I filmed them along with interviews. The night that piece was aired, I watched it at the Hilton, while what came to be called a "police riot" was going on right outside. It seemed incongruous to be running a piece like that when all hell was breaking loose, but the network decided to try to keep some semblance of balance in the coverage and not to overplay the role of the riots, as the networks were later accused of doing.

When the police went in to clear the park, they used tear gas and nightsticks freely. People, including delegates who were coming out of restaurants, were attacked indiscriminately. Passers-by in their cars were pulled out and beaten. Press photographers and film crews were particular targets. The report by the Walker Commission, which was appointed to study the event and which was filed as part of the report of the President's Commission on the Causes and Prevention of Violence, noted: "Out of 300 newsmen assigned to cover the parks and streets of Chicago during convention week, more than 60 (about 20%) were involved in incidents resulting in injury to themselves, damage to their equipment, or their arrest. Sixty-three newsmen were physically attacked by police. In 13 of these instances, photographic or recording equipment was intentionally damaged."[1]

The Chicago convention was a nightmare. We were shocked by the hostility of the police. The antiwar movement had not gained respectability yet, and it was a form of class warfare. This was apparent too in the relationship between film crews and correspondents. Many of the correspondents grew to oppose the war, while their blue-collar crews supported it. Opponents of the war had first surfaced on university campuses, where "teach-ins" against the U.S. involvement in Vietnam were common. Students and people regarded as intellectuals filled the streets with antiwar demonstrations, joining the more disreputable looking, long-haired hippies. The war had working-class support, and sons of blue-collar workers were not visibly taking off for Canada or going underground to avoid the draft. Covering antiwar

demonstrations with film crews who were openly hostile to the protests
meant that correspondents had to carefully monitor the filming, which
wasn't always possible. In covering stories, you had to be sure to tell
your cameraman to shoot the elderly, well-dressed protesters and not
concentrate only on the far-out hippies.

In those early days, the electricians and sound men came from
the theatrical unions. They worked Broadway shows as gaffers, and
their union jobs were passed from father to son. They were mostly
good-natured, hard-working men who had little intellectual rapport
with correspondents, male or female. The cameramen came out of
the old newsreel organizations, by and large, and were usually a cut
above the rest of the crew. Some cameramen studied film on their
own. Most could move rapidly and skillfully in the midst of mayhem.
Many years later, a new generation of men and women came along,
from colleges and film schools. They were nowhere to be found in
those early years and we tried to avoid discussing issues. Conversation
on the interminable drives from airport to story usually centered on
home repairs, cars, or union grievances.

After the 1968 Chicago convention a bitter school strike erupted
in New York in the fall, with most of the action in the all-black
Oceanhill-Brownsville section of Brooklyn. The dispute between the
New York City teachers and advocates of neighborhood control was
really between blacks who made up much of the school population
and the largely white and Jewish teachers union. My own eight-year-
old was out of class along with all the other public school students,
but with full-time help at home, I was luckier than most.

When the school strike was finally settled, I was again given what
was then the inevitable assignment of the few women in broadcast
news during a political campaign—an assignment to do stories on
the wives of the presidential candidates. This had been the lot of
Pauline Frederick twenty years before. The only sign of progress since
then was that unlike her, I was not required to do the wives' makeup.
Now, another twenty years have passed, and wives of candidates no
longer merit coverage unless they are personages in their own right.
Elizabeth Dole, former Secretary of Transportation, resigned that
post in 1987 in order to campaign for her husband, Senator Bob
Dole. She would merit some coverage by virtue of her status. By the
late 1980s, women themselves were running for the Senate, for governor, vice president, and as presidential contenders in primaries. In
1968, however, I knew it was hopeless to get a real candidate, and
was in no position to argue about being handed the wives. I resented

the assignment, but there was no recourse. The women's movement was still a few years down the road.

At least Muriel Humphrey was a real campaigner, better even than her Democratic predecessor, Lady Bird Johnson. Whatever she said, either in quiet conversation or before hundreds on a platform in the street, seemed sincere and from the heart. She was genuinely dedicated to the plight of retarded children, since she had a grandchild with Down's syndrome. Her personality was winning, and her genuine warmth always came through. When she did an interview, it sounded fresh and full of enthusiasm. Mrs. Humphrey's TV portrait went easily. She was on a heavy travel schedule, went to interesting places from a film standpoint, and willingly sat for an interview. She was not, however, destined to be the new First Lady.

Mrs. Nixon was another story. She was a silent presence next to her husband on platform after platform. She smiled and waved but did little else. Patricia Nixon was not going to campaign on her own. She accompanied her husband, and granted only group interviews to local press along the way. That was thought to be safe, and judging from some of the questions I heard the locals ask, it was. They tended to be of the "what kinds of hobbies do you enjoy" variety. I tagged along, but had been refused a sit-down network television interview. We had dozens of shots of Pat Nixon on the platform, waving and coming and going, but not enough substance for my story. I finally decided that if she would not cooperate I had to get an interview with her husband, the candidate. But he too was granting only group news conferences en route.

The opportunity for something more came in Detroit, where Mr. Nixon held a small news conference for local press and a few of the regulars who traveled with him. There were only about a dozen reporters in the room and, for some reason, almost no television except for my crew. There had been a major bombing raid on Hanoi around that time, and Nixon was grilled on his views for a long time. He was standing, rather informally, inside the circle of reporters, and was beginning to repeat himself. The subject, I felt, had been beaten to the ground. I knew it was my opportunity, but I felt like a terrible fool. There sat Homer Bigart, the esteemed political reporter from the *New York Times,* and several other top writers. Averting my eyes from the rest of the reporters and clearing my throat, I said, "Changing the subject for just a moment, Mr. Nixon, would you tell me what contribution your wife, Pat, makes to your campaign?" He looked relieved, to say the least, and I got the best answer one could expect, given the question. When the piece was edited, we ran it over shots of them traveling together and it worked just fine. I still feel embarrassment over the incident.

The trip continued, and there were ample "photo opportunities" at the last stop, Colonial Williamsburg. We duly filmed, and my persistence in requesting an interview finally paid off. With Mrs. Nixon defending her husband, and explaining her supportive role, the piece worked to everyone's satisfaction.

In January 1969, when the inauguration rolled around, neither Peter Jennings nor I were among the anchors this time. ABC's interest in the "youth movement" had dissipated. The old guard returned. Howard K. Smith and Bill Lawrence took on those chores, and since they were eminently qualified, it was hard to argue with that decision journalistically. I had a routine assignment on the White House lawn, reporting what is known as a "here they come . . . there they go" story, this time the departure of the Nixons and the Johnsons for the swearing in.

By the late 1960s, ABC was almost fully competitive with NBC and CBS by virtue of the addition of enough affiliate stations. It was also juggling staff, trying to find an executive who could drag the evening news out of third place. All correspondents were dependent on a set of executive producers in terms of assignments, frequency on the air, and thus new contracts. A reporter who was rarely seen or seen only on secondary broadcasts would be in jeopardy when contract renewal time came along. Anyone who did not get along with a key executive was in trouble, as I was to learn firsthand; it was another hard lesson in office politics.

In 1969, Av Westin, who had extensive CBS credits, was named to the job of executive producer of the "ABC Evening News." Just prior to his arrival, he had headed up the short-lived independent production unit called the Public Broadcasting Laboratory, an expensive, ambitious, magazine format failure, financed by the Ford Foundation.

There was no reason to think Westin's arrival on the scene spelled trouble for me. Before long, however, it became clear that a few correspondents became his favorites and got the choice assignments. The rest of us got the leavings. I continued to report on campus problems, and also did a number of reports on the government's Great Society programs like Head Start and the Job Corps. After the election, it fell to me to cover Pat Nixon when she finally found something to do. She adopted "volunteerism" as her project and I went on several of her desultory trips.

Story assignments usually came from the assignment desk, but at ABC, and even more so later at all the networks, the staff of the evening news determined who went where. When a routine story broke, any one of us designated "firemen" would rush out. But when a big story was in the offing, the recognized favorites were chosen.

Plainly, one had to learn how to cultivate those in power to become a favorite. When you were out of favor with the powers that be, it was awkward to hang around the evening news as some of my male colleagues did. I did try, and one day overheard Westin complaining about the shortage of correspondents for whatever the big story of the moment was. "What's the matter with me, I'm available?" I said. Westin replied, "I can't use you for stories like that. What do you want to be, another Liz Trotta?" Trotta was then an aggressive, often abrasive television reporter for NBC News. Her style made her unpopular with many in the industry, particularly with competitors. She was tough, and a very good reporter. Obviously, Westin didn't feel that kind of approach was suitable for a woman. Years later, after women proved they could be tough without necessarily being obnoxious, he changed his tune. It was too late to help me then.

On another occasion, in the fall of 1970, I was passed over on a story having to do with New York Jet's quarterback Joe Namath, who was returning to practice after being out for some time with injuries. When a male colleague, David Snell, came in, he was duly sent out. Snell was no sports expert, but he was male. So much for my experience in the 1950s writing Gussie Moran's sports interview programs. My family also happened to have season tickets to the Jets games. But no one bothered to inquire about my knowledge of the game. The desk told me Westin wanted a man sent on the story.

I had complained to both Lower and news vice president Bill Sheehan about what I considered to be discriminatory treatment. Both said they regretted it, but would not intervene with the executive producer's decisions. Lower suggested I should continue to try to work it out with Westin. And if I couldn't? "Well then," he said, "I guess you won't be very happy here." That laid it on the line.

Through Bill Sheehan, however, there was momentary relief from my dilemma. In March 1971 it was correspondent Sam Donaldson's turn to report from Vietnam. In addition to his Washington duties he also anchored a fifteen-minute Saturday night newscast from New York. I was asked to replace him for the three months he would be gone.

It was seven years since I had stepped in to anchor for ailing Ron Cochran. Press clippings nevertheless noted that it was "the first time a woman has anchored a network news show." It was, indeed, the first time a woman did the job for more than a few nights. There had been some progress during the intervening years however, on other fronts. Correspondent Aline Saarinen was named Paris bureau chief for NBC News, the first network to have a female bureau chief. NBC then led the networks in the number of women correspondents with four: Pauline Frederick, Nancy Dickerson, Aline Saarinen, and Liz Trotta. CBS had only one, Marya McLaughlin, in Washington. At ABC, Virginia Sherwood was in Washington, and I was in New York.

During the three months Donaldson was away, I came to work on Saturday afternoon to the second floor newsroom, enemy territory during the week. The weekend staff and I worked in harmony, and the atmosphere, while at times frenzied, was professional, without the tensions of the weeknight first-string staff. It felt completely different, and underscored for me just how ostracized I had been in the Monday-through-Friday operation. Reviews of my work were excellent in the press, and the management expressed satisfaction as well. It was not the first time the message would come through that it wasn't how good you were that counted, but how the key people in charge regarded you. Over the years, peoples' careers rose and fell not because they were less talented or hard working one year more than another, but because the hierarchy changed. One group's favorite was the other group's reject. Unlike other industries where employees are given regular evaluations, no such system exists in broadcasting for on-air people. For lower-level categories of people, there are salary reviews where the amount of one's increase is discussed, but that is by no means standard. Correspondents find out their status in contract negotiations and by rumor and innuendo, but rarely in direct confrontations.

It is not difficult, however, to tell where you stand. Air time is the broadcast equivalent of column space at a newspaper. If you are on the evening news regularly, the anchorman or executive producer is in your corner and you've made page one. If you are relegated to the early morning or weekends, fringe broadcasts or radio, then you are on the back pages. The favored correspondents, part of the so-called "A-team," get the major beats, while the workhorse correspondents, part of the "B-team," get the rest. If productivity were what counted, "B-team" players might actually be on the air more and get good marks. But if only the evening news figures in determining one's standing, then there could be problems. When CBS cut back staff in order to save money in 1987, it was members of the less expensive "B-team" that got the ax. The higher-paid semi-stars remained on staff and had to work harder.

The true stars of broadcast news, of course, are the anchors, and at the network level, in prime time, they are still exclusively male. In the 1970s and into the 1980s, on-air women found that if they were given a chance to anchor, it would be on the weekends or in the early morning hours.

Traditionally, weekends have been regarded as fringe time, and those news broadcasts were used to showcase supporting players. It was the opportunity to give a morale boost to someone who couldn't hope to inherit the weeknight star position. Later, it became a permanent home for women anchors. Since the second or third person who covered the White House or Congress tended to be female in the mid-seventies and into the eighties, weekends are their chance to get on the air while the main, male, correspondent had some time off. It was also the time when "shelf pieces," "features," or "takeouts" got on the air. These too often tended to be done by women. The statistics on the appearances of female correspondents soars if you include fringe time like mornings and weekends.

A study by DWJ Associates research firm found that in 1987, out of a total of 239 network reporters, none of the thirty-six women correspondents ranked among the top ten in terms of air time. Susan Spencer was twenty-second and Rita Braver was thirteenth. The top six men captured more air time than all thirty-six women put together.[2]

In a survey done for this book in November 1986, women correspondents reported 76 of the 609 stories that appeared on all three networks. This compares with the NOW Legal Defense and Education survey done over a two-month period the same year that points out that women report 10.5 percent of the stories on the three major nightly network news shows. This is only a 0.6 percent increase in women reporting since 1975. On the weekends in November 1986, 175 stories were reported, 27 by women. This weekend figure breaks down by network shows this way:

CBS: 30 stories—9 by women
ABC: 31 stories—17 by women
NBC: 15 stories—2 by women (NBC preempted many of their weekend newscasts for football)

Twenty-seven of the total 76 stories reported by women were aired on the weekends; that means 37 percent of women's stories were relegated to the weekends.

In the early 1970s there were too few women on the air to

gather statistics about the frequency of their appearances. The emerging women's movement, however, was about to change the number of women employed, and our status within the industry.

## Notes

1. Daniel Walker, Foreword and Summary of the report made by the President's Commission on the Causes and Prevention of Violence, reprinted in the *New York Times* (2 December 1968), p. 38.
2. Richard Zacks, *TV Guide,* New York Metropolitan Edition (13 February 1988): A-5.

Hilary Brown joined ABC News as a foreign correspondent after working as a reporter for CBS radio. She later became a correspondent for NBC in Israel, and is shown here in Jerusalem in 1978. (Photo by Catherine Leroy courtesy of Hilary Brown)

Hilary Brown returned from a ten-year stint overseas and in 1981 rejoined ABC News. She currently anchors a news hour for the Canadian Broadcasting Corporation in Toronto. (Photo courtesy of Hilary Brown)

Lesley Stahl became a Washington-based reporter for CBS News in 1972, and later worked as a national correspondent for the network. (Photo: CBS News)

The White House was Lesley Stahl's CBS beat for eight years. In addition to her work as a news analyst, she began hosting "Face the Nation" on Sundays in 1983. (Photo courtesy of Lesley Stahl)

Rebecca Bell's career in broadcasting has included work at NBC as a correspondent, and in management. She is currently with CONUS, a statellite news distribution system. (Photo: National Broadcasting Company, Inc.)

Liz Trotta became known as an aggressive reporter for both NBC and CBS News. (Photo courtesy of Liz Trotta)

Ed Bradley, Diane Sawyer, Lesley Stahl, and Bob Schieffer were CBS News floor correspondents covering the 1984 Democratic National Convention in San Francisco. (Photo: CBS News)

Correspondent Diane Sawyer's work on CBS's "Sixty Minutes" has made her one of the highest paid and best known of the television newswomen. (Photo: CBS News)

Martha Teichner's job as a CBS News foreign correspondent has taken her to Northern Ireland, Lebanon, and El Salvador. She was based in London, and in 1987 she began a three-year assignment in South Africa. (Photo: CBS News)

ABC News correspondent Carole Simpson was a veteran newswoman when she became a spokesperson for women at the network who sought to improve their status. (Photo: Capital Cities/ABC, Inc.)

Christine Craft, shown here in 1987 with Andy Asher at **KRBK-TV**, Sacramento, filed a landmark lawsuit against KMBC-TV in Kansas City in 1981, charging that she had been dismissed from the station because she was too old, too unattractive, and not deferential enough to men. (Photo: Sirlin Photographers, Sacramento)

Betsy Aaron has covered stories in Afghanistan, Lebanon, and Iran. In 1986 she reported from Siberia for ABC News. (Photo courtesy of Betsy Aaron)

NBC television correspondent Andrea Mitchell has covered the White House for several years and appears regularly on the "Nightly News" and "Today." (Photo: National Broadcasting Company, Inc.)

Mary Alice Williams anchors at Cable News Network and is also a vice president of CNN in New York. (Photo: Cable News Network)

Cheryl Gould, one of a relatively small number of women in upper management positions at the television networks, is the senior producer of "NBC Nightly News." (Photo © 1987, National Broadcasting Company, Inc.)

Marlene Sanders hosts "Currents," a public affairs series on WNET-TV in New York. The winner of three Emmy awards, she has worked as a reporter, correspondent, writer, documentary producer, anchorwoman, and vice president in network television. (Photo courtesy of Marlene Sanders)

# 6

## Women Make News

Although Betty Friedan's book *The Feminine Mystique* was published in 1963, it took years before its message began to sink in and help change irrevocably the lives of American women. Friedan noted that the message women had been receiving from the media at that time was

> how to catch a man and keep him, how to breast-feed children and handle their toilet training; how to cope with sibling rivalry and adolescent rebellion; how to buy a dishwasher, bake bread, cook gourmet snails and build a swimming pool with their own hands; how to dress, look and act more feminine and make marriage more exciting; how to keep their husbands from dying young and their sons from growing into delinquents. They were taught to pity the neurotic, unfeminine, unhappy women who wanted to be poets or physicists or presidents. They learned that truly feminine women do not want careers, higher education, political rights—the independence and the opportunities that the old-fashioned feminists fought for. . . . All they had to do was devote their lives from earliest girlhood to finding a husband and bearing children.[1]

The book provided the inspiration for the formation of the National Organization for Women (NOW) in 1967. Activist women were beginning to make news, and I began to cover the movement for the evening news and in documentaries. Until this time, women who had achieved anything had done it on their own by individual, personal effort. But now, women were supporting each other to find a public voice to advocate changes. Women were starting to discover the power of collective action.

Friedan observed that "by 1970, it was beginning to be clear that the women's movement was more than a temporary fad, it was the fastest-growing movement for basic social and political change of the decade."[2] By 1970, editors and reporters had routinely covered demonstrations for years. Civil rights marches dwindled, and were replaced by peace marches. Protest had been a media preoccupation over almost a decade. Women began to use the same techniques, marching on the Atlantic City boardwalk, sitting-in at a publisher's office, demanding to be served at all-male bars. These tactics prompted groans and sneers in newsrooms, as well as remarks casting doubts on the femininity of the participants. It didn't seem possible that the movement could change the complexion of newsrooms while it went about its major task of changing the status of women in the country.

It took several years before male correspondents were well enough informed about the movement to stop asking leaders like Gloria Steinem whether men were supposed to give up their seats to women in the bus, or hold open doors. Later they began to understand that women wanted equal pay for equal work, control over their bodies and the right to safe, legal abortions, and full equality with men in areas like insurance or in obtaining bank loans. In other words, when the men began to grasp that this was serious and not just fun and games, the few women covering the women's movement could relax and share the stories.

Because the groups of women activists were so diverse it was rare for women journalists to get advance word on what they were going to do, but in the case of the sit-in at the *Ladies Home Journal*, I was forewarned. The *Journal* was one of the many women's magazines with male editors in charge. On 18 March 1970 the women who worked there and a number of outsiders occupied editor John Mack Carter's office. We were the first network crew on the scene.

The publication had always billed itself as "the magazine women believe in," and women were now demanding a voice in running it. They called for serious articles on child-care, women's health, reproductive rights, job discrimination, and not just food, fashion, and homemaking. The end result was that a group of outside writers and editors created a special issue of the magazine that focused on those topics. There were also promises that changes would be made in the regular magazine. Some ten years later, almost all of the women's service magazines had women as editors, and new magazines like *Ms.*, *Working Woman*, and *Savvy* had come along to serve women who were no longer exclusively homemakers.

We provided ABC with an exclusive on the story, since only local crews were there. The sit-in was also covered by the wire services and the major New York dailies, which was fortunate for me. If we had been the only major outlet with the story it would have been taken less seriously. Television news management at the time tended still to be print oriented, believing that if print didn't have it, our exclusive might not be trustworthy, which was not exactly a vote of confidence in the staff.

The emerging women's movement needed straightforward television coverage instead of ridicule. The demonstration at the previous summer's Miss America contest was serious and also designed with humor. The demonstrators established a "freedom trashcan" on the boardwalk into which they threw what they called "women garbage," including false eyelashes and bras. It was there that the phrase "bra burners" originated, although the items never were set on fire because of boardwalk fire laws. It was the first anti-cheesecake demonstration, and it ridiculed the idea of beauty contestants showing off their bodies like so many sheep on parade.

While the women's movement was making news in bits and pieces, it warranted in-depth attention. The one thing a television documentary could do was to put the parts together and see what it all meant. So I pitched the story to the documentary unit, proposing that they let me produce a half hour on the subject.

The director of public affairs, Tom Wolf, was a man ahead of his time. He agreed to my proposal, thereby giving ABC the distinction, unheralded, of being the first network to examine the burgeoning women's movement in any depth. Our half-hour examination which aired 25 May 1970 was called, unimaginatively, "Women's Liberation." It was the first network documentary on the subject and served as a primer, exploring the goals of bra-less campus radicals and more socially acceptable feminist theoreticians.

One would have thought the production would give me credibility with the various groups of women in the movement, who ranged from radical feminists to reform-minded academics. But just as student radicals were hostile to the press who covered campus demonstrations, some in the women's movement distrusted women like me who worked for the male-dominated network news organizations. Worse, I wore makeup and traditional clothing.

In the initial phase of the women's movement, reporting on it was done mainly by men, and it was snide and hostile. Women's lib was treated with humor at best, and contempt at worst. The male reporters, at first, could not see the connection between women's charges of discrimination and the civil rights movement, where such concerns were easily discernible.

Therefore, some of the women involved in the movement were suspicious of reporters, with reason, and women reporters who worked for the "establishment" media were not immune. It was assumed we had adopted the prevailing values and could not be trusted. I was indignant, but went out of my way to guarantee that anything I did would be reported honestly and in a straightforward manner.

One event stands out. I had gone to film a meeting of a coalition group called the Congress to Unite Women for the documentary. After several preliminary negotiation sessions I agreed to certain rules, such as not filming anything but the speakers unless I had the agreement of those in charge. During the course of the event we checked out several rows of people for permission to get "listening shots," which are always needed as cut-aways in the editing. The organizers of the event either didn't know we had gotten permission from those involved or didn't care, since we almost immediately ran into trouble. We had finished in the auditorium, and had set up in a corridor to do individual interviews in the generally hostile atmosphere. Partly, the animosity was because I was with an all-male crew. It took years before enough women were allowed into the technical area, and there was simply no other way to shoot at the time. In 1976, when I produced an hour called "Women's Health: A Question of Survival," it was possible to put together an all-female crew, but even then it wasn't easy. It was not possible at all before that time.

At the Congress to Unite Women, when we began to pack up to leave, we found that one 1200-foot film magazine was missing. Usually one shoots 400-foot magazines, which is ten minutes of film, but for conferences sometimes the longer length is useful. We searched everywhere, but simply could not find the missing film. A friendly source at the conference whispered to me to give up because it had been stolen. The crew and I were thunderstruck. It was not the ordinary, run-of-the-mill mishap, and they razzed me about my so-called friends. That was nothing compared to the response the next day in the office. To say that I got a ribbing is an understatement. I really couldn't blame them. I was still fuming over the incident myself. Subsequently, we learned that the missing film had been unceremoniously dumped into the East River. I felt that the theft had done a great deal of damage and certainly didn't lend the movement any credibility in the ABC newsroom. It was indicative of the wide split among the various factions that continued for many years: the group that wanted to operate through the system, rationally and in terms the majority could understand, and the radicals, some of them lesbians, others left over from Students for a Democratic Society (SDS), who wanted to undermine the system, and who lost out in the movement in the long run.

As I look back on my career, the women's movement provided an exceptional point when time, place, and position all came together

to give me the power and focus to contribute to the country's awareness of the new status of women and also to vocalize that change for
my own industry. For once, I seemed to be in the right place at the
right time. I had come along too early to strongly affect the future
of women as anchors, and was too solitary a presence in the newsroom
to win battles to cover more of the important stories. The women's
movement came along as I was strategically placed in the documentary
department. Ironically, I had moved there largely because of my
inability to be part of the evening news "A-team."

ABC News was still in third place in the ratings in the early
1970s, and it was no great loss to the entertainment division to give
up time regularly to documentaries. Those half hours were inexpen-
sive to produce compared to prime-time fare. With ratings at night
so poor, substituting our product at least provided the network with
good reviews, if not with massive audiences. Documentary director
Tom Wolf knew a good story when he saw one, and the women's
movement had everything: controversy, pertinence to the general
population, and colorful characters.

The summer of 1972 found me at work on a half hour called
"The Hand that Rocks the Ballot Box." It focused on the efforts of
women to run for office, and many of the women who appeared
emphasized that one road to full equality was through political power.
My film reflected the ferment of the period. The National Women's
Political Caucus was in its second year, struggling to survive; Betty
Friedan said the time for consciousness-raising was over and the time
for action had come. We followed thirty-year-old Brooklyn lawyer
Elizabeth Holtzman in her successful campaign to win the New York
Democratic nomination from eighty-four-year-old Congressman
Emanual Celler, and also filmed the losing battle of a woman running
for office in Idaho. I couldn't be a participant, but I could draw
portraits of the movement. Critics had their say. Our vice president
for public affairs, Tom Wolf, was pleased with the results and so was
I. There was a slightly different reaction from news president Elmer
Lower, who was more perplexed than hostile.

The usual procedure on documentaries is to screen a rough cut,
usually an overly long version of the story, for the executive producer.
In our small documentary unit at the time, I reported directly to Tom
Wolf. We were on good terms, communicated easily, and while I never
looked forward to those sessions, knew him to be a reasonable man
whose criticisms would be useful. If we disagreed, we could argue it
out and reach a decision. In the case of "The Hand that Rocks the
Ballot Box," we had only a few minor differences. When Lower

screened a film, his comments were usually terse; if he liked it, he'd say "good job," and leave. If he had anything negative to say, he would generally exclude the producer from the discussion and talk privately to Wolf, who would bring back the bad news and the changes.

In the instance of the film on women in politics, Lower questioned me directly, but the conversation was brief. He couldn't understand why women wanted power, specifically political power. He thought they had considerable power, behind the throne, as it were. He didn't stay long enough to thrash it out, and I felt the best thing for me to do would be to try to explain more fully in writing. Lower's wife, whom I had met several times, was a charming, quiet woman who raised their two boys and as far as I knew had not worked professionally after the children were born. The women's movement must have baffled them both. In my note to Lower, I wrote:

> Now that the women in politics show is over, I feel compelled to answer more fully one of the questions you asked after the screening. You questioned my use of "powerless" as a description applying to women, and mentioned the "home" as a place where women have had power. This gets to the heart of the whole women's movement.
>
> When I was at your house about two years ago, I noticed a copy of Betty Friedan's *The Feminine Mystique*. That book reflected the frustration of women overeducated for their jobs. Power in the home means power behind the throne, or husband, indirect power. It also means power through one's children, often to their detriment. It means NO real personal effectiveness in the larger world. It means exclusion from lawmaking, from business, from the world outside. It means that women have had to be passive recipients of decisions made by others; it means that they have had no voice in legislating matters which concern them, ranging from abortion laws, to unequal social security payments, to child care, to war and peace.
>
> Women found themselves in this situation gradually. In the early days of this country, men and women worked side by side. As the industrial revolution took men away from farms and family-centered businesses, women found themselves isolated, out of the mainstream. Women have been educated to stay in those roles, and subtly told that it is unfeminine to do otherwise. Meanwhile, a lot of good educations were wasted.
>
> There is obvious puzzlement on the part of many men today about what women want. They have become used to seeing women in traditional roles and many older women would not want that changed. Younger women, however, in increasing numbers do want change. They are having to effect many of these changes by lawsuits, since attitudes change so slowly. They are angered by the condescension their aspirations provoke (certain newscasters are guilty of this very

frequently; women are treated with humor, people not to be taken seriously). If blacks, in the early stages of their emergence, were talked to and about in such a way, there would have been more violence. But people learned to tread with care. Women are just as serious, just less violent.

This note merely skims the surface but I hope is a more full explanation than I was able to give you the other day.

Let me put it one more way: would *you* trade your position for one of "power" in the home? Of course not. Neither would I.

Lower's manner toward me remained cordial and businesslike. For men of his generation, it must have been difficult to see us in the new roles we were assuming in the previously male world of news-gathering. It might have been easier for him to grasp if I had been single. The fact that I was married, a mother, and still persisted in this madness must have been nearly incomprehensible.

The women's movement had wide-ranging ramifications, including its effect on marriage, child-rearing, and women's roles in the workplace. It didn't take a lot of convincing to get the go-ahead in 1973 to do an hour called "Woman's Place" which examined sex-role stereotyping, among other things. We found that three-year-old boys had already selected fireman, policeman, doctor, or lawyer when asked what they wanted to be when they grew up. Not surprisingly, girls picked nurse, teacher, or mommy. Some adults, however, surprised us when they described their lives, and their fears about stepping outside proscribed roles.

Abigail McCarthy had become a public figure during the 1968 presidential campaign as she dutifully campaigned for her husband, Senator Eugene McCarthy. She had been a talented writer in college, but she had subordinated her personal goals to those of her husband and children. At the time we interviewed her for the documentary, her children were grown, and she was separated from her husband. She was just beginning to live on her own. Her description of some of the things she had to learn to do startled us. "You find really everything is a little triumph in a way. You learn how to handle your income tax return. You learn to cope with New York cab drivers on your own. You have some shocks too, because if you aren't protected anymore, you find that hotel clerks can be very aggressive and unpleasant, but if you learn how to deal with that, that's another victory."[3]

By now, Mrs. McCarthy has written several well-received books and evidently has learned to manage on her own.

The timing of the "Woman's Place" broadcast was ironic. It was to be aired on Saturday night, the same evening as the Miss America

pageant. The coincidence was not lost on some of the critics. Dorothy
Storck of *Chicago Today* wrote:

> "Woman's Place" was narrated by Bess Myerson, former commissioner
> of consumer affairs for New York City—and also a former Miss Amer-
> ica. It was an inspired choice by Marlene Sanders, who produced the
> show for ABC. . . . Bess Myerson's presence on the ABC hour—which
> came just before the Miss America by two hours—was a tacit an-
> nouncement of the psychological space that has come to separate the
> two concepts of womanhood. . . . I truly applaud ABC's courage in
> allowing Myerson, Sanders, et al. to take to task on the tube some of
> the more prominent sponsors, such as toy manufacturers, detergent
> sellers and hotel chains. "Commercials make women seem incomplete,
> silly and not too bright, and compulsive cleaners," Myerson com-
> mented. "Toy commercials are a rehearsal for domestic-
> ity." . . . Particularly noteworthy was ABC's effort to get in touch with
> women who were not singing, marching, liberators, but who had reached
> a life's dilemma and were somehow coping, asking until now, unasked
> questions of themselves.[4]

The growing focus on women's issues also opened up other
heretofore neglected areas for exploration. By the mid-1970s the
women's movement had begun to push harder for abortion rights,
as part of the movement to take control of their bodies as well as
their lives. Around that time both First Lady Betty Ford and Happy
Rockefeller, wife of the Governor of New York, had mastectomies
and the issue of breast cancer was being publicly debated. Women's
health was a timely issue, and I was given permission to move ahead
on a documentary on the subject, which aired on 5 January 1976.

One measure of progress since "The Hand that Rocks the Ballot
Box" aired in 1972 was that this time I was able to hire an all-female
crew. We were filming breast examinations in a clinic, and a more
intimate, self-examination at a feminist health center. There was no
other way to work. After the concern about breast cancer had surfaced
with the Rockefeller and Ford cases, local news programs began showing women doing self-examination (in what I felt was often an ex-
ploitive fashion), with most of the filming done by men. Just as some
documentaries have exploited subjects in the guise of deploring a
particular practice, I felt that much of the coverage of this new area
was salacious. By having only women work on these sensitive topics,
I knew we could do better, and I think we did.

In the early 1970s there began to be a clamor at universities
for speakers to explain the women's movement. Lecture agents searched
for visible spokespersons, and I was one of the few women on television

who could fill the void. In preparation for one of my speeches on the changing status of women, I called NBC's Reuven Frank. We had not spoken since I had first approached him for a job six years earlier. This time I asked him when a woman was likely to anchor an evening news broadcast on television. He told me it wasn't likely at all, for several reasons, "One, because broadcasters don't pioneer, they don't set trends, they follow them, and two, because a woman's voice is not authoritative."

It was almost ten years since Friedan published her book. Women's "voices" were beginning to be taken seriously. Television had covered the issues and events and thus voiced the concerns and victories of women. If broadcasters were followers, they had been given plenty of time to adjust. It was time for changes within.

Women in television, though, were not the first to challenge their bureaucracies on issues including equal employment and equal pay. In 1970 there were too few women employed in broadcasting other than secretaries. Not surprisingly, the places where women were most numerous — the magazines — were the first to move. There were researchers galore, frustrated at their inability to be promoted. They almost never were.

*Newsweek* led off. Forty-six women employees brought suit against the magazine in 1970, in the form of a complaint to the Equal Employment Opportunity Commission in Washington, charging violation of Title VII of the Civil Rights Act of 1964. They claimed they could not get promotions, were stuck in deadend jobs, and often did the work of other categories without getting commensurate credit or pay. Their suit was eventually upheld, and of course received coverage in the other media.

Soon after the *Newsweek* action, at Time, Inc. the women filed similar complaints, taking a different route — this time with the state attorney general's office. There an agreement was finally worked out that all jobs would be open to qualified candidates. Three women at *Life* were promoted to editors, at *Fortune* five women researchers were made associate editors, and *Time* hired a woman writer. The State Division on Human Rights was ordered to periodically review salaries of the men and women in the same job category.

Newswomen improved their status immeasurably by way of their 1972 Newspaper Guild contracts. Maternity leaves had been an issue for years, and didn't exist. Women had to take sick leave or vacation time and hurry right back. The *Newsweek* contract stipulated four weeks plus accrued vacation money for maternity leave. And, starting from the day a baby was born, a woman could take a one-year leave with the option of an additional six months. She was also permitted to leave work after six months of pregnancy, if she wanted to. What women asked for in terms of time is the equivalent to a man's military leave. In addition, the contracts allowed for a week's paternity leave with pay, so that men could be home with their wives and their new babies.

At around the same time, the battle of the National Press Club was being waged in Washington by women of the Washington press corps. Since informal contact over a drink at the club is often where news as well as trade gossip is exchanged, women writers wanted to belong. As things stood, they were only admitted at formal news conferences. It was too reminiscent of the back of the bus. After heated debate, in 1971, a two-thirds majority finally voted to admit women. The club bar was integrated, and the club became more financially solvent than it would otherwise have been. Financial need, not justice, was said to be the motivation behind changing the rules. At least that's what the women involved believe. Women were also fighting to be admitted to the press box at sports events, and later succeeded in having locker-room access as well, winning each time, but not without vocal opposition and a tough fight.

The women at the *New York Times* began to have their consciousness raised in 1969, when members of the National Organization for Women picketed in the street outside the Times building, as part of their campaign to eliminate separate classified columns for men and women. The good jobs had always seemed to be on the male side of the listings. Today, most people don't think twice about the desegregated classified section, but changing the former practice was a struggle.

There were threats of legal action over salary discrepancies and assignments inside the *New York Times*. The women began legal action in 1973 but there was no settlement until 1978. There has not been a case brought by women against a publication that has been resolved in court. Suits brought by women at *Newsweek*, the Associated Press, and the *Reader's Digest* were all settled out of court.

The *New York Times* was also slow in agreeing to use "Ms." as a form of address. It was not until June 1986 when it finally relented and the term was allowed to be used.

In broadcasting, pressure on the industry began back in 1970 when NOW filed a petition with the Federal Communications Commission (FCC), asking that broadcast licensees be required to file affirmative action reports regarding the employment of women. The National Association of Broadcasters opposed their claim, arguing that no pattern of discrimination against women in the broadcasting industry has been established. Those were men speaking, of course.

Change for women in broadcasting came through two government orders, one by the FCC, the other by the Labor Department. One affected local stations and the other affected the networks. In 1969 the FCC agreed to add the word "sex" to various antidiscrimination rulings they already had, and, to the satisfaction of women, in May 1971 a new requirement was added to the license renewal process: television stations were to file affirmative action plans for women with their application.

"Affirmative action" began to be the cry in the early seventies. It meant simply that employers had to take affirmative steps to bring themselves into compliance with earlier antidiscrimination laws. But they had to go beyond merely not discriminating on the basis of race, creed, or sex. Those who were government contractors or who employed more than a thousand people had to take steps to hire women and minorities to remedy the effect of past practices; there were "goals" and "timetables" established by computing the number of minority-group members or women in the work force in the particular area where the company was located. Statistics had to be submitted regularly listing the number of minorities in the various job categories.

But the National Organization for Women was not satisfied with that change and was concerned that there was still too little pressure on broadcasters. So NOW developed a legal strategy that would indirectly force the networks, the television decision-makers, to improve the status of women in the industry and to promote women's issues. The women did this by challenging the broadcast licenses of some of the network's owned and operated stations. NOW claimed that the stations did not act in the "public interest," and thus violated the stations' mandate by the Federal Communications Commission when awarded a television license. Attorney Nancy Stanley outlined the following violations in 1971: under the standards of equal employment opportunity, women on the staffs of the stations were underrepresented, underemployed, and underpaid; the stations' ascertainment process (evaluating the community's programming needs) was incomplete in their not including women as a significant community group; and the stations violated the Fairness Doctrine, a provision which stated that a licensee has an affirmative duty to present contrasting views of an issue in its overall programming, because the role of women in society is a bona fide controversial issue of public importance and licensees were not portraying contrasting views of that role in their overall programming.[5]

The first two license challenges were filed with the FCC by local NOW chapters and in cooperation with other women's organizations against WRC in Washington D.C. and WABC in New York City.[6] These two stations were chosen for the first battles because they were network owned, flagship stations in major markets, and their prominence would draw a lot of media attention. Litigation began in 1972.

The most serious charge against WRC was the absence of equal employment opportunity. The women used the U.S. Equal Employment Opportunity Commission study of WRC's record, published on 29 October 1971, which stated that it had "reasonable cause to believe" that WRC had discriminatory employment policies. "Specifically, the EEOC found underrepresentation of women employed in management, technical areas and sales. It found discriminatory policies on wages and maternity leave."[7] The FCC denied NOW's petition against WRC and renewed WRC's license, but with the condition that WRC improve its affirmative action program by posting all job openings.[8]

In May 1972, the NOW New York chapter challenged the license of WABC-TV, charging blatant sexism, including consistently failing to report serious women's issues and displaying a disparaging portrayal of women's role in society as reflected in overall programming and commercials. Preparation for the suit took nearly two years and involved over one hundred people watching the station night and day and noting what they saw. The suit was handled by the Center for Constitutional Rights, a group of lawyers who had worked together in early civil rights cases and specialized in public interest and unpopular causes. The lawyers handling the WABC case were all women. The petition to deny the license renewal eventually was turned down.

Both the WABC and WRC cases were appealed to the Washington D.C. Court of Appeals and were argued in 1976. The judges found that the FCC could "reasonably" have decided that NOW did not provide enough substantial evidence to withhold or revoke the licenses of WRC and WABC, but the court did find that WABC had erred in choosing to interview a low number of women during the ascertainment process. Again, this error was not grave enough to deny a license.[9] Although the four years of litigation resulted in victory for the stations, NOW and the women's groups were not disappointed. The legal challenges provided an opportunity for women's groups to air their grievances publicly. At WABC, women involved in the suit had a number of meetings with station executives, elaborating on the grievances that were clearly spelled out in the brief. Change thus came indirectly as a result of these legal actions. "Consciousness-raising," a new phrase in the language, was being forced on the television brass. They had begun to look around, not only at how their own companies were being run, but also at the articulate, able women lawyers facing them across the table. Interestingly, the station's legal departments became receptive to women and that was one area where changes took place rather rapidly.

At the network level, change came more slowly. Women did not have the legal avenue of license renewal challenges. Networks are not licensed by the government like individual television stations. But the networks were covered by a Labor Department ruling known as the Revised Order #4, which applied to all companies with government contracts.[10] Some network corporate divisions have government research contracts under which they are government contractors. Revised Order #4, called by some "executive lib" (because many of those who benefited from it moved into relatively high-level jobs), required that such companies draw up affirmative action programs to remedy the underutilization of women.

Organizing the women at ABC network was not easy, even with the Revised Order #4 on their side. The news division did not employ a lot of women and also it was located on West Sixty-sixth Street, twenty blocks away from the corporate headquarters on the Avenue of the Americas. The initial organizing efforts originated in the corporate headquarters where there were more women employed in reasonably decent jobs. Prior to a call to a meeting to devise strategy, there had been informal conversations among us. But the real impetus came about because of the license challenge of WABC-TV, the local ABC station, by the National Organization for Women.

Shortly after the NOW license challenge began, an article in *Broadcasting Magazine* examined the employment of women at the various networks. Most disturbing to the women at ABC was a statement by Marie McWilliams, then vice president of personnel, that no women at ABC in New York had complained about any problems. That comment was much discussed, and we decided that some of our grievances should be made known. A letter was drafted to Elton H. Rule, president of ABC Inc., requesting an opportunity to discuss what was on our minds. Even before the letter was sent, news leaked out via the grapevine, and a member of the ABC legal department called and invited the group to meet with management. I had to miss the first meeting in August, because of my vacation with my family.

The five women who did attend had been with the company between three and six years. They outlined and rehearsed what they were going to say and limited their complaints to six areas. President

Elton Rule was absent but other top executives did attend: Rule's right-hand man, Martin Pompadur, a vice president; the senior vice president and general counsel, Everett Erlick; and an attorney for ABC's owned and operated stations, Mark Roth. Those on the women's side included Susan Mitchell, then director of the now defunct Media Concepts (which marketed news broadcasts after they had aired, for nontheatrical distribution). She opened the meeting, emphasizing that the group was not there so much for themselves, but to help the company see its missed opportunities, pointing out how women were underutilized. She explained that no formal protests had been made (i.e., lawsuits) because more opportunities already existed at ABC for women than at the other networks; but there were still problems. She explained that when new job openings occurred, no announcements were made, so that no women could apply. "A few weeks later" she said, "we read in the releases that some nice young man had been promoted."

Jayne Ross, then ABC's manager of awards, brought out the need for an affirmative action plan; Mary Jean Parson, associate director of corporate planning, asked management to provide goals and timetables for implementing such a program, reminding the executives that ABC was a federal contractor and therefore was required to comply. News producer Pat Sides suggested the company establish a talent bank and asked whether or not the company had ever analyzed salary and job levels to see where the women stood; Julie Hoover, then manager of audience information, suggested the company prepare a questionnaire to survey women employees to see what they thought of ABC's employment policies. Several people discussed the fact that many of the unions covering workers at the network were hostile to women, and asked that the network put pressure on them to open up. Finally, a grievance committee was requested. Management said they would reply to the various points raised and would get back to the group. The message to them, loud and clear, was that things were not moving for women, and that this newly formed group wanted to "help" the network proceed in a way that would be useful to both the women and the organization. There were no threats. But the license challenge at the local station was fresh in management's mind; they knew how time-consuming it was for company lawyers, and how much negative publicity it had generated.

As soon as my vacation ended, I immediately got involved. Five of us then informally organized what we decided to call the Women's Action Committee (WAC). It was a chance to change things in our own backyard, to alter practices we had lived with all of our professional lives.

After a second management meeting, this time with ABC president Elton Rule on hand, it was decided that an employee relations committee be established to meet with us regularly. Everything was cordial. After a memo to all broadcast division heads from Rule reaffirming the company's equal employment policy, our joint meetings got underway, and took place every four to six weeks.

Before anything further could be done, we had to have more participation from other women to get a better idea about what they wanted and how much support we could get. How could the women in the company be reached, scattered as they were among four or more buildings, one a skyscraper? The only logical place that every women in the company visited was the bathroom. Thus began the system of bathroom notices, posted with the date, time (usually during lunch), and location of the Women's Action Committee meetings. Those of us in or near the various buildings had to find women we felt were sympathetic to be in charge of the posting in each floor's ladies room. Even when the system began operating, the notices were frequently ripped down. Later, once we were recognized as a company group, as legitimate as the credit union, we got official permission from the network to post them. We also were allowed to meet weekly with their permission in various boardrooms large enough to hold the twenty or so people who eventually began to gather. There were, of course, people who attended only to air their own grievances, and we had to find a way to prevent the meetings from becoming exclusively gripe sessions for individual complaints. A balance had to be struck. There were many grievances that were generic: women in line for promotions, who didn't get them, frustrated because outside men, often younger and with less experience, were brought in for them to train for jobs the women should have had; an unresponsive personnel department; the deep disappointment with being stuck in dead-end jobs; and salary discrepancies.

It was common for men to be hired from the outside for the same level job as a woman, but at higher pay. A woman, it was often said, didn't "need" the money. Perhaps her husband had a good job, or maybe she was single and didn't need that much, the myth went. Salaries, we felt, should reflect individual worth, not someone's uninformed speculation on one's needs. When men negotiate salary, no chart is made of their family obligations. How many single women support elderly parents, assist younger siblings in college, or are saving for their old age—or just plain deserve to be paid well?

Our group eventually began to sort itself out. A nucleus of regulars began to appear, and we tried to outline what kind of approach should be made at a forthcoming meeting with network division heads. The top men of all major parts of the company were to attend that meeting, and the women were nervous. Each member of the steering committee, now numbering eight, was given a particular area to discuss, and we divided up the responsibilities. Job posting, inadequate pensions and benefits, the grievance committee, and other specifics would be discussed after an initial statement of why we had formed and what we hoped to accomplish.

One of the most interesting developments was how the women in the group changed during those early months and years. Several who were insecure and nervous gained in confidence and poise. More professional-looking clothing replaced schoolgirl outfits. Before the scheduled meeting with the division heads, I gave a pep talk on how I felt we should conduct ourselves, and we discussed what to wear, which was a subject that worried a number of people. "Don't be afraid, don't be hostile," I said. "We are right and they may not like it, but they know it's true, and if we are reasonable and firm, we can make headway." Anxiety was rampant among our numbers. But despite the intimidating boardroom in the corporate headquarters, and the presence of top executives, the first meeting went well. A representative management group was appointed to meet with our steering committee on a regular basis, and those meetings did indeed begin.

The first concrete gain by the group took place only four months after the first meeting, and that was in job posting. As things worked out, job posting was never all it was cracked up to be, but at least it helped. Jobs were still frequently filled before posting, and some interviewing was pro forma only. Still, it was progress.

Another step forward occurred when Mary Jean Parson, one of the original women's group members, was made associate director of employee relations, and in addition, a manager of equal employment opportunities was hired. They had a mandate to recruit minorities and women, and they had the freedom to hire. The numbers began to improve.

We had no elected leadership, hoping that a group effort would successfully hold the loose collection of members together. Surprisingly the system worked rather well, although there eventually proved to be four or five people who alternated as leaders, myself included. I tried not to take on too much of that and served more as a morale booster, trying to encourage others to lead. On several occasions we met with women activists at the other networks, in sporadic tri-network meetings. Judging from CBS and NBC, we were making more rapid progress than either of them and could chalk up some rather impressive early gains.

An informal employee grievance committee procedure was finally established, wherein a woman (or a man for that matter) with a complaint against her boss did not have to face him alone, but could call on one of us to accompany her to a meeting with him or his superior. We always saw to it that the person who went along was from some other division of the company. In most instances our efforts were successful. My only assignment in this area was on behalf of a telephone operator who had wanted to change her shift by fifteen minutes because of a transportation problem she had been having. A female supervisor had been adamant in refusing her request. We went over her head, to the man one step further up the ladder, and managed to resolve the situation.

It became clear after that meeting that one of the problems was an unresponsive personnel department. The vice president in charge, Marie McWilliams, one of only two women vice presidents in the company at the time, had been on the job for many years. We later found out she was grossly underpaid herself and had been unwilling to make reasonable demands for increases from the management she was part of. She was old-fashioned; her efforts to change were too late and complaints about the past deficiencies of the department could not be overcome. Ultimately, she resigned.

The WAC group was at its most productive and active during the first two years. Women's issues were in the news, and the men we worked with saw what was going on outside.

The most difficult attitudinal problems to solve were deep-seated. Cronyism prevailed. Women were not members of the old boys club, were not on the lunch and golf circuit with them, had not come through the same employment route, and were therefore not considered for some of the top jobs. Management, after a protracted series of discussions with us, agreed that some kind of sensitivity training needed to be instituted, and a series of two-day seminars was begun, on a sporadic basis, at a conference center on Long Island. Representative women from different parts of the company were there, and some encounters that took place were not only candid, but emotionally charged. Several members of the WAC also attended. Men that I knew on the assignment desk seemed to have gained from the experience, and talked to me about it. The sessions didn't continue for very long, evolving into more traditional interpersonal relationship seminars, and later to standard job skills sessions.

There were several specific accomplishments by the WAC. In 1972, when our group organized, two women held the title of vice president and only half a dozen women exclusive of performers earned more than $20,000 a year. The female portion of the broadcasting division totaled just under 30 percent. By mid-1975, the proportion of women was up to 32 percent and approximately fifty women on the talent payroll earned more than $20,000 a year. There were still only two vice presidents but there was a female corporate officer and a woman put on the board of directors. Those gains were not astounding by any means, but were at least in the right direction, and the trend continued over the next several years.

By 1975, a new director of personnel was hired, but at the same time the people who had been charged with recruiting minorities and women lost their mandate to hire. The statistics dipped once again. The original impetus was gone.

The women's group no longer met with top executives but with three people involved in personnel, including a lawyer. Everything slowed down. Management had gotten to know members of the group, and a number of the women whose abilities had been hidden away in their departments were promoted. As they were promoted, in some cases their commitment to the women's group diminished noticeably. There were those who said the women were being co-opted, but after all, advancement was what we wanted, wasn't it? Women were being recognized and promoted. Undoubtedly some now saw that their best interests lay elsewhere. By 1981, ABC had twenty-one women vice presidents. In 1987 the company would give out no specific numbers.

Anyone who had been through the stress involved with this kind of group knows that it is not so much that the participants' commitment fades, but that they became worn down and weary of the battle. Strides had been made, and the hope was that they would endure. By and large, ABC management had been cooperative. At NBC, management resistance forced women employees to resort to legal action. At CBS, there was a more conciliatory leadership in the network hierarchy.

The most militant step taken by the CBS women's group concerned clothes. In 1970, when pantsuits were the latest vogue, a memo was issued by a middle manager in news to the effect that "it is not company policy nor the discretion of the immediate supervisor for female employees to wear slacks during the course of their normal working day. . . ." The women acted swiftly, and the next morning almost all of them appeared in pants. The event merited coverage in the *New York Times*. The rule was rescinded.

Following the pants revolt in 1970, no organized activity by the women of CBS occurred until 1973. Oddly enough, the women got together as a result of a "policy statement on women" distributed company-wide from network president Arthur Taylor. The memo seemingly came out of the blue, except that two weeks before it was issued, the women of NBC had taken legal action against their company. The memo declared that every employee at CBS should receive equal opportunity, that there was a policy of equal pay, and that five part-time women's counselors would be appointed to handle women's "aspirations and gripes." Obviously the memo was conceived to head off any activities such as suits that might follow in the wake of the NBC action. A group consisting mainly of newswomen got together and decided to reject the idea of only newswomen meeting with Taylor. They managed to gather together enough women from other divisions to present a more or less representative group. It took five months for a meeting to be scheduled. In July 1973, thirteen women, only two of them correspondents, met with the head of CBS and his senior staff. The women prepared presentations and conquered their nervousness enough to air their problems along with recommendations for solutions. The session lasted about two hours. In only three weeks, Taylor invited the group back and was ready with his responses. One was a firm rejection of goals and timetables, but he did agree to an advisory council consisting of women elected by women employees. That group began meeting with senior management every three weeks in order to resolve issues of equal pay, promotions, and other, discriminatory, practices. The meetings continued for two years.

Equally important were the meetings the women held with their own divisional management to work on their specific problems. That summer the newswomen met with news president Richard Salant and senior managers of the news division. By then, Salant himself was aware of the poor statistics. He had authorized the release of the personnel rankings rather than let the women's group try to compile a list from the telephone directory and Christmas card address list. The bad news was out, but because of Salant's newly developed personal commitment and his instructions to others, the numbers began to change. In 1972, only twenty-two women were in producers' jobs. By January 1979, there were forty more. Where there had been three female technicians, the number rose to fifteen.

The women met among themselves to try to devise a strategy. Occasional get-togethers of the tri-network group enabled us all to share our experiences. Some women felt that being identified as "women's libbers" would put off management and slow down the

progress. Others were afraid of being so identified and hurting themselves. The meetings were often heated and, in the interest of democracy, supposedly leaderless. Writing memos by committee was
difficult. Finally, practicality triumphed and four separate groups were
organized, each with its own steering committee. Priorities had to be
determined, and cries of elitism prevailed if, say, the problems of
secretaries were not addressed or put near the top of the list. There
were arguments about the group's responsibility to protest the image
of women as projected on the air in programming. (At ABC, we
quickly learned this area was off-limits. Employment problems were
the main focus of attention, and some progress was made.) The CBS
group felt that its major success was in getting "an absolute commitment at the senior management level to the issue of sexism."[11]
Second was "the establishment of awareness sessions for women and
men to help change long held ideas about how the two sexes should
and should not act in the business world." They also claimed credit
for the fact that in 1974, 36 percent of the promotions in executive
grades went to women, compared to 25 percent the year before and
13 percent four years before that. There was also a push to train and
promote women already in the company rather than hiring from the
outside. Short-term internship and training programs were begun.
Some salary realignments and job restructuring moved a number of
secretaries out of those ranks into better jobs. Job posting was begun
up to the director level. The women perceived a change in atmosphere
in many departments of the corporation. They also took satisfaction
in achieving changes without having to file suits or having to threaten
to do so.

The CBS women had failures as well, most significant of which
was that the new attitudes of top management did not successfully
filter down to most middle- and first-line men. The group had not
figured out how to get more women into the all-male unions, and
they had to fight a growing apathy among the women. They discovered that when progress begins, people tend to relax and become
complacent. The women who dropped back also believed that the
activist women would take care of things. This was a problem in 1975
and has gotten worse everywhere.

By the late 1970s, and well into the 1980s, the women's groups
at CBS had less and less power, finally dealing mostly with the personnel department. Arthur Taylor was no longer president. Others
appeared and disappeared. The national climate no longer placed
affirmative action and equality high on the agenda, but some of the
gains made in the early seventies remain. Women now have access to

the entry-level jobs, although many women on the way up lost their jobs in the firings at CBS in 1985, 1986, and 1987, stemming the flow of women into promotions to higher levels later on.

While the managements of ABC and CBS were by and large conciliatory in the 1970s, NBC was so hostile that legal intervention became necessary.

The women at NBC had not initially wanted a lawsuit. After meeting together toward the end of 1971 and defining their goals, they finally managed to have an audience with NBC brass, and quietly explained their position. One of their grievances was that secretaries were graded according to the standing of the men they worked for. A secretary to a vice president was paid more than a secretary to a lower-level person. No matter how well they did their jobs, they were treated as appendages, not as individuals who performed differently. Their initial appeals to personnel to change this practice were ignored. Money was not the main issue, however. What the women wanted was fairness.

After a cordial but inconclusive session with the NBC president, Julian Goodman, in September 1972, another larger meeting was promised. Some four months later, in January 1973, the women's group was summoned to what was then called the President's Council, consisting of network vice presidents. The women made a professional presentation complete with slides, a technique TV executives frequently use. The group's grievances went beyond employment; they charged that women's concerns were ignored on the air as well. They also documented their complaints about the lack of advancement, pay scales, and the image of women in the programming. Some time later, when they were called back, the men made a counterpresentation. As for the charges that soap operas, for example, did not deal with real women's issues, the network illustrated their virtues with statistics on how soaps did deal with adultery, abortion, rape, homosexuality, and incest—all, according to them, women's issues. These were certainly sensational subjects and surefire ratings grabbers, but they were not what the women had in mind.

The ABC Women's Action Committee knew that the NBC women had added to their difficulties when they criticized program content. That, we knew, was sacrosanct. Pressure groups of all sorts were always after the networks about entertainment programs. Other groups constantly complained that the networks violated their mandate to serve the public interest. The public interest? That, according to the networks, was what the public was interested in and was measured by the ratings. If people weren't being served, they'd turn to another channel or turn off the set. It was felt that those "cranks" from the black, women's, gay, or church groups should be placated if possible, but not at the cost of changing programming. The fact that blacks started to become more visible, that homosexuality began to be dealt with, and that some serious women's issues started to be included in programming came about because the society outside finally changed and not because of internal pressure. As Reuven Frank had told me years before, television doesn't set trends, it follows them.

There was a deliberate decision taken by ABC's Women's Action Committee not to deal with on-air programming, but to stick to employment. It was a wise decision.

The management's definition of "women's issues" underlined for the NBC women's group just how far apart they were from management in the comprehension of the issues. The group left, dejected. They decided to contact the New York City Human Rights Commission, and after thorough consultation, reluctantly decided that a more effective move would be to sue. They sought out an all-female law firm for help. Blank, Goodman, Rone & Stanley took the case. NBC had said repeatedly there was no discrimination, and therefore nothing had to be done. The women at NBC knew otherwise, and decided a class action suit was their only recourse.

Around one hundred women at NBC had been involved in discussions. When it came to signing the complaint, however, only sixteen were willing to become plaintiffs. Even though the women's law firm did not take payment, holding off for victory, there were many costs. All requests to NBC for documents or information were billed to them; xeroxing and other administrative charges mounted. Experts hired to analyze statistical data had to be paid as well. The sixteen women had to contribute from their own pockets, and the amounts grew. Some could afford only a few hundred dollars; others spent thousands, including one woman who contributed nearly six thousand dollars over the four-year period. These were lower-level management women, unit managers, secretaries. They were not network celebrities with big salaries. People like Barbara Walters kept their distance. She occasionally contributed small amounts to various fund-raising efforts. Most of the women involved tried to keep a low profile, going about their jobs as usual during the long ordeal.

A crucial development helped to conclude the litigation. The case was joined by the Equal Employment Opportunity Commission, which filed its own charges. This gave the case added stature, and with the government beginning to look closely, a settlement was finally reached.

NBC first tried to settle out of court for $500,000 but the women turned them down. Money, they repeated, was not the whole problem.

The settlement finally included a payment of $2 million, but much more was involved. The original sixteen women shared in a $200,000 fund, which they divided among themselves according to the severity of the employment complaint each had. Their costs were returned as well. Nonunion women at NBC divided $540,000, which was compensatory back pay. Female employees received either $500 or $1,000 each, depending on their length of employment. Pay increases were mandated as well, to bring women into line with men in the same job category. Some women ultimately received even more money than the men they worked with because of their longer experience and other factors. Provisions were made to pay the women's attorney's fees and expenses.

The bulk of the agreement involved a broad range of affirmative action designed to bring more women into previously male-dominated management and technical positions, to improve the salaries and job assignments in the primarily female clerical positions, and to provide a more open, documented personnel system. Twenty thousand dollars a year was set aside for monitoring compliance efforts, to end in 1981.

Some aspects of the agreement were broken almost immediately. One of the women's attorneys, Janice Goodman, reported that there were problems involving the status and salary of a number of individuals, mainly researchers doing the work of associate producers. They were neither receiving the salaries nor had the proper titles. Difficulties over filling technical jobs continued. The promises of allocating a certain number of those positions to women were not fulfilled. In some of those cases of violations of the agreement, arbitration was required. In others, suits were filed in federal court, but were settled out of court. There was never any satisfactory resolution of the technical jobs problem.

Under the decree there was a provision for a job evaluation to be done on all clerical, nonmanagerial positions, and for a committee composed of management and the women's group to review each job description and grade level. In six instances there was no agreement, and arbitration was again required. In four of those cases, the women's group prevailed.

Was it worth it? By the time of the settlement, only nine of the sixteen women were still at NBC. Some had left for better jobs elsewhere, or because they felt uncomfortable in their adversary roles. In 1980, only four remained in the company. One said yes, it was worth it because of the vindication of what they knew was right. She felt that it was a tremendous experience to see how sixteen disparate women of all ages and abilities could work together so well, under such trying circumstances.

I asked the "survivors" if the women employees who came into the company around the time the suit was settled appreciated what had been done for them. One of the remaining women, Gloria Clyne, doubted it.[12] In fact, she said, after the settlement was reached, and the money was distributed, the women's group received only two thank-you notes from recipients. "Only two?" I asked. "Out of how many?" The answer: more than a thousand.

It took some of us longer than others to make an unpleasant discovery. Women are no more virtuous or intrinsically better than men. Those who were leaders learned this, to their disappointment. Nevertheless, appreciated or not, the good fight has to be fought and there will always be a minority who will lead the way.

After the gains of the late 1970s, there was a decline in activism. Women had begun to be hired at entry-level jobs, and our numbers had increased on-air and in production. The movement had paid off, and at first we assumed our problems were over. Meetings with management were phased out. The pressure on business for progress, however, declined precipitously as the Reagan administration became entrenched in Washington. There were efforts to dilute affirmative action and equal opportunity, and the message sent out to management was clear. There would be no penalties for anything short of gross instances of discrimination.

By 1983, there was a growing realization, again at ABC News, that there was backsliding. By that time, I was at CBS News where there was an undercurrent of dissatisfaction among those other than stars, but no organized effort of any significance. The most shocking revelation to me about a newly formed group at ABC was that none among them knew about the group that had preceded them there by ten years.

ABC News correspondents in Washington began meeting among themselves in the fall of 1983 in what began as gripe sessions. At that time, there were nearly one hundred correspondents and only fifteen of them were women. They were not getting on the air as often as their male colleagues, did not have the major beats, and were not assigned the best stories. They decided that complaining to each other was not going to accomplish anything, and thus requested a meeting with management, going through the proper channels. The Washington bureau chief was not overtly hostile, but not responsive either, in effect telling them they were lucky to have jobs. George Watson, a new bureau chief, arrived at about that time, and gave them a more sympathetic hearing, saying he would take their message to ABC News president Roone Arledge. It was now February 1985. While the women waited for that meeting, they began to research how much air time women were getting. They examined logs, and used the computer expertise of Washington correspondent Carole Simpson's husband to compile their findings. As we had discovered earlier, obtaining numbers is difficult when company sources are not available. We had tried fairly successfully ten years before to find out what positions women held throughout the company in much the same way. The correspondents decided to be the spokeswomen in the early stages of the second ABC women's group because of their visibility and clout. No matter how poorly they were doing, they were a more prestigious group than lower-level women. Statistics finally ready, they waited to hear about their meeting with Arledge.

Two months later and no meeting as yet scheduled, all fifteen U.S.-based women correspondents were invited to a luncheon in New York at the corporate headquarters executive dining room to celebrate Barbara Walters's receiving the Silver Satellite Award from American Women in Radio and Television (AWRT) that night at a dinner. Since no meeting with management had yet been set, the organizers of the women's group thought the luncheon would provide an opportune time to raise their grievances. The top male executives were present, including executive producers of all news broadcasts. Arledge offered toasts to Walters, and she made a gracious speech, commending management on the presence of such a talented group of women. She did not then know about the women's group, mainly Washington-based, and in view of her remarks was embarrassed to learn about it shortly afterwards. (Years earlier, during the nascent women's movement in the industry, Walters had chosen to be aloof from its efforts.) Because she had a piece scheduled for "20/20," she had to leave the luncheon early, and missed the events that followed.

Carole Simpson, who had been chosen to speak after lunch, rose and went to the foot of the table. She looked directly at Arledge, saying that all present shared their regard for Walters and her award, but it seemed a good time to tell them that the women correspondents at ABC believed there was a pattern of institutionalized sex discrimination at the network. It was very quiet in the room. The women then passed out copies of their documentation of what they had found, and Simpson outlined some of it, pointing out, as we had done more than ten years before, that this underutilization harmed the company as well as the women. Carole Simpson was a twenty-year veteran of the business by then, a black women of forty-six, vivacious, charming, and able. She told me she could not bear the thought of her sixteen-year-old daughter having to go through this kind of thing, and had therefore chosen to act, even though the experience of being spokes-woman at the time was unsettling. Arledge expressed surprise, saying he had simply not given the matter of women's participation much thought. Back in the mid-1970s his department, exclusively sports at the time, had been a particular target of our original women's group, and he had been fully apprised of the same problems back then, but had done nothing to make changes. It had been the heyday of tele-vision sports, a lucrative and highly publicized department, and even though corporate management had been responsive to some of the original women's groups demands, sports appeared to be exempt. In 1985, Arledge was expressing surprise, saying he never gave the issue much thought. He said, however, that he would. The discussion heated, with the women saying that when a good bureau, or beat, or assign-ment opened up, perhaps Lynn Sherr would be considered, but no one else was.

At the time, Lynn Sherr was one of the more successful women on the air at ABC News. She had earned her way, working in public broadcasting, and before that at the local CBS television station in New York. She was fired from that job, for reasons, she believes, having to do with her appearance. A tall blonde, she is attractive, but not beautiful. No one told her why she lost her job. Sherr finds it shocking that there still had to be a woman's group in 1987.

At the AWRT luncheon meeting the women said they were not considered for choice assignments and were as though invisible. The producers present were defensive, making remarks the women con-sidered ludicrous, such as, "we didn't know you were interested in having a beat." The meeting became a free-for-all and lasted nearly three hours. When it ended, another meeting in the fall, five months from then, was promised. Notably absent at this first gathering was the one woman news vice president, Pam Hill, who had succeeded me in the job I left in 1978 as vice president and director of docu-mentaries. She also did not speak at subsequent meetings, either by her choice or by management's decision. She did not have a good reputation among the current women's group at ABC and had not shown any sensitivity to the issue since assuming her position. With rare exceptions, the few women executives in news at the networks in the late 1980s appeared to set aside any feelings of sisterhood they might have had, preferring to share the male values of the organization. They well knew but gave no signs that they had any concern about women's secondary positions at their companies. Perhaps the explanation is the "Queen Bee syndrome," a condition that makes many high-level women enjoy and want to keep their singular status. They are unwilling to share the limelight or to use their roles to help other qualified women succeed. They also feel that they are more readily accepted in the male power circle by not making waves. Whatever the explanation for Pam Hill's absence, she was not present at the first lunch meeting.

Of the eleven hundred employees in the news organization at the time, five hundred were women. That figure included secretaries as well as editors, producers, and correspondents. Mailings went out to all women, and when the group began to be formally structured in preparation for September, three hundred fifty voted. Some women, including young weekend anchorwoman Kathleen Sullivan, doing well for herself, remained aloof, having nothing to do with the organization. Others felt the women were rabble-rousers, and wanted to keep their distance from possible trouble.

Meanwhile, with a September meeting promised, the women and management went their separate ways after their first long lunch. The AWRT dinner that night held one surprise. Barbara Walters changed her speech, endorsing the women's efforts, and promising her support.

The September meeting did not take place. October, November, and December passed as well. Several small changes had occurred however. A woman, Joanna Bistany, was named vice president in the news public relations area, and women seemed to be getting on the air a little more. The women of the group wanted the promised meeting, however, and decided to write to Arledge requesting it. The letter was leaked to the media and got a considerable amount of space. Finally, a second meeting was scheduled for 15 January 1986, this time in Washington. Eight women were to speak, representing various areas. Again, the women were specific. Their research had revealed large wage discrepancies, and they asked for pay equity. They said women producers were paid on the average of 30 percent less than men. Management expressed disbelief and wanted to know where those numbers had come from. The women pointed out they were reporters and had found a way. The other major issue brought up was sexual harassment. Both were red flags to the network since they spelled possible litigation. The company had just paid a high price in a sexual harassment suit brought by Cecily Coleman. Salary discrimination could spell more trouble. The women believed management also paid close attention because on 3 January, Capital Cities Broad-

casting had taken over ABC, and management had new people to
report to. Capital Cities had a good reputation in its dealings with
women and minorities, in sharp contrast to its tough dealings with
unions. The women also knew you can't sue on the basis of not getting
enough air time, but that sex and money were valid issues. Once
again, the meeting lasted about three hours. The producers were once
again defensive. "World News Tonight" executive Bill Lord said producer jobs had been offered to two women who had turned them
down. One was a "Nightline" producer in London who traveled
extensively, had a fiancé there, and had no desire to move. The women
felt rightly or wrongly that jobs were offered to people who the men
knew would turn them down.

At the second session, the women presented five concrete pro-
posals: First was the establishment of a Woman's Advisory Board to
serve as a watchdog group and to meet on a regular schedule, perhaps
quarterly, with management. Second, a full-time recruiter was to be
hired who would locate qualified women, as well as minorities. Third,
job posting was to be established. This was the same demand made
by the 1972 women's group, and met. Job posting had begun in the
mid-1970s, but still does not include producer or correspondent or
high-level news jobs. Posting was needed so that women would be
able to apply for some of the openings that became available, although
no one expected top jobs to be filled in that manner. The fourth
proposal was that a system of employee evaluations should begin.
Instead of bad-mouthing people behind their backs, a common practice there as at other networks, the women wanted direct word about
how they were doing, on a regular basis. No one should be fired
unexpectedly for poor performance that she never knew about. That
demand was agreed to, and was scheduled to begin in December
1986. Correspondents were to be exempted from the evaluations,
however, because of their personal contractual arrangements, although the women wanted correspondents to be included. In the fifth
proposal, the women asked for a pay equity study.

The company responded positively to several of those demands.
In January 1986, a female news recruiter was hired. She has since
hired six new correspondents, five men and one woman. Why only
one woman, she was asked. She maintained that two women she tried
to bring in were pregnant and turned down the job offers. She pointed
out, in her defense, that two of the men hired were minorities. Job
posting did begin, but top jobs like senior producer are not listed.

In June 1986, six months after the salary study was requested,
the women were called to a meeting with the head of personnel and

Joanna Bistany. Much of the women's research, they said, was correct. They did not concede that any of those findings were caused by discrimination, but said discrepancies came about because of different hiring patterns. Women tended to rise within the company, restricted by the company policy of a 10 percent limit on raises. Men often came in from high-paying outside jobs. However, the company study resulted in substantial raises for more than forty producers, fifteen of them men. The company had averaged the salaries of all male producers, then raised everyone below it to that average figure. It cost the company about a quarter of a million dollars, and provided raises ranging from two thousand to twelve thousand dollars annually. A number of the women who benefited had been among those who felt the women's group was not needed and was unnecessarily making waves. As the women at NBC learned in the 1970s, not all women are deserving or appreciative. However, several were converts. As a postscript to these events, it should be noted that by 1988, the women's group was having difficulty arranging any meetings at all with management.

Young women will continue to enter the business with high hopes, assuming the barriers have fallen. They may find there is a limit to how far they can go. But it will not be because the Carole Simpsons of the world didn't work for change. The ABC women's advisory group may lose its impetus, leadership, and energy as did its predecessor. The 1972 group faded away not because we thought the battle had been won, but because a beginning had been made, and we thought that with enough goodwill, the pressure could lessen. We were wrong.

In the 1980s the local stations were hiring more women but discrimination was surfacing in a different form. Ratings had become increasingly important in local news. The early days of news as merely public service programming were gone. Television stations had discovered the public's appetite for news programming and the fact that the stations could make a lot of money from a news show. Instead of sharing profits with the network for network programming, profits for local news went directly into the local stations' pockets. Suddenly most local production was focused on news. Stations began to improve their technical capacities, hired large staffs, including attractive on-air talent, and covered action stories filled with fires, crime, and sex. Consultants appeared on the scene, decreeing that there should be shorter news pieces, that anchor people should look a certain way, that the weathermen should be "characters," and that political news was boring.[13]

   Christine Craft was hired as a local news anchor at a Metromedia-owned station, KMBC-TV, in Kansas City in 1981. She brought a discrimination suit against them in 1983. Her dispute with the station was based on her resisting the entertainment factors the critics accused Barbara Walters of embodying in 1976. Her complaint was indicative of the problems women were having in an industry where news is seen as entertainment.

   Christine Craft did not begin her career as a dedicated broadcast journalist, but rather was interested in TV news and took a job as weather girl in Salinas, California. She then moved on to do weather at KPIX-TV in San Francisco. There she experienced her first sexist demand in 1974 when her news director asked her to appear in a bathing suit. She agreed and came on camera wearing a trench coat. At a certain point in her report, she disrobed to reveal a turn-of-the-century bathing costume which covered her from head to toe.

   From weather she moved to sports, which propelled her to a network job when she was hired to work for the short-lived "Women in Sports" on CBS. She moved to New York. The CBS staff bleached her hair, applied bright red lipstick and dark eye makeup. When the show died, Craft vowed to never allow herself to be so physically manipulated again. She returned to California, opened an art gallery, free-lanced for a sports magazine, and engaged in her favorite sport, surfing. In 1979 she was offered a job at KEYT-TV, the 116th-size market, where she was a general assignment reporter and co-anchor of the 11:00 P.M. news with a salary of $18,000 a year.

   In 1980 an unsolicited offer came from KMBC-TV in Kansas City, the 27th-sized market, at a salary of $35,000. KMBC had hired a research consulting firm, Media Associates (now known as Audience Research and Development), to find them a female anchor who could bring "warmth" and comfort to the news. Media Associates went all over the country taping local talent off the air. They liked Craft because she looked "laid back with California energy." Because of that analysis, KMBC offered Craft the job. Media consultants became popular with local TV news stations in the early 1970s when local stations realized they could make money with their local newscasts. They hired media consultants to help them develop formats and news personalities who would attract an audience. "Happy talk" anchor chatter, along with logos like "Action News," was a result of consultants' advice.[14]

   Craft was wary of consultants and had disliked makeup artists since her experience at CBS Sports; she was aware that she was not "band-box perfection." In her negotiations with Ridge Shannon, news

director for KMBC, she stressed the fact that she wanted to be hired
for her journalistic abilities and not because her appearance would
fit into some consultant's categorization. But when the ratings did
not go up after she was hired, management sent in a consultant to
"help" her. They "helped" her with her makeup and developed a
clothes calendar for her to improve her image. Nine months after
she began she was called into Shannon's office and told that he was
taking her off the anchor position and assigning her as a reporter.
Craft's description of his reasons for demoting her was that she was
"too old, too unattractive, and not deferential enough to men." Shannon later denied making this statement.[15]

Christine Craft wanted to be evaluated on her journalistic abilities; she resented the emphasis on the look of her hair and clothes,
and on her audience ratings, so she decided to take her case to court,
claiming three things: "sexual discrimination in an advisory capacity,"
the violation of the Equal Pay Act (her male co-anchor was making
$52,000), and fraud in that KMBC said they hired her for her jour-
nalistic abilities but she was fired for her appearance. A major focus
in the trial was on the validity of the kind of research conducted by
Media Associates through the use of focus groups and surveys to
judge her success with the Kansas City audience. Focus groups are
small groups of people who experience something together and then
are questioned by a trained leader about their immediate reactions.

In the focus group organized to study Craft's presentation style,
the leader began the discussion by asking the group whether the
anchorwoman was a "mutt"; he is also reported to have said: "Let's
spend thirty seconds destroying Christine Craft," and "if we all chip
in we can buy her a ticket back to California." The leader claimed
that those remarks were meant to loosen up the group so they wouldn't
be afraid to criticize her.[16] The participants in the focus group had
not been tested for sexual preference, that is, for whether they liked
a man or a woman anchor better. The leader did try to find out what
*kind* of woman they wanted to see, whether they preferred a woman
with youth, beauty, and a nonaggressive style. Later, the lawyers defending Craft claimed that the method of testing violated Title VII
of the Civil Rights Act of 1964 because of the sexual stereotypes
encouraged in the testing setup. They said the focus group leader
encouraged a negative reaction to Craft's dress and makeup. Most
physical appearance requirements are illegal under Title VII. There
can be a dress code but not one grooming standard applied more
strictly to women than to men.[17] The focus group seemed to demand
more from her in terms of appearance than they did from her male

co-anchor. Craft claimed sexual discrimination because the reasons for her demotion were based on poor ratings in categories of appearance and demeanor. The news director is reported to have replied that "the audience perceived [Craft's] dress, appearance, makeup, and presentation as stumbling blocks." Craft claimed that this kind of reason for demotion was discrimination against women.

The first jury found in favor of Craft on the sex-discrimination and fraud charges, in favor of Metromedia on the equal pay count, and advised Judge Joseph Stevens to award Craft $500,000 in damages. But Judge Stevens threw out the jury's award and ruled that KMBC-TV had not been guilty of sex discrimination in insisting that she improve her appearance, that they demanded the same of men.

If the jury had viewed Craft's position favorably, Judge Stevens certainly did not. He said the only discrimination to be found in the case was the ironic one that, "but for the fact that she is female, [Craft] would not have been hired as a co-anchor in December 1980, regardless of her other abilities."[18] He also referred to her casual appearance and passion for surfing, saying, "Her affinity for casual beach life and her apparent indifference to matters of appearance required the defendant [Metromedia] to formulate and implement corrective measures appropriate to their unique circumstances."[19] Judge Stevens also rejected Craft's charge that the news director said she was too old, too unattractive, and not deferential enough to men, saying that Shannon had denied saying such a thing. Judge Stevens did order a new trial on the fraud charge (that Craft was hired under false pretenses).

The new trial convened with Judge Stevens presiding again. The second jury also found in favor of Craft and advised the judge to award her $325,000. Metromedia appealed the case yet again. Stevens declined to hear it a third time. Metromedia took it to the Eighth Circuit Court of Appeals where three judges read the arguments and briefs from both sides and delivered a verdict. They ruled against Craft, stating that they "didn't feel there was enough evidence for a 'reasonable' jury to conclude there had been fraud. The jurors had been 'unreasonable,' in the judges' opinion."[20] Craft was incensed by this, since two juries had found in favor of her case, and she felt that the three male judges—two friends of Stevens and the other, a recent Reagan appointee—all held anti–civil rights attitudes. She was further angered by the Eighth Circuit opinion which, she claimed, "read like the Metromedia brief. Its thirty-one pages bore only passing resemblance to my experience at Metromedia. . . . I read testimony attributed to me that was not mine, but rather the defendant's."[21] Craft decided to go the next step and take her case to the United States Supreme Court. On 3 March 1986 the Supreme Court refused to review the Appeals Court decision because of insufficient evidence on sex discrimination. However, the only female member of the Supreme Court, Associate Justice Sandra Day O'Connor, favored a hearing and said she would have heard the case.[22] Ironically, on the same day Craft was turned down by the Supreme Court, the California Senate approved a resolution praising Craft for her "outstanding achievement in journalism and her perseverance and courage . . . in advancing the cause of women."[23] During this same time, Brenda Williams, the anchor whom Craft replaced and who then replaced Craft at KMBC, filed a sex-discrimination complaint in January 1985 against KMBC's new owner, the Hearst Corporation. She settled out of court.

The Craft case highlights many of the issues affecting the status of women in television news. It is undeniable that television is an entertainment medium and that one's appearance does affect one's reception by an audience. Most women on television news are aware of that and do care that they look attractive. But that should not be the only criterion by which a female newscaster is judged. Sadly, the thing news directors may have learned as a result of the Craft case is to be careful about what they say; as Reuven Frank commented when he was president of NBC News in 1983, "What will happen is legal departments will instruct news executives on what to say."[24] In other words, news directors will just tell more lies about why someone is being hired or fired. Others are more optimistic about the effect of the case on the news business. CBS News correspondent Lesley Stahl "hopes the people who are pursuing policies like that will sit up and question their method, and that a person's ability to write and get a story and convey the story to the public will be considered first."[25] But can the entertainment aspect of news be separated from the informational function?

There is no doubt that women face more pressure than men do on television in terms of appearance, age, and demeanor. Judy Mann in her 9 September 1983 article in the *Washington Post* also noted the huge effect television has on the way society views women:

> Television, whatever else it does, is a mirror of society.
>
> The Craft case shows that the mirror does not come close to reflecting the presence and interests of half of society. It is as distorted a picture of America as an amusement hall mirror.
>
> The finding in Craft's case should make it easier for current

newswomen, most of whom are now in their late 30's, to grow older
on the air, just as say Dan Rather has done.

Many women want more than the illusion of credibility. They *are*
credible, and they are more than mere announcers. They've served
their time, chased stories all over the nation and the world, and earned
the lines in their faces and the authority in their voices. Craft observed
that wrinkles are "seasoning" in a man but "disqualification" in a
woman. Perhaps that is not sex discrimination, but it is a sad statement
about how women are viewed in our society. In local television, more
than a third of the nation's anchorpeople are women, but only 3
percent are over forty. Only three of these women are believed to be
over fifty (Ann Bishop in Miami, Pat Harper in New York, and Sylvia
Chase in San Francisco). As for the men, half are over forty and 16
percent are over fifty.

Men are usually not fired because of age, nor asked to appear
in a bathing suit, and are not evaluated according to their wardrobe,
makeup, and hair. Men are under pressure, but it is not a pressure
based on their sex. Sex discrimination can be blatant, as described
by Christine Craft, or it can surface in the much more subtle and
destructive form of sexual harassment. Some women try to ignore it,
others are forced to leave their jobs because of it, and some women
go to court over it.

Sexual harassment is difficult to deal with because it is so difficult
to define. The harassment often occurs without witnesses. A woman
must get someone in power to believe in the complaint. Then there
is always the question as to whether the woman is overreacting. Even
worse is the underlying suspicion that the woman is inviting the "attention." The law has not helped much in defining sexual harassment
because of inconsistent laws and the emotion surrounding the issue.
Under Title VII of the 1964 Civil Rights Act, employers may not
discriminate on the basis of sex, and sexual harassment is a form of
sex discrimination. In 1980 the Equal Employment Opportunities
Commission (EEOC) clarified its definition adopting the following
guidelines: "Unwelcome sexual advances, requests for sexual favors
and other verbal and physical conduct of a sexual nature constitute
sex harassment when (1) submission to such a conduct is made a term
or condition of an individual's employment, (2) submission to or rejection of such conduct is used as the basis for employment decisions,
and (3) such conduct unreasonably interferes with work performance,
or creates an intimidating, hostile, or offensive working environment."[26] Clause 3 was used as the basis of the 1986 Supreme Court
case of *Meritor Savings Bank, FSVB* vs. *Vinson* in which Mechelle Vinson

claimed that she and other female employees worked in an atmosphere that was pervaded by sexual aggression on the part of her supervisor, ranging from fondling to indecent exposure. Vinson was pressured to have sexual intercourse with her supervisor forty to fifty times because he threatened her with being fired from her job. The Court decided the bank was responsible for this environment of sexual harassment and that employers are liable for the action of their supervisors even if they have not been notified. The decision gave Vinson the right to sue and enforced the concept that sexual harassment is a form of sexual discrimination. It also affirmed the fact that businesses are liable even if they have a policy against sex discrimination and a grievance procedure that is not used.[27]

Harassment cases do not have to be carried to the extent Vinson's was to fall under the protection of the EEOC guidelines. But the definitions are hazy because one man's sexual flirtation can be one woman's harassment. Sources such as the Women's Rights Program of the American Federation of State and Municipal Employees (AFSME) and a brochure on sexual harassment printed by Channel 17, in Philadelphia, advise that when you cannot freely choose to say no to a sexual request or demand and your job may be at risk, you're experiencing sexual harassment. Employers are responsible for their supervisory employees regardless of whether officials of the company knew or should have known of the incident or whether it was forbidden by company policy.[28]

The National Organization for Women further defines sexual harassment as "any repeated or unwarranted verbal or physical sexual advances, sexually explicit derogatory statements, or sexually discriminatory remarks made by someone in the workplace which is offensive or objectionable to the recipient or which causes the recipient discomfort or humiliation or which interferes with the recipient's job performance."[29] The Mayor of the District of Columbia issued an order defining sexual harassment this way:

1) verbal harassment or abuse;
2) subtle pressure for sexual activity;
3) unnecessary patting or pinching;
4) constant brushing against another employee's body;
5) demanding sexual favors accompanied by implied or overt threat concerning an individual's employment status;
6) demanding sexual favors accompanied by implied or overt promise of preferential treatment with regard to an individual's employment status.[30]

Harassment is usually a demonstration of power, but it can take the form of demanding sexual intercourse, eyeing a woman employee in a suggestive manner, requesting a uniform of a sexually revealing nature, displaying pictures of nude women, commenting about one's body, or telling dirty jokes. Harassment is persistence in the face of clearly saying no.

The EEOC and the National Organization for Women suggest that when a woman thinks she is the object of sexual harassment she should first say no to the offender. They suggest that writing a letter to inform the harasser of her discomfort is often effective. She should keep a written record of the harassment, discuss the incident with co-workers to see if they were witnesses to the incident, and ask for past work evaluations. With that in hand, she should go to the employer, supervisor, personnel office, and union, asking them verbally and in writing to solve the problem. If the complaint cannot be resolved that way, the employee can go to a women's resource organization and with its help file a complaint to a local, state, or federal agency.

Women in television news have used many of these methods to deal with the problem of sexual harassment. Some have even gone to court. There have been three major cases of sexual harassment which were won by the women involved. One was the case of Cecily Coleman against ABC, another was that of Elissa Dorfsman against CBS Inc., and the third case was brought by seven members of the latenight "Nightwatch" staff against CBS News.

Cecily Coleman worked on several voter registration projects for ABC News in 1983 and was rehired early in 1984 at the recommendation of the ABC chairman of the board, Leonard Goldenson. Coleman's title was Executive Director of the Advisory Committee on Voter Education, at the salary of $60,000. Her job was to promote voter education through the production of public service announcements and campaigns for voter awareness at ABC and at its affiliates. She was abruptly fired from her Washington office on 1 May 1984 after making a confidential complaint to the company's personnel manager about James Abernathy, vice president for corporate affairs. Coleman responded to her dismissal with a multimillion dollar lawsuit against ABC charging Abernathy with "sexual harassment retaliation, intentional infliction of emotional distress and defamation." Coleman claimed that Abernathy repeatedly touched her, brushed up against her, and demanded sexual favors coupled with implied threats about her job. He demanded she admit him into her hotel room when on business trips. He called her into his office, shut the door, and made unwelcome sexual advances. When Coleman did what she was supposed to do and informed superiors of this behavior, she was isolated, and co-workers were discouraged from being witnesses. When she asked for written assurance and protection for herself and other ABC women, urging ABC to develop a program to protect female employees from sexual harassment, officials of ABC ransacked her office while she was away on company business and then fired her. When she asked for reinstatement ABC allegedly offered to buy out her contract in exchange for silence. Coleman refused.[31]

She took the case to court with the help of the National Organization for Women's Legal Defense and Education Fund, asking for $15 million in damages. The case was settled out of court on 2 July 1985. Coleman received an estimated $500,000. Since then she moved to WETA, the Washington public television station, where she has been working as associate producer on a two-hour documentary on the Supreme Court to air in 1988.

Elissa Dorfsman brought her case against CBS-owned WCAU-FM radio in Philadelphia. She worked at WCAU for twelve years, the last four as general sales manager making as much as $80,000 a year and supervising ten people. She filed a $1 million suit against CBS Inc. and a male veteran sales executive on numerous charges, including sexual harassment, because of the behavior of that sales executive at a company sales dinner in 1982.

Dorfsman described the incident this way: "The next thing I know is that he's running his fingers all the way up my leg. . . . And then he took the fur tail from my shawl and made like he pulled it out from my crotch."[32] She says he then whipped the tail around above his head and shouted an obscenity about her. She was further angered when she reported this incident and CBS privately reprimanded the sales executive but would not do so publicly. Dorfsman believes that implied approval of the incident. She filed her suit and kept on working but was faced with "disgusting things" happening to her, reporting that anti-Semitic remarks about her were made by WCAU general manager Vincent Benedict, Jr., and that she was subjected to "discriminatory and retaliatory" suspension for a week in April. She also claimed that she was warned by a top CBS executive that she could not successfully sue a network and that he would destroy her career if she tried.[33]

Dorfsman settled the case out of court, receiving $250,000 from CBS Inc. She says it is now clear that it is unacceptable for a woman to be humiliated when she hasn't consented to being touched. She left WCAU-FM after the settlement and has been selling syndicated shows in Hollywood.

In September 1986 seven women employees of "Nightwatch,"

the overnight news program produced by CBS News, sued CBS Inc. They charged that John Huddy, the executive producer of "Nightwatch," caused the "intentional infliction of emotional distress" and "sexual assault," both violations of the District of Columbia Civil Rights Act.[34] They said that Huddy created a working environment offensive and hostile to women. The women claimed the harassment ranged from unwelcome sexual advances, gestures, and comments to actually touching the women. They said Huddy made cooperation with and tolerance of his actions part of the condition of their employment. He also was charged with encouraging other men in managerial positions to behave in a similar fashion. The women notified CBS officials of Huddy's behavior but CBS did nothing to alleviate the situation. The suit also said that when Huddy found out about the complaints against him, he retaliated by firing four of those involved and forcing another out by assigning her extra duties at no increase in pay.[35] Women not involved in the suit who worked on the show while Huddy was there said that he would always make comments on their physical appearance, frequently in the form of derogatory remarks. It was not until the management changed at CBS News that the company finally listened to the complaints and conducted an internal investigation. Huddy left soon after that in June 1986. In September, the seven women filed suit and asked for $14 million in damages. They settled out of court in September 1987, but neither they nor CBS would discuss the settlement.

The key point in this harassment case is that when women went to management with their problem they found it was loyal to Huddy and sided with him against the women. That kind of feedback made the women feel helpless and defeated. It was a risk to complain; there was the real fear of retaliation—two of the women lost their jobs after the first complaint and attributed their dismissal to their involvement. A male employee and a former senior producer of the unit noted that Huddy's verbal abuse directed at both sexes created a depressing work environment for men as well as for women.

If management had responded to the women in the first place, they might not have had to face a lawsuit. All three networks have organized sexual harassment training seminars for management in an attempt to improve their awareness of the problem. But there is also a need for the creation of women's groups that have credibility with and access to management. This is not the case at the networks at present.

There have been other less publicized cases. In 1985, twenty-three-year-old Pam Golden, a weather forecaster for a Duluth TV station, filed an $8 million suit in Superior, Wisconsin, claiming that KDLH-TV made dress and behavior requirements which were not included in her job description and which exploited her sexuality. Golden had been fired in May 1983, four months after her promotion to full-time weekday weather forecasting. She says she was fired because she refused to wear revealing clothing, stand and sit in a suggestive manner, wear a microphone in a way that accentuated her breasts, and entertain an influential salesman.[36] Her case was settled out of court a year later, in June 1986.

Although only a few women have taken their cases of sexual harassment to the courts, women in television news often face incidents of harassment. When Mary Alice Williams, vice president and anchor of Cable News Network, first came to New York City looking for a job, she went for an interview, with shocking results. She reported, "It was as though the whole staff was involved in this sort of public harassment and humiliation. At one point, with I don't know how many people in the room, the news director actually asked me, 'Do you fuck?' "[37]

But harassment in the newsroom or out in the field can be much more subtle. It can stem from the old buddy system, resentment of women taking on jobs men feel should be filled by other men with families, and a sense that a single woman working must have something wrong with her in that she can't find a man or doesn't want to settle down and have a family. This attitude surfaces often in the technical areas where women are having a harder time breaking in and proving themselves. They must be twice as good as many men to get respect and must contend with constant humiliation. Young women today are sensitive to this issue. Female college students see male chauvinism and male dominance in the supervisory and management positions in TV news as major obstacles to succeeding in broadcast journalism.[38]

At ABC harassment used to be most prevalent in the sports department. It was an area where women weren't welcome in the first place and rarely had the top jobs. Sexist comments, mostly regarding anatomy, were routine. Anyone in the control room during events heard frequent references to "boob shots." This problem at ABC was taken on by the first women's group, to no avail.

Informal complaints of harassment now come most often from women working cameras or from women editors who work long hours in a small area. In these close quarters attitudes become more blatant and the testing never ends. It is not unusual for men to try to intimidate women by telling dirty jokes around them, keeping pornographic pictures visible, using obscenities, and even showing favoritism to men over women. There is pressure on women to become "one of the guys," which means putting up with all of this. Perhaps women are easily intimidated by these tactics. A woman editor at one of the networks, who asked that she not be identified because of the harassment that would bring, observed that when a new male comes into the department and has a good attitude toward women he soon discovers that is not acceptable, so he changes. He starts to tell dirty jokes and put women down in order to fit into the power group. Unfortunately, the supervisors are the worst offenders because they have the most power. If a woman does complain, she cannot usually go high enough to save herself from retaliation or even sabotage of her work. There is often pressure on women not to talk to each other because they will be suspected of plotting against the men. So the harassment can take on the form of a negative work environment— not necessarily a physically aggressive harassment but that of a more psychological nature.

There are several ways to combat this kind of endemic attitude problem. According to AFSME, first, the company must make it clear to every department in its organization that sexual harassment will not be tolerated. The unions should also reinforce this. The next step is to educate employees. Many companies are producing films on sexual harassment. The personnel departments of all three networks, ABC, CBS, and NBC, have commissioned a thirty-minute film as part of a larger training package. The film is not enough. It must reach the people who need it and company policy must clearly state punishment for the offense. There must also be an effective mechanism in the workplace to stop the harassment. This is particularly difficult. As seen in the cases of Coleman, Dorfsman, and "Nightwatch," the companies immediately sided with the executives and not with the women. How can a woman complain if she will not be taken seriously and is doubted, or even punished, for making the problem public? Another way to combat harassment is to assign a management person to deal with harassment problems confidentially. A much more subtle way is to try to change the portrayal of working women as sex objects on television and, for women in broadcasting, on television news. Young anchors on local news who are hired for their looks and not their reporting skills only reinforce these stereotyped views of women. It is obvious that the men whose wives stay home and whose daughters get married and have children and never work do not have any role models for working women. They see women as sex objects first and as workers second. They feel that their male domain of power has been invaded, challenged. Many men feel more comfortable with women in the bedroom than in the boardroom or newsroom. As long as men choose to spend their leisure time with each other, on the golf course, fishing, or at the poker table, or at all-male clubs, women will remain outsiders. Women need to organize, to petition for their rights, and not give in to intimidation. A women's group needs women from the very top levels to be involved because they have the most power and will be the least intimidated. Such women also rarely face sexual harassment so they are the least likely to take up the cause. Cecily Coleman was not supported by female witnesses at ABC because of their fear of reprisals, but on the other hand the "Nightwatch" group found strength in numbers, even though many were fired or were forced to resign. CBS has a Women's Advisory Council (WAC) whose five-member steering committee constantly receives anonymous phone calls complaining about the offensive behavior of male colleagues or superiors. They devised a questionnaire for women in the company and also conducted in-depth interviews. WAC then presented their findings to the vice president of personnel and other managers. One result was the production of the film on sexual harassment. WAC also hopes to influence the highest level of CBS executives to back up the company's policies with concrete actions. There is no discernible evidence that this is happening. The women's group, by 1987, was composed mainly of low-level employees with little clout. No well-known correspondents or producers were involved, and most women employees view WAC as largely impotent.

Would women in management have put a stop to sexual harassment by their very presence? The question of how much things would change with women in charge is, so far, academic. Few believe that one woman, outnumbered by male colleagues, could make much of a difference. The women's movement had provided us with mobility, to a degree, but we have not yet managed to break through what has come to be known as the "glass ceiling." That glass ceiling can be described as a barrier that allows women to see the top jobs of their professions but somehow bars them from getting there. In order to break through, women will have to find a way to eliminate the male resistance that holds so many of us back.

## Notes

1. Betty Friedan, *The Feminine Mystique* (New York: Dell, 1963), p. 16.
2. Ibid., p. 389.
3. "Woman's Place" aired 8 September 1973, on ABC-TV.
4. Dorothy Storck, *Chicago Today* (10 September 1973).

5. Nancy Stanley, "Federal Communications Law and Women's Rights: Women in the Wasteland Fight Back," *Hastings Law Journal* 23 (November 1971): 15–53.

6. ABC, 33 RR2d 305 (1975), and NBC, 33 RR2d 244 (1975). Referred to by Maurine Beasley and Sheila Silver, in *Women in Media: A Documentary Source Book* (Washington: Women's Institute for Freedom of the Press, 1977), pp. 126–27.

7. 33 RR2d (1975), pp. 261–65 of document.

8. Cherie S. Lewis, "Television License Renewal Challenges by Women's Groups," Ph.D. diss., University of Minnesota (Ann Arbor: University Microfilms International, 1986), p. 129.

9. NOW v. FCC, 40 RR2d 679 (D.C. Cir. 1977).

10. Executive Order #11375, Revised #4 (17 October 1967), and Federal Register 32, p. 14303.

11. Judy Hole, "CBS and Women: An Experiment That's Working, (Knock on Wood)," Speech at the Massachusetts Institute of Technology, 24 February 1975.

12. Interview with Gloria Clyne, May 1987.

13. Ron Powers, *The Newscasters* (New York: St. Martin's, 1978), pp. 79, 89–91.

14. Ibid., p. 35.

15. Christine Craft, *Christine Craft: An Anchorwoman's Story* (Santa Barbara: Rhodora/Capra Press, 1986), p. 68. The summary of Craft's story was taken from this source unless otherwise noted.

16. Ibid., p. 127.

17. Leslie S. Gielow, "Sex Discrimination in Newscasting," *Michigan Law Review* 84:443 (December 1985), p. 444.

18. *Broadcasting Magazine* (7 November 1983): 62.

19. Ibid.

20. Craft, p. 194.

21. Ibid., p. 195.

22. *Broadcasting Magazine* (10 March 1986): 74.

23. Ibid.

24. *New York Times* (9 August 1983), p. C17.

25. Ibid.

26. *Federal Register* 45, no. 72 (11 April 1980), p. 25024.

27. *Meritor Savings Bank, FSVB v. Mechelle Vinson*, no. 84-11979 (argued 25 March 1986. Decided 19 June 1986), 106 Supreme Court Reporter.

28. "Sexual Harassment on the Job . . . What You Need to Know" (brochure published by Channel 17, WPHL-TV, 5001 Wynnefield Ave., Philadelphia, Pennsylvania, 19131), p. 2.

29. NOW Legal Defense and Education Fund, "Facts on Sexual Harassment," "Facts on Women 1986," June 1986.

30. American Federation of State and Municipal Employees, "Sexual Harassment, On-the-Job Sexual Harassment: What the Union Can Do" (April 1983), p. 19.

31. "Media Report to Women" (July–August 1984), p. 7.

32. Howard Rosenberg, *Los Angeles Times* (28 June 1985).

33. Ibid., p. 33.

34. Complaint filed in the Superior Court of the District of Columbia Civil Division of Susan Balsam, Amy Jeanne Gutman, S. Beth Homan, Anita M. Lemonis, B. Rachel Ray, Laura J. Schwartz, and Marylynn Vosburgh against CBS Inc. for violation of the District of Columbia Human Rights Act, D.C. Code 1-2501 *et seq.* The lawyers for the plaintiffs were Jacob A. Stein, Robert F. Muse, and Patrick A. Malone, from Stein, Mitchell & Mezines, 1800 M. Street, N.W., Washington, D.C.

35. John Carmody, "The TV Column," *The Washington Post* (5 September 1986), p. B6.

36. *Duluth News-Tribune & Herald* (June 1985).

37. Geoffrey Stokes, "The Eyes Have It All," *New York Women* (September, 1986).

38. Results of an informal survey of female journalism students at New York University, May 1987.

# 7

## Women in Management

Despite the activism of the 1970s, few women were promoted into management in broadcasting. Since there are a limited number of power positions in any system, including broadcasting, questions of promotion are inherently questions of politics. The established system had promoted men into high-level positions. The same men who had benefited from the old system were being asked to change that very system to include qualified women. Only a male executive with some vision would risk upsetting the status quo for some societal gain. A political power struggle at ABC News provided the climate to make the timing right for such a move.

It was 1973, and I was at the final stages of producing the hour-long "Woman's Place." All documentary producers got a call to report to vice president Tom Wolf's office immediately. We rarely met with him as a group, and wondered what was up as we walked the few blocks to his office. He closed the door behind us. There were several bottles of liquor on the table. He announced that he was being replaced by Av Westin. Bad luck for me, I thought. Everyone poured drinks, amid protests of his situation. Apparently Westin failed to unseat Bill Sheehan as news president, and was shifted to documentaries, out of the mainstream. His mandate, we learned later, was to tackle more hard subjects, rather than the softer features and sometimes cultural stories the unit was alleged to have been doing. The unpredictability of the business had struck again. Just when things seemed to be going well, another executive shuffle had taken place. There was nothing to do but finish "Woman's Place," and worry about my status later. It was August and no time to job hunt.

As my documentary neared completion, the executive switch

took place, and Westin, who seemed friendlier than I had expected, asked to screen the hour. I waited it out, wondering what the reaction would be. The subject, I thought ruefully, was apt. Much to my shock, after the screening he stuck his head in the office and said, "very nice, I liked it. I would have made a few minor changes, but it's a good show."

For reasons that could not be credited entirely to that documentary, Westin's attitude toward me changed. His divorce had come through, and he was about to remarry. He made no sign that I was to be booted out of the unit, although one of the other producers was immediately fired. The staff was thin, and gradually new people were hired, among them a woman from NBC, an associate producer named Pam Hill. After my September hour, the new series, called "ABC News Closeup," began with much hoopla. Westin was still good at getting his name in the paper and he had something to crow about—a time commitment of twelve hours a year for documentaries—a decided improvement over the past.

With the clout of an energetic, ambitious executive, ABC News documentaries began to get more publicity. Since such hours were known to get low ratings, the advantages of doing them were for prestige and good reviews. Even controversy generated by the broadcasts was not entirely unwelcome, since it showed the station's willingness to tackle hotly debated current topics. At that time, before deregulation by the Reagan administration, affiliate stations still needed to schedule public service hours for their license renewal ascertainment review.

My next documentary, called "The Right to Die," examined for the first time at any length on television the new subject of euthanasia, living wills, and the issues that improved medical care had just begun to raise. Westin and I were getting along for reasons not entirely clear to me. The whimsicality of the business had struck once again. There was no predicting one's standing, and an entire career could be brought down or made to flourish with one shift in command.

The executive shuffle continued. Elmer Lower relinquished his title of news president and moved to corporate headquarters to serve as vice president of corporate affairs, where he remained until his official retirement. Bill Sheehan, an old friend, became president of news. For the time being, things seemed to be going my way. However, in early 1975, a further reshuffle took place. It was announced that in addition to Westin's responsibility for the "Closeup" documentary unit he would also return to the job of executive producer of the floundering evening news, and be elevated to a vice presidency. The evening news was then anchored by Harry Reasoner, who had left CBS when it became clear that he would not be the successor to Walter Cronkite. ABC's news ratings improved for a time after his arrival, largely because more affiliates began carrying the broadcast. However, the addition of Howard K. Smith as co-anchor in Washington failed to get ABC out of third place in the network news ratings war.

A strange phenomenon started to develop. Despite the cost of crews, travel, and AT&T lines (before the days of satellites), network news started to become profitable. Corporate types started paying closer attention to the news operation, and could not be described as overjoyed by the poor ratings on documentaries, hour-long efforts that ate up profits from the evening news program and helped put news in the red.

The fun had begun to go out of the business. Getting to be number one became the main preoccupation. Personnel musical chairs became the rule, not the exception.

There were no repercussions from Westin's dual authority immediately. Productions went along as scheduled, with Westin approving new subjects as before but simply not appearing in our offices as often as he had. Most of his activities were centered on the evening news in the Sixty-sixth Street building. He did come back for screenings, however, and his imprint was still in evidence. For my part, I was just as well satisfied. Beyond the professional contacts with him that each show required, we had little communication anyway. In fact, the only social contact that had developed between him and anyone else in the unit was with newly hired producer Pam Hill. While at NBC, she had married producer Fred Freed, who had divorced his wife of many years. Hill shortly divorced him and married *New York Times* columnist Tom Wicker. The Westins and the Wickers began to socialize. Westin liked Hill's flashy production style, and though her budget overruns drove other administrators crazy, he didn't seem to care.

At the time, their friendship was a matter of indifference to me, but the form of networking that was going on had serious consequences for me later.

"Women's Health: A Question of Survival" aired on 5 January 1976. While I was involved in its completion, the power struggle between Westin and Sheehan was being played out in what appeared to be its final stages. Again, Westin's name was in the papers regularly; this time, he was passing the buck on why the evening news had not taken off, blaming it on a "new format" forced on him by others. I don't recall what the new format consisted of; there were always changes, and often they involved a new set or other cosmetic alterations. His campaign against Sheehan had intensified at corporate headquarters.

There were rumors that Westin's days were numbered. Everyone was concerned because of his wide-ranging responsibilities in both news and documentaries. If he left, who would replace him, and how would his partisans survive? Around that time, I was called into Bill Sheehan's office for a talk. He told me he was thinking about a replacement for Westin in documentaries and there were several names that had surfaced, people I knew. He said he'd like my opinion of them.

Three names were mentioned. Two I knew quite well, the other only slightly. None was at the company at the time. The first, I told him, I felt was a hack who wouldn't bring anything to the department. The other was a decent, able fellow whose work had always been routine. I really didn't know the third well enough to comment on. There was a pause. "Could you do it?" he asked. "Could I? Yes, I could," I replied. We talked for a few minutes more, and he said he would talk to me again the next day, that there was no commitment just yet, and to keep quiet about our conversation.

In many ways, it seemed like a logical progression. I had long experience in news by then. I knew what made a good story and how to put one together. My shows always came in on budget, and there was no evidence that I could not manage people. An executive producer needed all of those qualities, plus the ability and poise to deal with corporate management, meet with potential sponsors, and be a spokesperson for the unit. I assumed I would be offered the job of executive producer, since there were no women news vice presidents at any of the networks.

The next day, Friday, 23 January 1976, Sheehan's secretary called again, asking me to come over at 5:00 P.M. When I left the office, I told my secretary I would not be back, that I'd go home from there.

Sheehan was all smiles when I came in. He closed the door. "I've talked to them downtown," he said, "and have full approval to offer you the job of Vice President and Director of Documentaries." I thanked him, and said I would do my best to justify the decision. Overnight I had thought of the possibility and was not entirely unprepared for the decision, although I honestly didn't think it would be a vice presidency. Sheehan then outlined to me just what that meant: First of all, a change in salary, a meaningful upward move.

Then I heard about the annual bonus, based on Hay points awarded by the division head, which could be significant. "No wonder," I thought to myself, "men have always wanted these deals — lots of goodies to go with the title." The value of each Hay point was determined by company profits. The higher level the job, the more points it was awarded. Then there were the stock options. I scribbled notes hastily on a scrap of paper, silently cursing my mathematical deficiencies, and not quite sure what all this meant until I figured it out later at home. Sheehan asked me not to say anything about it until he could make an official announcement on Monday. I assured him I would keep quiet.

I left the office elated, and headed home to celebrate with my family. I could not think of any other women news vice presidents. It turned out that I was indeed the first. CBS appointed three women news vice presidents in the next few years, but by the 1980s, that number had shrunk to one. With the departure of Richard Salant as president of CBS News, and as the pressure to hire and promote minorities and women lessened, there was considerable backsliding.

I thought again about how impossible it had always been to plan anything in this business. There was no way to aim for that job specifically, and only someone else's miscalculations provided the opening this time.

Management had seemed like a possible route for me but I had not been able to see how that could be achieved. Even though the TV news business had grown enormously in the number of people involved since the early days, still it was not an industry top-heavy in management. There was the news president, and then the vice presidents in several specific areas of responsibility: hard news, documentaries, business affairs, special events, the Washington news bureau, and someone who coordinated general news gathering, crews, and the assignment desk. Turnover in those areas was then rare, unless there was a total housecleaning, usually the result of a new man as president. ABC News management had been fairly stable for many years, reflecting Elmer Lower's choices. As I had mulled over possible future courses of action for myself in the past, I usually was stumped. Fortunately, circumstances provided me with a new direction, for the moment at any rate.

On Monday morning, no one except a few of Sheehan's associates knew of the decision, and I tried not to look like anything unusual was going to happen. In the late afternoon, rumors about Westin's imminent departure spread and a call came to the documentary department to gather everyone together — producers, researchers, film

editors, and secretaries—in the large screening room, to hear an
announcement from Bill Sheehan. At 4:00 P.M. Sheehan and Martin
Rubenstein, vice president and business manager, strode briskly into
the room. Sheehan was quick and to the point. "Av Westin has resigned
as of today," he said, "and the new vice president in charge of documentaries is Marlene Sanders." There was an audible gasp. I knew
who Westin's friends were, of course, and they did not look particularly
happy. Others, however, were. As the room emptied, I was swamped
with congratulations. Word had leaked out by then and the phones
began ringing. I had a small office, the same as the other producers,
and I had to close the door to try to take the calls that were pouring
in. Among the first to phone were Walter Cronkite and Barbara
Walters, and congratulatory calls continued for several days. On Monday, 26 January 1976, a memo was sent out to be received in interoffice
mail on Tuesday. It was from Bill Sheehan to the ABC News Staff,
and it read in part: "The Board of Directors of ABC Inc. this afternoon
elected Marlene Sanders Vice President and Director of Television
Documentaries, effective immediately. Marlene replaces Av Westin,
who resigned from ABC News today. . . ." People in the office began
immediately trying to discuss assignments, but I put them off by saying
that it would take me a while to get organized. Notes began arriving.
Many came in from my male colleagues, but the letters from women
were particularly gratifying, with comments of "it's about time" and
"great for you, great for women." Andy Rooney's note said, "I thought
you might like to hear from someone who isn't looking for work."
There were, of course, job applications among the letters. Another
friend wrote, "I have a strong feeling you're stepping into a mine
field, but I can't think of anyone who is more deserving of the opportunity to demonstrate survival techniques." And the tri-network
committee, the women still plugging away at all three networks, wrote,
"You have served as a role model for many of us . . . and we deeply
appreciate your untiring efforts in behalf of women." Notes came too
from executives at the various affiliates, many of whom knew me from
my years on the air, wishing me luck in continuing to provide them
with the excellent documentaries the Closeup unit had been producing.

The changeover period was not without awkwardness. Westin
was slow to clear out of his office, and was finally offered space
elsewhere for a while. His previous quarters were now mine, the
proverbial corner executive office, directly across from the Metropolitan Opera with wide windows facing Lincoln Center. In the winter
months, as dusk fell, you could see the Chagall murals and the glit-

tering chandeliers in the opera house and the lights of the Lincoln Center fountain.

There was bad news as well as good that went along with my promotion. Instead of the twelve annual documentaries we had been used to, we were cut back to six new ones, making a total of seven for the year, if you counted "Women's Health" which aired in January. It, however, was in the budget from the previous year. The 1976 budget had been cut, and I was not pleased with the news. The cuts were attributed to the election year and the need for additional hours for political coverage. Activity had come to a near standstill in the months prior to Westin's departure. Shortly, however, producers were at work again, and we had most of the year's productions mapped out.

Life changed in several ways for me. I began attending regular meetings with Sheehan and the five other ABC News vice presidents. We reported on what was going on in our departments and mutual problems were discussed. I felt comfortable enough, after the first meeting, when I found out how things worked. The others attending were longtime ABC News employees that I had known, at least casually, for many years: Bill Lord, Walter Pfister, Nick Archer, Martin Rubenstein, Washington news bureau head George Watson, and on occasion, whoever was executive producer of the evening news, a job that offered even less stability than most.

Much of my time was spent in conversation with ABC entertainment executives, the people who doled out air time. They tended to play with the schedule, moving our air dates to suit their competitive needs. Then there were regular meetings with the sales department, occasional lunches with potential sponsors, and discussions with press and promotion people. Producers were never involved with the sponsors, but it was not a violation of news ethics for the executive in charge to help persuade a prestigious company to sponsor the series. Documentaries have a classier look if there is one distinguished corporate sponsor rather than separate spots touting a variety of products. The agencies or sponsors had no say in what programs we produced. They had the right, however, to decline to sponsor documentaries on subjects they objected to for some reason or another. Getting sponsors, by the late seventies, was no longer a problem. As ABC grew and began to become more and more competitive with the other networks, its air time became more and more desirable, and time could always be sold. Documentary rates were lower than those charged for entertainment programs that had a greater audience potential.

One of the perks of the job was the use of the executive dining room at corporate headquarters. Rooms could be closed off, according to the size desired, and excellent lunches were served to one's guests by the company chef. Vice presidents, of whom there were over one hundred by then, also could use the company limousines, if they were not already called for by the very top brass.

I upgraded my clothes, producers not being famous for haute couture. I had never been one of those who wore jeans around the office, as did some of my female producer colleagues. Men do not usually wear jeans to the office. Women who do are not taken seriously by their bosses. It looks too much like Off-Broadway television, not quite serious work somehow, not grown up. It's hard enough to get ahead without looking like an amateur. Upgrading dress for me simply meant paying more attention to looking businesslike and more chic.

Relations with my colleagues in the office changed perceptively. People were now drifting in with complaints, and I found that personnel problems were taking a good deal of my time. A producer would not work with a certain film editor; an associate producer did not want to work with a particular producer; film editors, producers charged, were cheating on their time sheets, etc. One had to try to deal as diplomatically as possible with such issues. At Christmas, just as Sheehan was responsible for recommending the amount of bonuses for vice presidents, I was responsible for the raises in our department. Surprisingly, below the level of producer, everyone knew what everyone else was making, and if one person received a 7 percent raise and another 9 percent, gripes soon followed. Personnel records showed a surprising range of salaries of the various producers, which seemed to have less to do with their abilities than with how long they had been under contract and how many renewals there had been.

Their pay went from a low of around $35,000 a year, to a high, then, of $60,000. Producers' salaries jumped later, when Roone Arledge took control of the news division. He raided other networks for both correspondents and producers, and the escalation of salaries was part of the reason for the large increase in news budgets, which eventually led to massive cuts and layoffs. Some hard-news producers in the 1980s made as much as $200,000 a year. We had an adequate number of associate producers, researchers, and technical staff. Women were fairly numerous in most documentary units, since those operations were not considered the most important areas of a news division. However, I was concerned over the absence of blacks in the department, and was determined to improve the numbers on that score, which I managed to do.

Creatively, the job was more interesting to me when I fulfilled the job of show editor, at the rough-cut stage of production. It took considerable tact, but since I was fresh from being on the receiving end myself, I tried to handle the chore with care. One of my most unpleasant tasks was to fire one member of the staff, because of a budget problem. He was a young associate producer whom I liked personally, and I found the job of explaining why he had to go simply awful. Perhaps executives get used to firings, but I was relieved that in my two years in the job I did not have to repeat the process often.

When Westin left ABC he went into business with a colleague as an independent producer, selling some documentaries to non-network station groups like Westinghouse Broadcasting and Capital Cities, but he could never be counted out for long. He returned to ABC a few years later, becoming executive producer of the successful "20/20" series, as well as being in charge of numerous special projects. Luck was with him when ABC merged with Capital Cities Broadcasting, his major client during his brief independent producing period. Talent is an undeniable asset, but it is just as important, if not more so, to have the right friends and professional connections. However, Westin was temporarily suspended in 1987 after overreaching in what appeared to be an effort to unseat news president Arledge.

In terms of advancement into management, traveling in the right circles is vital. Often promotions come from within and occur among friends. Women are not usually part of the in-group. Those few women who do advance are often not particularly anxious to help or identify with other women. They have absorbed male values, and tend to play the game the same way as the men. If women are going to change corporate structures, they will only do so when their numbers increase to a critical mass—then, if so inclined, they can act without fear of being overruled or mustered out.

After a relatively peaceful first year for me running the ABC documentary unit, 1977 dawned along with new rumors of change. ABC Sports had been successful under the leadership of Roone Arledge, with his innovative "Monday Night Football" and imaginative coverage of the Olympics. There were whispers that he was growing restless, and that other networks were making offers. It was known that he wanted to expand his activities. There had been a short-lived experiment where he produced an entertainment series with Howard Cosell as host. That digression was a flop, and with no further encouragement from programming boss Fred Silverman, then ABC's entertainment impresario, Arledge turned his attention to news. One thing was certain, and that was that ABC could not afford to lose him. It was in this atmosphere that Pam Hill agreed to go with two other women to discuss the woman problem in sports with Arledge. It took a while to set up the meeting, but it was finally scheduled. Each of the three who attended had lists of items to discuss, and as usual in such circumstances, they were well prepared. The session was reportedly polite on both sides, and while the threesome stressed employment problems and the lack of job mobility for women in sports, they also mentioned the sexual pressures on the road. Arledge seemed most interested in that, deploring the practice and promising to attend to it. He made no other commitments. As far as the number of women in sports was concerned, there was only one woman sports producer then. The route for promotions for female production assistants was well known in the department: a sexual liaison with a sports vice president.

There were no noticeable changes in those practices as a result of that meeting. Pam Hill, however, had a chance to meet Arledge and get to know the man soon rumored to take over in news. My assumption, later, was that since she had not been particularly active in the women's group, her main goal was to meet him. Arledge was known to be impressed by celebrities, sports or otherwise. Hill's marriage to *New York Times* columnist Tom Wicker would surely have been a plus for her with Arledge. Whether she had by then decided to go after my job I don't know, but when Arledge did take over, that was plainly her intention.

By early 1977, it appeared that peace in the news division was once more about to be disturbed. Apparently the wave of the future would be the increasing frequency of top staff changes in network news. Until early 1977, the president of ABC News reported directly to top network brass, namely, Elton Rule, president of ABC Inc. But early in 1977, network president Fred Pierce, a young, energetic man who had worked his way up in the company, was given added responsibilities—including news and engineering. This posed serious problems for Bill Sheehan, who had gotten along well with Rule. His direct protector was now a step removed. Pierce had a tacit go-ahead to do whatever needed to be done to move news up along with the rest of the network. Shortly after he took on news, he was largely responsible, and best known, for hiring Barbara Walters from NBC at the expiration of her contract there. Pairing her with Harry Reasoner was part of the effort to boost the ratings on the sagging evening news. There was a good deal of negative publicity over her million-dollar-a-year contract, only half of which was to be paid by the news division. The rest of the money came from entertainment for the six specials a year Walters would do. Although I had anchored the evening news in 1967, filling in for Sam Donaldson, the press regarded that as a temporary innovation, but not a major change, as it did when Walters assumed the co-anchor job. The press reacted noisily, and the reaction was negative.

The *Boston Globe* had a cartoon caption: "Barbie's Evening All Newsy Show." Tom Tiede, a syndicated columnist, wrote, "In years to come, Ms. Walters will be a nightly suggestion that neither life, nor freedom, nor domestic security is sacred in the nation anymore, only money." Richard Salant, then president of CBS News, said, "Yeech!" The criticisms then moved to her request that a hairdresser, limousine, and press agent, which were already a part of her "Today" contract, be included in her ABC contract. The press stereotyped her as a prima donna.[1] Ron Powers commented about these reactions in his book *The Newscasters*: "The curious thing about women's ascendancy in television journalism is the degree of hostility they have encountered among critics as well as their male colleagues. . . . [M]any critics react as though women alone are the interlopers, as though the very *presence* of a woman on a newscast constitutes selling out to show business."[2]

All of the flurry over Walters may seem odd a decade later. Female news anchors are provided with hairdressers, and network anchors often get limousines; most network evening news anchors make well over one million dollars; and most news directors hope their talent (the television term for the persons in front of the camera) care about the way they look. To examine some of these changes in a more positive light, today, nine out of every ten network affiliated stations has a female anchor. In 1985, 36 percent of anchorpersons were women, compared to 11 percent in 1972.[3] News teams are considered "old fashioned" if they don't have a woman. Of course there is a big difference between local and network newscasts in terms of numbers, audience, and pressure. There are more local than network news programs; the network reaches a greater number of people and a network news anchor is the embodiment of the network's identity, one that then carries over to an identity for the affiliated local news programs. So while local news shows have incorporated women into their newscasts, the networks have not, except on the weekends and in the early mornings.

One of those who made the transition to network news was Jessica Savitch. A former local reporter, by 1977 Savitch had joined NBC News. She anchored regularly over the weekends, and because of her blonde good looks and audience appeal was assigned the News Updates in prime time. Rumor had it that Savitch was being groomed for the weeknight anchor job, and in fact she did substitute from time to time in that slot, the first woman at NBC News to do so. Savitch's star declined, however, as news management changed and Connie Chung arrived on the scene. Additionally, rumors of Savitch's drug use and her declining performance clouded her future. She died in an auto accident in 1983 at the age of thirty-six.

The critical attacks on Barbara Walters, forecasting gloom and doom for the television industry, were based on the fact that she had little journalistic experience and was hired for her "star" quality. They said that although she could do a good interview on the "Today" show, the evening news was different. It was serious and she was not. Her hiring was a red flag that TV news was turning into "show business," and the culprit was a woman. Even Walter Cronkite's first reaction was that "all our efforts to hold television news aloof from show business had failed."[4]

There is no denying that Barbara Walters was and is a star, that she was chosen because she was a known personality and thus could attract an audience; ABC was looking for some attention. There is also no denying that she did not work well with Harry Reasoner. He so resented sharing the stage with her that the teaming turned out to be self-destructive for the show and all involved. But it must also be remembered that TV news began fighting the battle against show business in the days of Edward R. Murrow, who reacted as Walter Cronkite did when Murrow first saw the game show, "The $64,000 Dollar Question." He intuitively knew that his news program, "See It Now," was doomed. It's reported that "Murrow looked up at the control room monitor, saw a new CBS show called 'The $64,000 Question' shoved into the time slot just preceding theirs, and knew the game was up. (To Friendly: 'Any bets on how long we keep this time period now?')."[5] But in 1976, the symbol of destruction was a woman.

Further, it could not have been good for Reasoner's male ego to have to bring in a woman to help get the show back into the ratings race. After the initial publicity, the ratings showed no improvement.

In 1977, the Arledge rumor was disquieting to people involved in TV news. While everyone acknowledged his success in sports, it was clear that the same razzle-dazzle approach to news could be a disaster. Would we have instant replays? Technical tomfoolery with the news itself as victim? No one knew. Besides, most, although not all, network news presidents until that time had come up through the news ranks, if not in broadcasting in the early years then from print.

Finally, in early May, Arledge was named head of both ABC

News and Sports in an attempt to improve news ratings and to keep him at the network. Pierce told the *New York Times*, "I've picked the man whom I believe to be a super broadcasting journalist." He went on: "Sports and news have a common challenge, dealing as they do with the transmission of events." He acknowledged that Arledge lacked formal news credentials, but cited his handling of a "world crisis," the mass murder of the Israeli team by Arab terrorists during the 1972 Munich Olympics.[6]

When ABC put out its formal statement, Bill Sheehan was "named to the newly created position of Senior Vice President, ABC News, reporting to Mr. Arledge." It was a humiliating move and Sheehan must have accepted it only so that he could take his time in relocating and not lose the various company perks that he was entitled to as president.

A few days after the announcement, all news vice presidents and managers, and a rotating group of producers and correspondents, were invited to a weekend at a resort at Montauk, Long Island. Nearly forty people were involved in all. Meetings would begin on Saturday afternoon, 14 May, and run through the next two days. The purpose was loosely described in a memo from Sheehan: "to give Roone Arledge and Fred Pierce a chance to meet you and to exchange ideas about our path to success in the coming months, and for you to hear their ideas and plans."

There was a choice of transportation: limousine or seaplane. Those coming in from Washington were expected to transfer to the small plane at La Guardia and it undoubtedly impressed them. Money was no object, a hallmark of the new ABC news style of the immediate future. I went by limo, by my own choice.

My first glimpse of Arledge at the Montauk Inn revealed a short, pudgy man with blonde curly hair and aviator glasses. He was wearing a navy-blue-and-white polka-dot shortsleeved shirt, one he subsequently favored in the office as well, open to mid-chest. Around his neck he sported several gold medallions on chains. News presidents tend not to be so trendy. True, it was an informal weekend, but nobody else dressed like that, the rest looking more conventionally sporty. He was however, cordial, equally friendly to all, without bestowing more than a few words on any of us however.

He circulated, but the scene was more like an Arab sheikdom, with various petitioners coming to plead their cases before the chief. No one was quite that abject, but you could see people angling for position, trying to get a few words with him. I was the only woman there for the entire event although correspondent Ann Compton was rotated in, as was Win Rowe of business affairs. Only one black was on hand for a portion of the sessions, Tony Batten, a documentary producer I had hired.

The sessions were held in a long conference room, with a U-shaped table. Sheehan, Pierce, Arledge, and Tony Thomopolous, a programming executive, sat at the head. Sheehan ostensibly ran the meetings. Whatever issue was being discussed, whether it was the evening news, elections, or the assignment desk, Arledge's response to staff suggestions was "good idea," or "I couldn't agree more." He made no suggestions of any substance whatsoever.

On the last day, during one of the sessions, I decided to ask a question that I thought might provoke a revealing answer from Arledge and give us some hint as to what he thought about news and news gathering. "What," I asked, "do you think of Geraldo Rivera?" My associates were alert. Our feelings about Rivera were shared. He was like a red flag to people working in the field. A young lawyer turned advocate of liberal causes, Geraldo Rivera had earlier become a local reporter for WABC-TV in New York and later also did a latenight program for the entertainment network which was produced by his own production company. At the same time, he used his film crews to do local news stories and a highly praised documentary on Willowbrook, a mental hospital on Staten Island. This was an unusual and unorthodox way of working in news. Everyone else used news crews and news department producers. No one knew how he got away with it. But it was his editorial style, his theatrical dress complete with jaunty neckerchief, and his flouting of objective journalism that most annoyed other reporters. The heavy exposure he gave himself in his stories on the air also irked correspondents. He was not considered a trained or responsible journalist, and while he might have a following because of his flamboyant style, he was not taken seriously by network correspondents. My question, therefore, was of interest and might reveal Arledge's thinking about news. He didn't know that, it was obvious, and he replied without hesitation, to the effect that Rivera was very talented and the kind of fellow he would like to use much more; he conceded that Rivera might need a little guidance, that he needed to be kept under control, but that he was a terrific journalist and would play a larger role than he had in the past in news.

I knew I would have to leave as soon as I could, not solely because of that response. I could see it was unlikely there would be any grounds for rapport between us.

The so-called news seminar wore on, the sessions interspersed with drinks, sumptuous meals, and time to watch gulls soaring above a still wintry-looking sea. It was, for me, a melancholy weekend. Evenings we worked late, and when the sessions ended, I took a dip in the indoor pool, while many of the men played high-stakes poker. Jock. It was all jock. I hated to think about the future. Summer was coming. I would take my vacation and think things over then.

Shortly after our return from Montauk, on 29 May, Arledge announced that Av Westin would be coming back as executive producer of the evening news, and would become a vice president. Bob Siegenthaler, who had been in the job, trying to navigate the treacherous waters of the Reasoner/Walters twosome, was moved into "other duties." He was a survivor and lasted out the transition. The Westin development came as no surprise to any of us who had been watching the backstage maneuvers from afar.

After eighteen months away, Westin was back. Our paths rarely crossed, but he was no less cordial than he had been in the documentary unit.

Meanwhile, office furniture was being moved around at Sixty-sixth Street, and responsibilities began shifting as well. A former executive assistant to New York Governor Hugh Carey and a close Kennedy family associate, David Burke, was brought in as an aide to Arledge. Burke was unofficially tabbed as Arledge's hatchet man. He was obviously intelligent, and could be friendly when he wanted to, which didn't turn out to be very often. His total lack of knowledge about television was an obstacle he overcame because of his access to Arledge and the power he held.

Shortly after my return from the Montauk meeting, I thought it would be a good idea to have a talk with Arledge. I wanted things to go smoothly as long as I stayed around. Would he be screening the rough-cuts of the broadcasts? How would daily business be conducted? I had had easy access to Sheehan whenever necessary, through frequent phone calls, or by checking his secretary to see when he was free and just dropping by. Business had been attended to with dispatch.

A short time later, after repeated failures to reach Arledge, I asked my secretary to compile a log of her phone calls to Arledge's secretary, and to make notes on my various efforts to see or talk with him. He had a reputation for not returning calls or answering mail, and stories of his ignoring top executives at the network level were common. I found that conduct infuriating, insulting, downright rude, and totally unprofessional. The incomplete record registered four broken appointments over a three-month period, nine phone calls that were not returned, and ten memos about documentary business to which there were no replies. He was informed when programs were ready for screening, but he never asked to see them. Planning nearly came to a standstill, since approval of future subjects was not forthcoming. Howard K. Smith had been our narrator on most of the documentaries, and we had to assume this would continue.

Arledge did act, however, in the area of salaries, and the effect of the escalation that resulted had long-range implications for the industry that were not fully felt until the late 1980s. Several correspondents were added to the staff, a few from CBS News. Word of their salaries leaked out, and in several cases the reporters hired away from other networks were offered inflated contracts. It was not common then for producers to have contracts at all. Only union personnel, such as on-air correspondents, covered by AFTRA, had personal contracts. AFTRA members who were hired at minimum were covered by the union agreements, but over-scale people customarily had additional written arrangements. Arledge had a reputation as a big spender as head of sports. Now, apparently, he wanted his news organization in the big leagues. Later, when he was involved in a bidding war with CBS for Dan Rather, he directly affected the multimillion dollar contract that Rather extracted from CBS. The publicity surrounding some of the salaries being offered caused a near mutiny among ABC staff correspondents. Many of the new employees were hired for the Washington bureau. Ted Koppel sent in a letter of resignation in August, protesting his replacement as anchor of the Saturday night news by one of the newcomers. That resignation was withdrawn after reconciliation efforts by Arledge. There were other protests as well. Howard K. Smith and half a dozen other Washington correspondents sent a joint letter to Arledge around the same time, complaining about the "Son of Sam" coverage masterminded by Arledge himself. The news president had rushed to New York City's police headquarters to oversee the coverage of the arrest of the long-sought murder suspect. Geraldo Rivera, now a full-time network newsman, was the chief correspondent on the scene, and while the suspect was being taken in, Rivera used such inappropriate words on the air as "fiend" and "killer." Experienced correspondents would be unlikely to do that, even if the man had been tried and convicted. Neither was the case. Further, nearly the entire newscast that evening was devoted to the story, a highly unusual practice to say the least; it was roundly criticized by a number of critics as well as by people in the business as purely sensational coverage.

Many within ABC News were embarrassed by Arledge's presence at the police station. CBS News president Dick Salant was quoted at the time as saying he slept peacefully that night knowing his producers and correspondents could handle their jobs very well without his personal direction. Arledge's "playing reporter" was out of line, just not needed, and unacceptable in a news president.

My own situation was becoming increasingly intolerable. Once again, some strategy had to be devised to survive within the organization. Given my disapproval of Arledge's taste and style, I did not see an obvious solution, and since I could never meet with him, the problem seemed insurmountable. I thought, however, it was worth one more try to talk to him, to see if any rapport was possible.

ABC president Fred Pierce and I had been on friendly terms, at Montauk as well as before. He was close to my age, I respected him, and found him easy to talk with. Toward the end of August I decided to call and ask to see him. On the phone (I could get through to him) I told him it had to do with my relationship with Arledge and I wanted his advice. He agreed to meet me on the Wednesday before the long Labor Day weekend. We met for breakfast and I told him that I had tried to see Arledge ever since Montauk without success, to learn what he had in mind for the documentary department. Here I was, running a large operation, one of his six vice presidents, and for more than three months I'd been trying, unsuccessfully, to talk to him. What did he suggest? He looked displeased with my report, and agreed that I certainly should see Arledge. He said he would take care of it.

Later that afternoon (Wednesday, 1 September) my secretary, Ellen Barr, reported with some amusement that Arledge's secretary, Carol, had called and wanted to know what my schedule was like for that day. Anytime was okay, my secretary told her. There were no calls back from her. Monday was an official day off, and I had given the staff the Friday before the holiday off as well; I intended to leave by noon myself. Most of the company was closing down. That afternoon, after I had gone, Arledge's secretary called, wanting to know if I could see him. My secretary explained that the unit was deserted and people had been given the afternoon off. On the day after the holiday, much to my shock, I found a handwritten note from Arledge saying, "Communication works two ways: I expected to spend time with you today (Friday) as relayed yesterday. It is now after 11:00 A.M. and you have gone to the country without even a call. FYI had asked Carol to set aside whatever time you wanted." Of course none of this had been communicated, and the fact that he picked late in the day before the holiday weekend was typical of what could only be interpreted as his contempt for others.

My telephone log for the next week indicated seven phone calls back and forth with Arledge's secretary, with several appointments scheduled and then broken. When our meeting finally took place, it was anticlimactic. We spent half an hour together discussing future hosts for the documentary series, and his wish that the programs be hard edged. Nevertheless, the rumor mill reported back to me that he had been complaining about the programs, saying the recent subjects had been too soft. I responded by sending him a list of the documentaries done during 1977, not one of which could be called soft.

Plainly there was no way we were going to be able to work together. The atmosphere had deteriorated, I no longer enjoyed the work, there was increasing tension, and I was forced to face the fact that I could not survive any longer at ABC News. Changes at the top of the business inevitably bring staff shifts all the way down the line. Although the concept of mentors was not much discussed at the time and came into vogue later, the Arledge episode was a good illustration to me that tying one's career to one person has to be a mistake. If I had been totally dependent on my first boss at ABC, Jesse Zousmer, or even on Bill Sheehan, my career there would have ended even earlier. Zousmer's death was a blow in that he had picked me, and had a stake in promoting my success and in advising me on how to do better on the job. Sheehan appointed me to an important job, and rightly deserved credit for promoting a woman. All of his appointees were going to suffer under someone else. He could be of no help and had to look out for himself. I had to do the same. I had seen, and continued to see, several women tie their careers to their bosses, and move with them from one company to another. When the men's careers thrived, so did theirs. But when the men's fates declined, the women had to go it alone, much later than they should have. I had done well under several regimes at ABC, but the Arledge reign was clearly not going to be one of them. After nearly fourteen years, it was not pleasant to think about starting over someplace else. Nevertheless, it was clear I had to leave.

In the past, I had found that when confronted with an impossible situation, there were several courses open. First off, one should try to analyze the problem and solve it directly by confronting the people involved. If that fails, next one can go over their heads and try to solve it as diplomatically as possible through their superior. That failing, there is only one course of action left, and that is to leave, not necessarily the company, but one's particular untenable situation.

Women tend, by and large, not to be fighters. One hears over and over again from female colleagues that they would rather stay in their middle-level positions than risk being shot down on their way up the ladder, that it isn't worth it. Others who could probably advance find that the assertiveness needed is simply not in them. Neither view was my own.

Back in 1977, CBS had a stable management, the best reputation for news coverage, and a documentary unit, CBS Reports, with a distinguished history. CBS was, it seemed to me, the logical place to go. NBC had slipped, and was doing almost nothing in the documentary area. The Murrow legacy was still alive at CBS. I contacted Dick Salant, president of CBS News, saying I would like to talk. Within a few days, Bob Chandler, vice president and director of public affairs, called, and we arranged an appointment and soon worked out a deal.

There was an almost two-month lame duck period before I could leave ABC and still receive the annual bonus. I wanted to try to protect the integrity of the projects that were in the works, and I was determined to stick it out no matter how sorely tempted I would be to leave right away. In the weeks ahead, I was often put to the test.

That fall our documentaries were doing well, in terms of reviews, and, surprisingly, even in the ratings. I made sure that Arledge received copies of the reviews and ratings on our October program, "Teenage Turn On: Drinking & Drugs." My memo came back with a handwritten note from him stating: "Congratulations to you and Tom B. [Bywaters, the producer]. The reaction was outstanding."

There were a few other favorable contacts, but too late to matter. What he really wanted became clear to me a few weeks later, not through him, but through an emissary. Arledge liked to deliver good news, not bad, and that was apparently one of the reasons his aide, David Burke, was hired.

A phone call summoned me to Burke's office. Pam Hill, I found, was also present. In his most Teutonic manner, Burke informed me that "Roone would like Pam to become executive producer of the unit," he said, "to work on increasing the production values of the shows, for one thing. You will continue to administer the department but she will also have hiring and firing power. . . ." I was outraged, but decided I had too much at stake in that bonus to quit on the spot, remembering I had only a few weeks to go. It was clear that Hill had been conniving all along to get my job, and this was step one. What kind of person would stay in a job like mine with the hiring and firing capability removed? It was an untenable situation. I left the office, tight-lipped and grim, grateful that I'd be out of there in only a few short weeks. My sympathy for what Bill Sheehan must have been going through all those months increased; his power was chipped away, bit by bit. The next day I went to see him. He knew what had been coming, but could do nothing about it but offer consolation. I broke my word not to say anything about my CBS job, swearing him to secrecy for a few weeks longer. He assured me that he too was making progress in taking steps to get out.

My relations with Hill were strained. She mentioned some public relations kinds of projects she thought I should undertake in Washington. I was vague, saying that planning on anything would have to wait until after the Christmas holidays. The remaining project, a two-hour special on hostages, was begun under my supervision and completed under Hill's, with constant interference and meddling by Arledge. The hostages in question at the time were not Americans. There had been, in the late seventies, increasing incidents of hostage-taking by disgruntled South Molluccans in the Netherlands, by the Palestine Liberation Organization, and by other disaffected groups worldwide. The program also dealt with efforts to train police forces in how to handle the growing number of incidents. I considered that the program was ruined and felt sick about it, but could do nothing. Getting through January presented itself as a dreadful ordeal.

It was still early in January when I got a call from Les Brown, television correspondent for the *New York Times*. I had become acquainted with Brown when I did a documentary about prime-time television on which he had been interviewed, and we had become friends. "Listen," he said, "I hear you're leaving for CBS." I tried to be cagey. "Come on," he said, "I'm going with the story. I have to go with it tomorrow. You'd be better off telling me about it than letting me get it wrong."

"Look, Les," I told him, "the only reason I've kept quiet this long is because I thought my bonus money might be in jeopardy."

"I sympathize with you," he said, "but word is out and I can't let someone else go with the story before me."

I understood the situation, and decided the best thing to do would be to level with him, telling him I had signed with CBS as a correspondent/producer to work with Bill Moyers on "CBS Reports" and planned to leave by late January.

I placed a call to Arledge, deciding to talk to his secretary myself. "Carol, I don't want any run around this time. I must see Roone tonight and I don't care if it's midnight, because I'm quitting and I want to tell him myself."

She called back and said to come over at 7:30 P.M. I arrived a few minutes early and visited with Bill Sheehan in a nearby office. He told me I had been silly about the bonus, that I would have gotten it anyway, but I felt somehow that it would have been wrong of me to leave in November and expect a January bonus. He wished me luck and we promised to keep in touch. I went to Arledge's office at 7:30. Of course he wasn't there yet. Across from his desk was a comfortable sofa, coffee table, and several chairs. His secretary asked me if I'd like a drink, and I said yes. She opened up a wall bar and filled my order, and then started setting out large hunks of cheese with assorted crackers on platters. "What's all this?" I asked, since it looked like preparations for a cocktail party.

"Oh, every night he has staff people in, after the news, and they sit around and chew the fat," she informed me.

"I see," I replied, picturing the cluster of hangers-on that must gather nightly around the chief before he took off for more celebrity-studded camaraderie and a late dinner at "21," a favorite hangout of his.

Before too long, Arledge appeared, cordial as always face-to-face.

"Roone," I said, getting directly to the point, "it's not my style to have you pick up the *New York Times* tomorrow morning and read about my resignation. I just wanted to tell you personally that I am quitting and going to CBS."

He said, "I'm sorry to hear that," or words to that effect. He made a feeble attempt at trying to tell me that Hill's promotion in no way indicated he wanted me out, and there was more about "production values" being added to the documentary unit. I told him it was a totally unacceptable situation, but that I had decided to leave long before that particular development. Our conversation was brief, and I left for home, relieved.

Now, it was final. Even though I knew I would be going, it had more reality to it now. More than thirteen years at ABC were coming to an end. I had mixed feelings. Regret certainly was one of them. I had seen the news division grow from a handful of people crowded in one narrow room to a large, competitive network operation. There were people there I had known and worked with over all those years. Some were young and relatively inexperienced in the beginning. They were mature men now, with grey in their hair, people who survived the battles and were gearing up for more to come.

The 1960s were great years to be a correspondent as years of trouble and tragedy always are—the Kennedy and King assassinations, civil rights, Vietnam, student unrest, the peace marches, and the start of the women's movement all took place in that period.

It had been a break for me to come to ABC when I had; I joined a loosely structured, growing organization that had not yet developed the killer instinct of a real competitor. That came, and somehow I had survived that, too.

Moving into an executive job had been a big step forward for me, and for women. I knew that. I had developed reservations about staying permanently in management. Much of the work was routine compared to the more creative work of production. I tried to remind myself of something I had so often told young women: "Management is where the power is. People in production or on-air are a dime a dozen. That's not where it really counts." Still, a part of me wanted to return to it.

After so long at one place, I wondered how it would be at CBS, but I felt sure it would not be very different. Starting over again did not appeal to me. I had started over so many times already.

The next day's *New York Times* had it on the back page, with a large picture. The headline was: "Marlene Sanders Quits ABC for CBS." The article went on:

> Marlene Sanders, vice president of documentaries for ABC, is resigning to join CBS News as both producer and correspondent concentrating on documentaries. Miss Sanders, who became a vice president two years ago, gives up the distinction of being the only woman to hold that high a title in a network news division.
>     . . . She is scheduled to work primarily with Bill D. Moyers on documentaries for the "CBS Reports" series, but Mr. Moyers may be leaving CBS next fall to return to public television.
>     . . . Pamela Hill is expected to be Miss Sanders' successor at ABC News. Miss Hill recently was promoted to the position of executive producer for documentaries by Roone Arledge, president of ABC News and Sports. Miss Sanders has worked for ABC 13 years, as a reporter, newscaster and documentary producer, before becoming an executive. In a telephone interview yesterday, she said she was changing networks because she had become bored with administrative work and wished to again produce and do the reporting for documentaries of her own.
>     Then she added: "Besides, I feel much more comfortable with the news philosophy at CBS."
>     She explained that actions taken by Mr. Arledge since he became head of ABC News in June gave her the feeling "that my interests may not be the same as those of the new management."
>     Miss Sanders said that Mr. Arledge rarely spoke to her and that he had not screened any of the documentaries from her unit before their airing, except for the latest one, a film on hostages scheduled for this month. From this she concluded that the new president had little interest in the network's documentaries.
>     Mr. Arledge could not be reached for comment yesterday.[7]

As I sat on the bus that morning on the way to work, my picture stared back at me from several newspapers across the aisle. I saw people reading, and I wondered what they thought about another change in the fickle world of television. Some glanced at the story and never read it at all. People in the business, I knew, would be very interested indeed.

As soon as I got to work the phones were ringing. I had told Bob Chandler at CBS that the story was coming out. A release had been prepared by CBS and was ready for the same day. Friends in the business were on the phone, and many of the people in the department stopped by to congratulate me and say how sorry they were that I was leaving. Some genuinely were. Others, already sniffing out the impending change of command, had already made overtures to Hill, making points and laying the groundwork for their own careers, now that their fates, for the moment, were in her hands.

The CBS job looked promising; I was not laboring under the illusion that my troubles were over, but at least for some years to come they would be located elsewhere. I was grateful for the new opportunity. I looked forward to the future, to more directly covering the news again. Many of the people I had begun with had left the business by now, tired of the struggle and ready to try something else. I could understand that; that day had not arrived for me, not yet, anyway.

I had been the only woman news vice president at ABC, but when I arrived at CBS News there were four women with that title. One, Pamela Ilott, was in charge of religious and cultural broadcasts, not a powerful job. Three other women replaced men. Kay Wight was named vice president of news administration, and assistant to the president, Richard Salant. Margery Baker was made vice president, public affairs, and Sylvia Westerman became vice president of election and convention coverage. By 1987, three of the women were no longer at the network and there was only one woman news vice president, Joan Richman, until November when Beth Waxman Bressan was made vice president of legal affairs for news.

Joan Richman became vice president and director of special events in 1981, serving as executive producer of all special events broadcasts. That category included instant specials at the time of disasters, election coverage, and political conventions. At the time of her promotion, she had been in the department for a number of years, a department run originally by a man she considered her mentor. She feels he was very valuable to her progress, which evolved gradually.[8]

She was hired as a junior researcher, number two of two. After eight years she had risen to senior producer. That happened, she says, not only because she was in the right place at the right time, but because the department head knew her well enough to stick his neck out, even at a time when it was unusual to give women a great deal of responsibility. He knew she was ready to take on more of a challenge, and it was a risk he willingly took. Looking back, she says her advancement could have come out of a book on management, even though she felt her experience then was unique. At the time of her promotion to vice president, she had been executive producer, and it was agreed by top management that there was a certain redundancy, two people in effect doing the same job. So it seemed a natural progression when the jobs were consolidated. An older man left as vice president, and she was promoted.

By early 1987, Richman was still the only woman news vice president at CBS. In the mid-seventies there had been several. She feels the change represented something positive, in a backwards sort of way. Two of the women vice presidents were not in powerful jobs, she says; in effect, they were non-vice-presidential vice presidents, and it meant something only on paper. The job she holds today "is much more powerful, a more integral part of the management structure than any of those women vice presidents held, because they weren't real." As for the future, she thinks there will be more women vice presidents because the women are now in place. "There are lots of women in middle management, and every day they're proving that they're ready, and there's going to be, there already is, a large pool to draw from." Several of those people presumably are among the women bureau chiefs who work in Miami, Dallas, Los Angeles, and Atlanta.

As for male clubbiness, Richman says it still exists, always has, and probably always will,

> because there are occasions when men are more comfortable with men, just as there are occasions when women are more comfortable with women. . . . I have always taken the view that you just accept that as part of the deal, you work around it, you acknowledge it as a reality. I don't feel that it's critical. I don't think crucial power decisions get made in the men's room or on the golf course or fishing, but there's no point in denying that those relationships exist and that you're not a part of them. . . . I do not feel that I'm left out of major things that I should be a part of. I don't feel I'm forgotten about or anything along those lines.

The measure of her success was that in March 1987, prior to the purge of more than 215 correspondents, producers, and other CBS News personnel, Richman was one of the group of half a dozen who participated in the selection of those to be fired. She was also named vice president of news coverage in the reorganization that followed the cataclysmic changes within the news division at that time.

Earlier, in 1986, after a previous change in management at CBS News, a new, younger group of men took power. Richman says that group is different from its predecessors, partly because

> we now have a group of people on a senior staff that have known each other for a long time and have been colleagues for a long time, who are very good friends, . . . professional and in some cases personal friends. . . . We've got some very sensitive guys in this group now. They couldn't be any more sensitive about women, about women's issues. They all have working wives. We're all about the same age, remarkably similar in age when you consider management over the course of time, and it's really different.

The current group are all in their mid-to-late thirties and early forties, but their impact on more mobility for women has yet to materialize.

Affirmative action may be gone, Richman says, but she feels they now automatically keep moving women in. A greater priority, she feels, is the slippage in minority hiring, which needs more attention. Hiring, however, has been curtailed, with all of the networks doing more firing than expanding. Richman feels that another factor that had changed is the influence of a Harvard Business School kind of management style. While she feels there is a downside,

> it does have one upside. I think there really is a more formal management here, and presumably in the news business in general. There used to be things done very informally; it was very small and it was very intimate and everybody knew everybody, and you could stand in the men's room and say "let's hire Joe." You really can't do that anymore. The division is too big, there are too many people in it that everybody doesn't know. . . . Decisions like that get made in management committee meetings and they get hashed through and you get a much more formal structure and that makes the formal part of it much more effective and it makes those informal things much less crucial than they used to be.

Mary Alice Williams has a unique role in broadcasting. She co-anchors at CNN during prime time as well as being vice president of the Cable News Network in New York. At CNN the anchor teams are almost all composed of one man and one women. She points out that, "CNN started with a clean slate. We began in 1980 with the

values of 1980. It's not fair to generalize, but men over forty have
to be educated. Men under thirty-five are used to us. They've had
women bosses, their favorite professor in college was a woman, or
something. So they have some experience with this. The men over
forty have not. We don't have a problem with that because we tend
to have a young group. At thirty-seven I'm one of the older people
at the network."[9]

Williams's management responsibilities sometimes seem to have
little to do with news gathering. "Much of it frankly gets you so far
away from journalism. I spend most of my mornings doing budgets. . . . Why is the taxi cab budget for this month so high? Do we
have enough copy books? Have people overrun their sickday limits?
You know, there's a lot of that. I have two hundred people. That is
small relative to the rest of the world."

As for the age factor, on-air, Williams says, "I'm looking at twenty
years ahead of me and I'd like to prove that we are not different
from men and that we can be on the air up until our mandatory
retirement age." She is admittedly ambivalent about continuing to do
on-air work, which she began in the early seventies.

> You know that being on the air is no great shakes. I like my anonymity
> which is less and less the case for all of us now, and I don't particularly
> like that part. But boy, when a shuttle explodes in the sky I want to
> be sitting there talking about it. That's what I like about the business,
> watching the machine work to gather the information and to do it.
>      . . . The dual roles I have sort of enhance one another. It closes
> a circle every day. At the beginning of the day . . . these are the stories
> we're going to cover and how do we juggle these crews around so that
> we get financial and entertainment and news stuff covered in one day.
> And then at the end of the day I present the ones that they did all
> day.

With the pluses of management come the unpleasant tasks as
well. Joan Richman of CBS says firing people is one of those. "It has
got to be the single worst thing in life, in business life. I consider it
to be real hell. It's the worst thing and I've had to do quite a bit of
that during the last two years as we all have had to, and certainly you
never get used to it, maybe a little more graceful, but it's horrible.
But those are the things, along with pushing a lot of paper, and
budgets, that just sort of come with the territory, that you just have
to do."

Whether more women in management will advance the cause
of women on the air and in other jobs is debatable. Most women
think it will help, but the evidence so far is not favorable. There are

too few women to make a real difference now. Betsy Aaron at ABC says that "we expect more of them, we want them to be Mother Teresa. In most cases they are just ordinary, no worse, no better."

Some women bend over backwards to show that they are not favoring women, with the opposite result. Joan Richman's mentor was a man, but she says she tries to be a mentor to both promising young men and young women. She feels the presence of more women at the executive level would not change the kind of coverage editorially, but she concedes there "might be a receptivity to ideas about women or from women now that there didn't used to be. What you might have is something more organized. I think women are more organized on the whole." As for the decline in the number of women news vice presidents at CBS, Richman points out that "there was an effort when the legal issues arose, to put women into jobs and jobs were created to put women into, and those are the jobs that have been eliminated."

At ABC, following my departure in 1978, Pam Hill assumed what may now be the woman's slot. Joanna Bistany was named news vice president in 1986, and is in charge of public relations. Neither of those jobs represents significant power within the organization.

No matter how important or insignificant women's roles in management are, once having reached that level, one's relationships with former colleagues and with other vice presidents, usually men, change. While Joan Richman says she felt comfortable, by and large, as the only female vice president among eight male colleagues, on the professional level there are awkward sides to that minority relationship. At least there were in 1976–78 when I was an ABC News vice president. The informal friendships that my five male colleagues established among themselves, even if they did not extend to after working hours, were somewhat different from my own relationships with them.

Lunch could be a bit awkward. There were no women of my own rank in my own department, or any other. I frequently had business lunches, but often ended up eating at my desk, sometimes because I needed the time there, and sometimes because there was no one to go out with informally at the last minute. My male colleagues, the other vice presidents, were in another building. We occasionally did go out, but always at my instigation, when I called one of them. We would talk shop, and it was perfectly comfortable, but it apparently never occurred to them to call a female colleague in the same casual way as they did each other.

Many years later, one of those former vice presidents, Wally Pfister, was surprised when I questioned him about this. He said he was not aware of excluding me. He said he thought it was because I was in another building, and when lunchtime came, he just didn't think of me.

But examine the scene in any company cafeteria: People tend to eat with their professional equals, and if women are not on an equal footing, they separate. Women sometimes go to lunch with male colleagues who are peers, but don't often feel comfortable insinuating themselves into a male lunch group without invitation. Usually women have to take the initiative in extending a lunch invitation in advance, even in a casual way. Male resistance in some cases reflects male discomfort. The problem has been given a name: the comfort factor.

Professor Richard L. Zweigenhaft, of Guilford College in Greensboro, N.C., is credited with coming up with the phrase in the course of a study commissioned by the Institute of Human Relations of the American Jewish Committee. In his 1984 report called "Who Gets to the Top?," he examined executive-suite discrimination in the 1980s through a study of the Fortune 500 companies. He interviewed graduates of the Harvard Business School as far back as the 1960s, and included women, blacks, and Jewish men.

One Harvard woman MBA from the class of 1975 told him that management now knows the right things to say. She said the problem surfaces when one wants to advance beyond the assistant vice president level. She said,

> Outwardly, there are a lot of unbiased opinions expressed. But when people are reviewed, all the subconscious things really are at play. Way up at the top, a lot of business gets conducted in non-structured ways, over a golf game, or even in the men's room after a meeting. It's not really the old boy's network, but a lot like that, and women just aren't in it. It's hard for them to get into it because people at that level still are born and raised with the belief that women belong at home. They might make an exception, but they don't do it in general. They don't have the same comfort with women.[10]

A 1980 graduate told Zweigenhaft, "They've only dealt with wives or daughters, and they're not sure how professional women will react. They're so used to dealing with women in a teasing sense, or in a non-business sense. Socially, it's still difficult to be a woman in management. Men still perceive you either as their daughter or their mistress. They find it difficult to relate to you as a co-worker."

"60 Minutes," for years an almost exclusively male preserve, has recently added women to the staff. Until the mid-1980s there was one female producer in Washington and one in New York. Now, out of twenty-six producers, nine are women. When I asked senior producer Phil Scheffler why he thought women were kept out of so many male inner circles including top jobs, he said he felt it had nothing to do with professional skills, but rather with the kinds of friendships men tend to form with each other. Men, he said, are not intimate or very personal, even with someone they consider a best friend. They talk about externals. They view women, probably correctly, as more comfortable with intimacy, more personal, demanding more of people. He felt that men, by and large, like keeping work relationships on an impersonal level in terms of emotional content. Admitting women into their midst would therefore threaten the kind of casual, comfortable relationships the men have with each other. Possibly it does not occur to them that women can be impersonal and cool on the job and will not necessarily transfer their out-of-office conduct to the workplace.

CBS News correspondent Susan Spencer, a rising star in Washington, has no complaints about getting along with the new, youngish CBS News management. She went to journalism school with some of them and they all came up together. They are peers and hold each other in mutually high regard.

Cheryl Gould, in her mid-thirties, is the senior producer of "NBC Nightly News." She also feels optimistic about being a woman in television news today. She is one of the very few women in an editorial/managerial position in television news, but that was not her goal in the beginning. She was a history major at Princeton and after graduation moved to Rochester with her husband, who was studying for a Ph.D. Looking for work, she stumbled onto a part-time job at a radio station. She moved from part-time to full-time, learning interviewing and tape recording techniques. As she went from story to story she got to know members of a local TV crew who told her about an opening for a TV reporter. She got the job.

Things were going well, but when her husband decided to study at the Sorbonne she went along and hooked up with NBC radio as a stringer in Paris. After leaving her husband and Paris, she arrived in London and worked free-lance for "Weekend Nightly News," doing TV field producing. She was sent to North Africa because of her fluency in French.

When she returned to New York, she was hired as a newswriter for "Weekend Nightly News." The executive producer, Herb Dudnik, had spoken to her in London every weekend and knew she could do the job. When he was asked to be executive producer of the experimental program "Overnight," anchored by Linda Ellerbee and Lloyd Dobbins, Dudnik took Gould along as a producer. After Dudnik left,

Gould became senior producer. There was a real team effort on that show, which was staffed almost entirely by women, and it was a highlight in Gould's TV news career.

Sometimes one moves more quickly through failures than through successes. When "Overnight" folded after seventeen months Gould was asked to work on "Summer Sunday." This reinforced her senior status. When that show folded at the end of the summer, she knew a lot more people in the organization and also refused to take a demotion. She says,

> I was a senior producer on two programs and I felt I had proved myself and I didn't feel I had to keep proving myself. It may have been an arrogant position to take but I held fast. Ultimately they gave me the job of foreign producer on NBC nightly news, and then domestic producer. And then an opening developed and I was made senior producer. That was two years ago.[11]

Gould sees her success only partially attributable to the fact that she was a woman in the right place at the right time.

> It didn't hurt me to be a woman. But if I hadn't been someone they wanted for it I don't think it would have been something to tip them. [Tom] Brokaw and [Bill] Wheatly [executive producer] are real champions of women and they're sensitive to the issue. Perhaps in the beginning with Brokaw, he might have felt that we don't have enough women here and she's talented and that solves two problems, and that's to his credit. But I think at the point of the decision for senior producer [being a woman] wasn't a question. I don't think of it as a factor in that decision.

But when she looks around her newsroom most of the women are production assistants, associate producers, or secretaries.

> And when I fill in for the executive producer and I have to go to the daily editorial meetings with all the executives and vice presidents of the news organization there are a couple of women there but for the most part it's the boys' club. I'm ever conscious of that.

Gould finds that having been in the second coed class at Princeton helps her cope with all-male situations.

> The whole place was a male club and yet it was an extremely exciting time to be a young woman pioneer at an all-male institution where anything was up for grabs. I was only eighteen but you pick up what's going on in society. If I could go to Princeton I could do anything. It gave me an incredible sense of confidence. But what was most important about it was being among so many men and having that be

the norm and feeling you have just as much a right to be there as they do.

But skill and confidence are not the only attributes one needs to move up in an organization. Networking is the other key. Herb Dudnik, Linda Ellerbee, and Bill Wheatly are Gould's NBC role models. They also helped her get to where she is today. In turn, Gould feels committed to helping other women and minorities. "With the way the news is going, I'm going to be stuck with what we're left with. Some of these fellows at the show are there for five to ten years. I'm thirty-five; it's important to me to have the right kind of people as my colleagues." But she is networking on her own. Like many of the women working in news today, she is unaware of the legacy of the earlier women's action committees.

Gould is optimistic about the men coming up through the ranks. She feels that men in their thirties don't think it's a big deal if a woman is the boss. The older men feel awkward, and she remembers that "one correspondent was always condescending to me, always calling me 'dear' and saying that I reminded him of his daughter. I made a conscious decision not to object. My approach was to ignore it." But she doesn't hesitate to be critical when appropriate, regardless of age or sex.

Giving criticism is part of the responsibilities of being number two on the nightly newscast. She sees the best part of the job as being able to direct information and news to millions of people each night. She enjoys "being a boss and having that leadership role and setting a tone that is a healthy working environment."

In Cheryl Gould's position she can also affect the kinds of stories and treatment of those stories by the news department. She is proud of NBC's coverage of the Supreme Court affirmative action decision on 25 March 1987 that allows women and minorities to be promoted over a man in order to achieve a better balance in the workplace. NBC followed that story with an update on the status of affirmative action in this country, giving the lead story some context. Examples like that prove that a woman in a position of authority can have a real impact on story choice, giving stories that men might play down the important focus they deserve.

## Notes

1. Judith Hennessee, "The Press's Very Own Barbara Walters Show," *Columbia Journalism Review* (July/August 1976): 22.
2. Ron Powers, *The Newscasters* (New York: St. Martin's, 1978), p. 168.

3. Vernon Stone, "Women Hold Almost a Third of News Jobs," *RTNDA Communicator* 40, no. 4 (April 1986): 29.

4. Excerpted from a speech by Walter Cronkite to the CBS affiliates conference held in New York, May 1976. See also, Hennessee, p. 24.

5. Ann Sperber, *Murrow: His Life and His Times* (New York: Freundlich, 1986), p. 484.

6. *New York Times* (3 May 1977).

7. *New York Times* (5 January 1978).

8. Interview with Joan Richman (4 December 1986). All the quotes and other information from Ms. Richman in this chapter were taken from this interview.

9. Interview with Mary Alice Williams (4 December 1986). All other quotes and information from Ms. Williams in this chapter were taken from this interview.

10. Richard L. Zweigenhaft, "Who Gets to the Top?" (Institute of Human Relations, American Jewish Committee, 1984).

11. Interview with Cheryl Gould (29 March 1987). All other quotes and information from Ms. Gould in this chapter were taken from this interview.

# 8

## Looking Back, Looking Ahead

In 1978 when I joined CBS News, the organization was somewhat arrogant about its preeminent position in the business. It had led the ratings with Walter Cronkite at the helm, and prided itself on the distinguished "CBS Reports" series and the depth and strength of its news organization. Much of the staff had been on board for many years, and an outsider coming in was bound to feel like something of an interloper. Still, the organization was stable at that time. Richard Salant had been news president for nearly seventeen years, and the major managerial staff had been in place for some time.

Relieved as I was to be going to CBS, there was one sign of trouble from the beginning. My hiring had been done by news president Salant and his vice president of public affairs, Robert Chandler. Bill Moyers, my husband's former colleague and close friend, was happy to have me on board, to lighten his load at "CBS Reports." My status, it was clear, would be secondary to his, but that posed no problem to me because I expected to do some of the hour-long "CBS Reports" on my own. I was also to contribute to the proposed multi-story format that was about to be adopted.

Because of my peculiar problem in leaving ABC immediately, my contract at CBS had been settled well in advance of my arrival. However, weeks passed and I had no communication whatsoever from the executive producer of "CBS Reports," Howard Stringer, later to become president of CBS News. This disturbed me and, finally, I called him and suggested we meet for lunch. It seemed to me we had a good deal to talk about, but he was rather taciturn, decidedly cool but polite. He offered no explanations about why he had not been in touch, and we had a desultory conversation about what I would be doing.

When I finally moved into CBS, my office was directly adjacent to his. There was little time to worry about our relationship as I went on the road immediately and began doing stories at a fairly rapid pace for a documentary department. The short segments, as well as an hour I produced and reported on the handicapped rights movement, were well received by the critics. Two of the hours on which I was correspondent, "What Shall We Do About Mother?" and "Nurse, Where Are You?," both produced by Judy Reemstma, won Emmies. Nevertheless, there continued to be a distance between Stringer and myself, not animosity, but more precisely, indifference on his part. The few women in the unit were open in their remarks to me about what they considered to be his lack of regard for them as well. This apparent sexism seemed unaccountable, as he was married to a medical student, later a practicing dermatologist, a woman of charm and intelligence.

In the three years he ran the department while I was on staff, he never made a personal gesture of any kind, nor did he ever suggest an informal lunch. Male producers and other male colleagues joined him routinely. One more time I asked him to lunch with me, in an effort to establish better rapport. At lunch he seemed glum, mildly denying that there was a problem. Shortly thereafter, Stringer moved up the ladder to executive producer of the "CBS Evening News with Dan Rather." When he wanted to court those in power, Stringer could be as charming as the best of them.

During the course of my early years at CBS in documentaries, "Sunday Morning with Charles Kuralt" debuted, and I began to contribute stories regularly to that broadcast. Additionally, news vice president Bud Benjamin asked me to do the Friday evening TV "Newsbreak" in prime time, and radio began to call on me to substitute on the network hourly broadcasts. I was busy and satisfied, although there were increasing rumors of change. Richard Salant had retired as news president, and Bill Leonard was holding the job on an interim basis. Van Gordon Sauter then moved into that position in what appeared to be a revolving-door presidency.

Sauter's style was not remotely like that of the gregarious Salant. The news division was Salant's baby, and he guarded it from interference by the network brass and, as best he could, from commercial considerations as well. Bill Leonard, then beyond retirement age, had the unenviable job during his brief reign of finally accepting Walter Cronkite's resignation as anchor of the "CBS Evening News," and presiding over the expensive assumption of the post by Dan Rather. Under Sauter, that broadcast began to change, with an emphasis on more emotional, colorful stories, and a search for stories with "moments," a euphemism for emotional grabbers of some sort. Sauter, unlike Salant, did not mix with the general staff, keeping himself aloof. My few conversations with him were held at my instigation, with the view to contributing from time to time to the Rather news. He said I should talk to Rather, which I later did. Although I did two stories for him, the one high-ranking woman on his staff explained to me that the broadcast's first priority was to use the correspondents specifically assigned to that program. The system previously in operation at CBS, like the one at ABC News, was one in which correspondents were, on paper at least, equal. Some had specific beats, but breaking news theoretically was covered by whoever was available. Under the new system, several highly paid, favored correspondents worked only for the Rather news, and were not available for morning, weekend, radio, or "Sunday Morning" assignments. A caste system, in effect, was instituted. What became known as the "A-list" and "B-list" was informally established. While I was busily engaged in documentaries, it was clear that I was on the "B-list" in hard news. While irritated, I did not view it then as a threat to my status. My first three-year contract had been renewed for another five, with adequate raises in compensation. Plainly, I was productive and well enough regarded in at least some quarters.

Before Sauter had been in place two years, another executive change put his deputy, Ed Joyce, in charge. Joyce continued Sauter's policies, but apparently did not get along with Rather, and he left, to be replaced once again by Sauter. While that game of musical chairs was underway, the documentary division began a precipitous decline. Bill Moyers returned to public television and I was reassigned to the Northeast bureau. Housed in New York, it was the jumping-off point for stories in the northeast. I was doing an increasing number of "Newsbreaks" at night, and had a busy schedule of "Sunday Morning" and weekend assignments as well as radio. I was not a fireman, not sent routinely to cover breaking stories, and I had no desire to return to that.

I felt, however, an undercurrent of dissatisfaction, but no alternatives came to mind. My husband had become ill and this had begun to affect his behavior; he talked frequently about retiring. Under the circumstances, my income was more important than ever. Neither of us knew at the time that his increasing fatigue and withdrawal was due to a brain tumor that had been developing slowly over the years.

Our son was by then in law school, and at least the end of tuition was in sight. At work, I tried to ignore my second-class status as much as possible, as did others who were not part of the "A-list" star system.

A series of company cutbacks and forced early retirements were signs that the news division was not immune from an increasing concern over profits. Management indifference to the network's responsibility to serve the public interest was reflected in the cuts. Documentaries were downgraded and rarely surfaced. When they did, they were used as vehicles to promote Rather or other news stars.

I was well paid, but misused, and became increasingly angry. I was also over fifty, even though I didn't look it. On network news, Barbara Walters was the only other woman my age still appearing on TV within a news-oriented format. Betty Furness, in her seventies, was still on local WNBC-TV in New York and reporting consumer news on the "Today" show. She had her own unique set of qualifications. My options, it seemed, were limited.

One would think that age and experience would be a valuable asset to a correspondent. On the network level, most anchormen are over forty and so are most of the respected male correspondents. Whether the same standards will apply to women should be resolved in the 1990s. The age question was one of the factors that drove NBC's Rebecca Bell to leave her correspondent's job for management. She had been overseas for NBC News, and during one of her trips home turned on the television set and thought she saw the future.

> I came home on home leave and started watching local television and network TV and I noticed something very strange. The blondes had taken control, and I don't mean the Diane Sawyers of the world who have earned their stripes. I mean young, fresh-faced, very pretty women who just didn't seem to have writing ability, or delivery. I suddenly came back to a country where everything seemed to have gone bland. My problem was these people seemed to be fluff heads. I saw the handwriting on the wall. I was a forty-year-old woman and I'm not terribly photogenic. So how do you remain authentic and true to yourself when the industry is making something else of you? The time would pass and I know many women who have become sidelined, who you see as microphone stands, doing stake outs, women who have been years in this industry, who still write well, observe well, and I thought, I don't want to stay in a career where I'm looking down the barrel of a gun with a time deadline. I want my years and my experience to matter for further growth.[1]

Correspondents, at least the new ones, seemed to be getting younger, and so, in the 1980s, was news management. As Elmer Lower, once president of ABC News, left his job in his sixties, a new generation took over. His replacement, Bill Sheehan, was a decade younger, and some years later, was displaced by a still younger Roone Arledge. At CBS, news presidents Richard Salant and Bill Leonard were replaced by younger men: Van Gordon Sauter, Ed Joyce, and forty-five-year-old Howard Stringer. The men surrounding Stringer, making choices about personnel for the evening news and other broadcasts, were all around forty or younger. It may well be true that this is a young person's business, but the lack of a mix of age, race, and sex in a management team tends to limit the breadth of their decision-making. It is not surprising that they are inclined to hire people in their own image. This leaves women, minorities, the middle-aged, particularly older women, in a kind of limbo.

Rebecca Bell felt that aging would affect her career: "You are not rewarded for aging on television. . . . If I were a female version of Charles Kuralt I would not be on the air. . . . You know what my first news director told me when he hired me? He said I'm hiring you for two reasons. You're a terrific writer and you're not threateningly attractive. You look okay, he said. And I said that's great because that fit my self-image. When the cosmetics became more important than the content, well, I hope it's a phase."

Lesley Stahl sees it differently. She told me:

> I don't think women are going to have any more of an age problem than men. I've always laughed at people who say women aren't going to last because the women who were there early have lasted. You. Barbara [Walters], Aline [Saarinen], and Marya [McLaughlin]. Who else was there? Who did they throw away? When they began to hire women, the ones they hired, the great bulk of us have lasted, and I'm almost forty-five. . . . I'm not saying there isn't age discrimination. I'm just saying the women are treated the same as the men. Age is a problem but not because I'm a woman. Because I love this job, I will try not to age, but what can I do? Some men age and they let them work, Walter [Cronkite], Mike [Wallace]. . . . I wear gobs of makeup, I get my hair done twice a week, I diet. I knew it was part of the qualifications and I damn well was going to do it because I wanted this job and it is part of the qualifications, sadly; it's also a part of it for the men. They are facing the same thing as time goes by. They have to be good-looking too. They're getting their hair styled and they get blow dried. If I need hair spray I'll ask a male colleague the same as I would ask a female colleague, and they've got it.[2]

That view is shared by the most successful women on the air, such as ABC's Lynn Sherr: "There are a group of us now in our low forties. Those who are good are too strong and firmly established to get the heave-ho that men got away with in the past. And the audience is growing up with us, getting older. Demographics keep going up. TV news managers go with what works. If we work, we stay."[3]

CBS's Susan Spencer doesn't seem worried about the age issue and says she hasn't even thought much about it. "You reach the point where you hope we'll be too valuable to drop. It would be unfair if they did."[4] NBC's White House correspondent, Andrea Mitchell, also feels that quality work will count: "I think the value of what we can bring to their broadcasts, having covered these issues a long time and having developed sources, it's too important to them so they're not going to get rid of us."[5]

Betsy Aaron feels that women who are not particularly good-looking have a better chance of lasting. Those who depended on their good looks will not survive because their beauty will inevitably fade. For the rest, if their work is up to par, and their appearance does not change dramatically, she is hopeful that they will last.[6]

While Judy Woodruff was White House correspondent for NBC News, she registered a growing concern about aging. She noted that "the age barrier may be the most significant hurdle women will face on television. If we're hired because we're pretty and young, we will be put out to pasture once the wrinkles emerge."[7] She was then in her mid-thirties. A highly respected reporter with blonde good looks, Woodruff cannot be said to be just another pretty face. At forty-one, her work on public television's "MacNeil/Lehrer NewsHour" reveals a quick mind and solid intelligence. It is still not known, however, whether those qualities will shine through the inevitable wrinkles.

Veteran anchor Walter Cronkite reflects on the double standard:

> It's an unfortunate fact of life that men as a group are more likely to age gracefully than women are, as far as authority goes. It's probably a false concept, but I think it exists nonetheless. It's unfortunate. . . . As more and more intelligent broadcasting executives continue to use the talent and wisdom of older women I think the barrier will break down. I think it just takes a little while for people to get used to it, and for some courageous executives to go ahead and use the women. I don't think there's anything women will be able to do about it. I don't think the public concept is as harsh as the executive concept in this area.[8]

Joan Richman, who is in her forties, participates in executive staff meetings, and says no one there discusses age.

> I think the country is finished with the sort of youth craze. . . . The demographics of the country are different; there is no great "where

are the young dazzling blondes of twenty, we want to put them on CBS News." There is no feeling like that. I really think there's a much greater concern with the professionalism of broadcasting. There certainly is more concern with performance than there used to be, but that's equally true with men and women. I really believe the same standards apply and I don't see any change. I never heard anyone say, "is she, or is he, getting too old?" I never heard that said. I've heard people say, "his hair, or her hair, looks like hell," or "he or she doesn't know how to dress; he's putting on, or she's putting on weight." I've never heard any distinction made, and I've never heard any discussion of age except the other kind: "Isn't he or she too young for this assignment?"[9]

Correspondent Diane Sawyer of "60 Minutes," one of the highest paid and probably best known of the newswomen, has a contract with CBS News that takes her to age forty-six.

I think the possibilities are almost unlimited at this kind of work. I don't know whether on "60 Minutes" or what, at least for the next ten years. We all base that on part on Barbara [Walters] and what she's doing, but we all know she's a special case. . . . I guess I feel the verdict is out and in a lot of ways it will be up to me if I have Mike's [Wallace] stamina, his energy, his sense of the quest. Maybe I can keep doing it another ten or fifteen years. . . . It depends a lot on what I do. I'm still defining here what my stories are, what my way of doing my stories here is. If I come up with something distinctive, if you come up with something distinctive in the way that Mike is distinctive, with something that is uniquely your voice, which is what we all hope to do when we do our stories, I think they'll give you the benefit of the doubt at that age. I'm realistic enough to know that it's uncharted territory, and maybe I'm naive in thinking that in another ten years that management is going to be more sophisticated than it's been in the past about women and the way women think, and again, I never underestimate demographics.[10]

The real stars of broadcast journalism will be the anchors, including the anchor team of the popular "60 Minutes." Women, when they anchor, do so on the less desirable weekend broadcasts, on the brief newsbreaks in prime time, and in the morning when they co-anchor, usually with more highly paid men. Lesley Stahl on CBS anchors "Face the Nation" on Sunday, a highly visible, respected slot, but not the nightly "CBS Evening News."

No one, however, has ever accused Stahl of lacking ambition. She is satisfied with her own progress, and thinks, in general, that women have few grounds for complaints, given when they entered the business at the network level. "They hired us all in 1972, that was thirteen, fourteen years ago." As for why there hasn't been more progress, Stahl believes there has been a great deal of progress and that the charge is unfounded. Citing her own White House responsibilities, as well as those on election night and "Face the Nation," she goes on:

> And we have a woman covering the Justice Department, Rita Braver; Susan Spencer has her own beat, and a major candidate. Joan Richman runs a unit and is a vice president. . . . Your generation was pre-affirmative action, and we still don't have a critical mass, but once they began to hire us, CBS gave us opportunities and the women did well. Susan Zarinksy is running the evening news in Washington. You want to know why she isn't a vice president? She's thirty-two years old. We're moving up. I think we're where you would expect any man to be at this stage. I just don't think we can go out there and bang CBS on the head. The other networks aren't doing that well.

Unless Diane Sawyer joins Dan Rather or replaces him as "CBS Evening News" anchor, the sole female occupant of the evening anchor chair will have been Barbara Walters. Ten years after that failed effort, the idea is taken far more seriously.

There are more experienced women anchors available whose images are not sullied as being only celebrity interviewers, no matter how successful that form of journalism has been and remains. Walters and her co-anchor, Harry Reasoner, were a poor mix, but the male-female anchor team is now routine at local stations. Local anchor teams often look as though they had been picked by casting directors: one young blonde woman, co-starring with an attractive older man, an image not unlike many men's second marriages. Consultants continue to take surveys, measure audience pulse rates, weigh their reactions with buzzers and bells, and come up with the combination they hope will work. Supposedly, this didn't happen at the networks, although some of the women who have anchored the weekend editions of the evening newscasts have not put in much time reporting. Those short on experience always make up for it with their good looks.

To its credit, when CNN began in 1980, its policy from the beginning was to have male and female co-anchor teams for its nonstop news programming.

Walter Cronkite, who anchored the "CBS Evening News" from 1962 until 1981, believes that for a half-hour network broadcast, co-anchors are superfluous: "I'm opposed to dual anchors. It doesn't matter whether they're men, women, blacks, Chinese, Japanese, whatever. I just think dual anchors are a dumb idea. I don't see any reason for them. It's a show business gimmick, Mr. Gallagher and Mr. Sheehan. It's not needed, it gets in the way, it delays the production of the broadcast, it complicates the production of the broadcast. There's no reason for it except show business."

During Diane Sawyer's well-publicized contract negotiations in early 1987, one of the areas of speculation was whether she would be offered a co-anchor job on a rival network. She does not admit to seeking such a job, but disagrees with Cronkite's co-anchor theory:

> Did Huntley and Brinkley get in each other's way? Each brought something different to it. It wasn't a co-anchor, it was more of an anchor and a person who was different. . . . I didn't lobby in my contract to be co-anchor or to be anchor. All I was talking about was that if anybody is looking down the road, what are you thinking of? The idea that I was in there muscling these guys out of their jobs is a little unsettling to me and I'm sure to them because it didn't happen that way at all. But we all know that evening news is evolving toward something different, that it's been a wonderful thing for the country.
>
> The division of labor between network and local news has become more ambiguous in many ways. Evening news will redefine in order to strengthen. If you do it differently at some point, would you want to free up one of your anchors to go do other things? Would you want to have the anchor less tethered to the chair all the time? I don't know. I don't know that it couldn't be useful.

Cronkite and Sawyer are closer to agreement on the eventual anchoring of a woman, alone, on the main evening news. Cronkite sees a woman anchor in the future:

> Fine, why not? I think it likely. . . . You've got three fairly young people in the anchor positions now. I see no particular indication, at least at this particular moment, maybe tomorrow, but no indication now of serious trouble. So we're looking fairly far down the line. . . . I think by the time the next change comes, the next generation of anchor people, I would think that the barriers would be down and that women would have as good a chance as men. And there will certainly be a pool of them out there. Local stations have a whole lot of dual anchor positions.

Sawyer thinks the public is ready now:

> At this stage I don't think it has to do with being female or male or whether you have co-anchors. There are three really good journalists, those three guys. I think it has more to do with how you build a really good broadcast and if there is caution and nervousness about changing the broadcast, I think that's probably justified. I'm not sure that there's resistance to female co-anchors. I don't know about a single woman

anchor. I don't know what that will be like, or when that will come. . . . It will come, sure.

Women are taking charge of broadcasts on non-network programs. When it came time for gavel-to-gavel coverage of the Iran-Contra joint congressional hearings in the summer of 1987, Judy Woodruff of PBS was the logical anchor. Her in-depth reports filled the "MacNeil/Lehrer NewsHour" nightly while the hearings were on, and led to a little-noted innovation during the long hours and weeks of daily coverage. For the first time, all of the major commentary was done by women. Woodruff's co-anchor in the booth, who did analysis of the unfolding events, was Elizabeth Drew, a longtime political reporter for *The New Yorker.* Additionally, there was a need for someone to comment and secure interviews from members of the bipartisan committee members. The logical choice was National Public Radio congressional correspondent Cokie Roberts. The choice of personnel, Woodruff says, just fell into place, and neither executives nor staff made an issue of the all-female contingent. Viewer response was reportedly excellent, with many women writing that they were bursting with pride because of the outstanding work the three female television correspondents were doing.[11]

Could it have happened on one of the major networks, where the traditional anchormen held forth with only an occasional woman correspondent putting in an appearance? Conceivably the talent was available, but it is unlikely network executives would have dared to give such responsibility and star billing to their staff newswomen.

Roadblocks at the top continue to be a problem for women. As more doors opened for entry-level positions over the years, and women began to work their way through the system, it was natural to expect them to continue to move up. The route varies, but one road might be to begin as a researcher, moving on to the assignment desk, or to news editor or a logistics person; from there one might go to night news manager, which means being in charge in the evening and contacting executives if a major story breaks. It also involves producing the latenight newsbreaks, and making sure affiliates get late feeds of breaking news. It's a minor managerial job with a good deal of responsibility but with long hours over the weekend and long stretches of boredom. The route out of that job could be a promotion to field producer for a bureau or working for the weekend news as an associate producer. If one is well connected and makes the right friends, bureau chief is another avenue out. There are a limited number of those jobs available. For years there were few women above the level of researcher. While that has changed, the amount of frustration for those who do not move ahead has driven many people out of the business altogether.

Young women contemplating the future, at least those who have been forewarned, seem to have developed a grasp of the problems that lie ahead. An informal survey of female journalism students at New York University in May 1987 revealed that the young women perceive TV news as dominated by men. They feel that one has to prove one is equal to if not better than a man, but they feel a woman does not get equal pay. They notice that women are seen more in the less desirable time slots and that few women have made it to the management level. They think women are not taken as seriously as men, and they see sexual discrimination as a problem. One student gave her own example of discrimination: A young woman who was working as a weather girl in Minneapolis applied for an anchor position and was told she didn't get the job because she had nice legs and the producers didn't want to lose viewers by seating her. The students realize that there is more pressure on women than on men to look young, and that it is difficult to juggle marriage, children, and work. They also see the more positive side: Women are more visible as anchors in local news, and broadcast journalism is important to our society. They want to be a part of that, and prove they can do the job.

Network news has lost its charm, for me at least, and by all accounts, it has changed in many ways that are apparent to veterans of ten years or more. Hilary Brown would warn potential correspondents of the favoritism that seems to prevail in an increasingly competitive industry. She calls it the "flavor of the month." A producer or anchorman will latch onto a correspondent, and feature him, reducing others to covering secondary stories or feeding material into his spots. Correspondents fall in and out of favor. If someone wants to pursue this work, Brown would say to go for it, but be forewarned. It's wonderful if you are the flavor of the month. The overstaffing of the 1970s created difficulties for reporters in that while they were hired for what they could do and were rewarded with high salaries, they did not get to do what they were capable of doing.[12] The veteran correspondents who survived the 1980 cuts find the lack of good assignments debilitating, humiliating, and depressing. It's bad for morale. Veteran correspondents at the peak of their experience, even if still employed, are filled with self-doubt, wondering what else they can do with their lives.

The practice of promoting star reporters as well as star anchormen will undoubtedly grow and their usurping of other people's material will continue. Walter Cronkite remembers his days with United Press International. Star reporters would come into another person's territory and "take the cream off the story." He notes: "In newspaper work there were politics too. I'm thinking of the Hearst organization, Scripps Howard, some of the others, who made the star reporter. . . . There were by-line names. You wanted Bob Considine on the story. He picked everybody's brains, he talked to his fellow correspondents, but he wrote every word himself." Cronkite is not sure the star system is so detrimental in television:

> I'm not sure it's all as bad as it's made out to be. It's not comfortable for the correspondent obviously. But on the other hand I've always thought, why shouldn't TV networks operate for heavens sake like newspapers or press services, and that's that people work for the company and if you're in the position of being a leg man or leg woman reporter, or a second-ranking correspondent, or whatever, I think you ought to expect it to work that way. The business isn't made in order to promote individual ambitions. It's meant to deliver a product, and if delivering that product is best organized into the fashion that seems to have developed, with three or four or five or a dozen people who can command public attention and have gotten that position because the company thinks that they're able to command public attention, I don't know why the organization shouldn't be mobilized in support of that. People ought to expect that and hope that they're the ones that are struck by lightning or by the luck of the draw, or talent, or looks, or whatever it is that makes it worthwhile, that makes it work.

And if they don't like the system? Cronkite adds, "well then they ought to go elsewhere. I think it's kind of brutal to put it that way, but I think that the ego trip involved in television news is one of the great problems that this business has. I'm afraid that people get into it because of an ego trip. People are going through communications schools and trying to get into television. There are people, who, if it weren't for television would be in drama school. . . ."

NBC's Cheryl Gould is concerned also that young women come into the TV news business for the wrong reasons.

> The first thing I always do when they [young people] tell me they're interested in getting into TV news is to try to get their real interest in going into the business. If they say "TV production" I don't know what they're talking about. Do they want to get into TV news or do they want to be journalists? When they think TV is glamorous and see news as a vehicle I don't have much to say.
> They need to be interested in critical judgment and analysis. They need a good liberal arts background: history, English, philosophy,

the classics, government, sociology, science. In the beginning they don't
need a specialty but a well-trained mind that thinks and asks questions
and that wants to know why things are the way they are and not just
accept.[13]

Gould suggests that the best way to get into the network is by first
finding a job in local television where one can fall but not get hurt.
Working one's way up through the network, moving from page to
desk assistant to associate producer to producer is a slower route and
doesn't necessarily provide the depth of experience one can get by
working locally. Gould believes, "it's good personally to go out into
the field where you don't know anybody and tackle that kind of life.
You learn self-reliance and build self-confidence. You learn how to
make a story interesting and become a generalist. You also learn what
you like to do and what you're good at." Gould thinks appearance is
also important, especially for on-air work; neatness and not distracting
the viewer from what you're saying is important. But the best thing
is to try to make contacts in an organization. "The best recommendation is to do a lot of good work and then be recognized for it."

Network news may still hold an aura of glamor and adventure
to many young reporters, but local stations will most likely win them
over. The hours of air time are longer, travel is not a problem, and
local celebrity is one reward. Many local stations will continue to do
mostly tabloid news as competitive pressures continue. Reporters who
are in the business for the money and fame are unlikely to understand
the differences. There will be some on the staff who will be able to
handle politics and the more serious fare, but the meat and potatoes
of local news will continue to be crime and natural disasters. Local
stations more and more have the capacity via satellite to pick up foreign
and national news from networks and other sources. Some of the
local news teams of the future will have to be able to provide appropriate commentary and they will need staff adequately qualified to
do that. Many of those staff members will be former network correspondents, like former CBS newsman Bill Redeker, a victim of the
1987 cutbacks who found work co-anchoring a one-hour evening
newscast on KTTV-TV (a Fox-owned station) in Los Angeles. Satellite
technology, he says, means local stations "are trying to find people
who have that experience. . . . That's where the opportunities are, in
local and syndication work."[14] It seems doubtful that women will
advance rapidly to the top echelons of news management or to the
major network news jobs in the predictable future. Without pressure
from women in the industry, and without support of the government,
it is unlikely the statistics will alter greatly in the years ahead. Women

are making inroads into cable news, and a new generation of male managers in the commercial institutions may make a difference.

A major fear is the direction the industry itself is taking, as businessmen who now run the networks worry more about profits than about their obligations to the public. As CBS chief executive officer Laurence A. Tisch told a convention of the National Association of Broadcasters in March 1987: "The numbers no longer seem to work. . . . For the first time the question has been seriously raised whether the bottom line and public service are now mutually exclusive claims, whether in fact we have reached a point where we can no longer serve the public and stay in business."[15] If the networks curtail their coverage of world and national news, while cable reaches only half of the television households, the availability of information will decline. There will also be fewer jobs for broadcast journalists.

Correspondents fired from CBS News in 1987 did not have an easy time relocating. Six months after the March layoffs, several still had not found work in the field, veteran reporters Jim McManus, Ike Pappas, and Chris Kelley among them. Several responded angrily to print reports quoting Tisch saying that no one had been hurt in the firing process, and that the CBS pension and severance policies were more than adequate.[16] In interviews with the former staffers, *Variety* reporter Elizabeth Jensen found one saying, "We're not going to wind up in the streets, but that's not the same as being a journalist," and another claimed that "every time Tisch says publicly CBS News was not hurt, it doesn't help any. It means we're effectively being described as deadwood, that my departure meant nothing to CBS."[17] Chicago correspondent Karen Boros commented, "The idea that nobody was hurt, I find that appalling. . . . To be a reporter one day and then the next day you're not, it's frustrating, it tears at your stomach."[18] Several network correspondents relocated and joined local news organizations, one as anchor, others as street reporters. Legal correspondent Fred Graham returned to his hometown to anchor. He says he would "never go back to CBS, it's a very unpleasant place and had been for some time."[19] David Andelman, who worked at the *New York Times* before joining CBS, left the news business to become a vice president at Burson Marsteller, a public relations firm. Andelman expressed the hope that "there's still room for the upper-middle-level correspondent who is very good and very smart . . . that there's room for the journeymen not just the stars or the entry level people."[20]

When the broadcast organizations were small, there was more of a family feeling, and a sense of real participation. Growth changed that, and all of the networks became impersonal organizations where individuals were interchangeable. When my own time to leave CBS came in 1987, it was far less of a trauma for me. I had been there ten years but had changed jobs often enough before that to be immune to the psychological shock at least.

When the third wave of firings began at CBS News in March 1987, news president Howard Stringer asked me to move to radio. That proposal was unacceptable. It was not so much the job reassignment and the dreadful hours involved, but the blow to my professional pride and self-respect that could not allow me to stay. My husband had died three years earlier. I hoped there was still time to rebuild my private life and establish a new professional life as well.

I did not fit the profile of the "A-team" television correspondent of the eighties. Middle age was no asset, but there was an even more pointed observation passed on to me some five years earlier by my agent. The business affairs lawyer negotiating my contract, basing his comments on instructions from management, had said that I was regarded as "good, but not a star."

It was heartening to see that my work of more than thirty years was respected by many on the outside. I no longer needed the kind of income network news provided, and could accept several assignments from public television to do the kind of work I continued to care about. The pressure to climb some invisible ladder, to reach some new professional heights, was gone. I had been there already, and now simply wanted to do solid, serious work for its own sake.

Former ABC news president Bill Sheehan, who rose from the correspondents' ranks, often expressed frustration at the lack of options for older correspondents. They could, if they weren't fed up with travel, work as field producers, but that has less status and a lower salary. Another possibility is to run a bureau. That job however is regarded as a stepping-stone toward management, and most often goes to a promising former producer. It is also demanding, requires travel, and is a sure route to burn-out after a few years. Many departing correspondents seem to end up in public relations, teaching, or running university journalism schools.

And most newspeople, when they do leave a major network job, are angry and disappointed. People dismissed after many years of service, as so many were during the waves of firings in the 1980s, could not be expected to be happy about it. But the major feeling was that of resentment—that years of dangerous assignments, long hours, and work well done could be discarded with the flick of a pen. The message is clear; we can all be replaced. There are no guarantees of longevity, and no obvious destination where news professionals can translate their experience and knowledge into new and satisfying careers.

Far too many women see their work as extensions of their families, even as substitutes. The women, most of them single, who had spent as much as thirty years at CBS, were shocked, even grief-stricken, when they were fired in the purges of 1985, 1986, and 1987. This was home, this was where they had expected to spend their entire careers, and they were stunned to find that the ever-changing management didn't know them or care about them.

To the women involved, their work, their careers, represented more than just a paycheck, though that of course was important. They were not biding their time until marriage, like many women in the fifties had done. They had made personal commitments to their work, found it satisfying and rewarding, and considered their contributions to the company's success important. Many had worked their way up from secretarial or research jobs, attaining a stature and salary beyond their mothers' dreams. To find their efforts swept aside was a shock for which they were ill prepared.

Dedicated women and men will always come along who want to report and explain the increasingly complex world we live in. Those of us who have had that privilege have led interesting lives, and have done good work when we've been allowed to. To those who follow, the challenge to continue to do so remains.

The problem of meshing one's life with demanding work exists, not only for women in broadcasting, but also in the other professions to which we have gained admission during recent years. Striking a balance is not easy, particularly when society has not yet placed child-care as a high priority.

Ambition propels us along. We want recognition, good salaries, and involvement in the world. Virginia Woolf put it this way: "Women have sat indoors all these millions of years, so that by this time the very walls are permeated by their creative force, which has indeed so overcharged the capacity of bricks and mortar that it must needs harness itself to pens and brushes and business and politics. But this creative power differs greatly from the creative power of men. And one must conclude that it would be a thousand pities if it were hindered or wasted."[21]

We have much to offer to an indifferent world. To all who choose to meet the challenge, one final word. Do not mistake a job for home and family, or trusted friend. It cannot be counted on. It can turn you out in an instant. However you decide to live your life, it is important to have personal involvements separate from your profession that will sustain you when, for whatever reason, your work comes to an end.

## Notes

1. Interview with Rebecca Bell (18 November 1986). All quotes and information from Ms. Bell in this chapter were taken from this interview.
2. Interview with Lesley Stahl (19 November 1986). All other quotes and information from Ms. Stahl in this chapter were taken from this interview.
3. Interview with Lynn Sherr (23 February 1987).
4. Interview with Susan Spencer (17 October 1986).
5. Interview with Andrea Mitchell (18 November 1986).
6. Interview with Betsy Aaron (14 October 1986).
7. Judy Woodruff and Kathy Maxa, *This Is Judy Woodruff at the White House* (Reading, Pa.: Addison-Wesley, 1982), pp. 199, 200.
8. Interview with Walter Cronkite (18 December 1986). All other quotes and information from Mr. Cronkite in this chapter come from this interview.
9. Interview with Joan Richman (4 December 1986). All other quotes and information from Ms. Richman in this chapter come from this interview.
10. Interview with Diane Sawyer (15 January 1987). All quotes and information from Ms. Sawyer in this chapter come from this interview.
11. Interview with Judy Woodruff (27 August 1987).
12. Interview with Hilary Brown (23 November 1986).
13. Interview with Cheryl Gould (29 March 1987).
14. Elizabeth Jensen, *Variety* (19 August 1986).
15. Speech given to National Association of Broadcasters, 31 March 1987.
16. Jensen, *Variety*.
17. Ibid.
18. Ibid.
19. Ibid.
20. Ibid.
21. Virginia Woolf, *A Room of One's Own* (New York: Harcourt Brace and World, 1929), p. 91.

# Index